STEPPING STONES
SUCCESS
EXPERTS SHARE STRATEGIES
FOR MASTERING BUSINESS,
LIFE, & RELATIONSHIPS

Stepping Stones to Success
Copyright © 2010

Published in the United States by
INSIGHT PUBLISHING
Sevierville, Tennessee • www.insightpublishing.com
ISBN 978-1-60013-473-9

Cover Design: Emmy Shubert
Interior Format & Design: Chris Ott

Disclaimer: This book is a compilation of ideas from numerous experts who have each contributed a chapter. As such, the views expressed in each chapter are of those who were interviewed and not necessarily of the interviewer, Insight Publishing or the other contributing authors.

A Message from the Publisher

There are many things I've come to understand throughout the many years I have been in this business. I've learned that it's never too late to grow and learn, to change course, to expand perspectives, and to admit I don't know everything.

Because I know it's important to learn from the experience of others, I reached out to many experts when putting this book project together and I gained some valuable information from them. The people I talked with have presented some insights that will expand your horizons and make you realize that you can be the key to your own success.

This book, *Stepping Stones to Success,* is your golden opportunity to profit from the knowledge of others. It will give you the facts you need to make important decisions about your future.

Interviewing these fascinating people was a unique learning experience for me. And I assure you that reading this book will be an exceptional learning experience for you.

—David Wright

The interviews presented in
Stepping Stones to Success
are conducted by

DAVID WRIGHT
President and Founder
ISN Works and Insight Publishing

TABLE OF CONTENTS

CHAPTER ONE

Consciously Creating Success in Business

An Interview with . . . **Karen Coffey**

DAVID WRIGHT (WRIGHT)

Today we're talking with Karen Coffey. Karen is the Founder and Facilitator of The Million Dollar Success Circle Programs, the first and only approach to consciously creating six and seven figure incomes. She is also an internationally sought-after speaker, the author of two books, and the CEO of The Hope of Humanity Foundation. In her quest for passion and meaning in her own life, Karen lost everything but kept her connection to what she calls her "intuitive source." In a little more than a year, she went from losing everything she owned to making over a half million dollars following the guidance and direction of this intuitive connection.

Karen, welcome to *Stepping Stones to Success.*

KAREN COFFEY (COFFEY)

Thank you, David; I'm glad to be here.

WRIGHT

Wow, half a million dollars in one year from nothing! How did that happen?

COFFEY

Well, lucky for me it happened very successfully. I've always known that I had a gift for earning and attracting large sums of money into my life—I've done it repeatedly. However, it wasn't until May 2008 that I realized what this gift actually was and how it truly worked in my life. I'd been doing work that I loved and was passionate about for two years—coaching individuals one-on-one to find their passion and make money at it.

I was what we describe as a "success coach". I was able to coach my clients' on how to overcome roadblocks to their success in all areas of life—love relationships, finances, business, family matters, life purpose, and so on. I would 'get still', almost as if I were in a state of meditation, and I would receive intuitive guidance on processes and steps they could take in their own lives to create highly successful outcomes.

I later realized that although I was assisting my clients, I had fallen into the same trap so many people experience—I was helping everyone but myself. I had left me out of the equation and created a huge imbalance in my life. I wasn't taking the time to 'be still' and follow this intuitive source for myself. As so many do, I found myself doing all kinds of ineffective marketing, talking to all the wrong people, wasting time and throwing good money after bad.

The result was that I lost everything I owned—my car, my house in the Blue Ridge Mountains. I even had to sell my clothes and my jewelry just to put food on the table for my son and me.

The defining moment for me was reminiscent of a scene from *Gone with the Wind*. We had about two hundred acres surrounding our home and I was lying in the field in the fetal position, crying. I was just screaming in pain because I had to give up this home I loved so much. I swore in that moment that I was going to figure out exactly how my connection to this intuitive source would work for me because I knew that it worked for other people.

In my effort to bridge the successful concepts of intuitive guidance for others to myself, I realized that the problem was due to my attachment to the outcomes in my life. Being human, we become so attached to what is going on in our own lives that we find it difficult to discern and then follow the guidance we receive. We sense, we feel, and we connect in many ways to intuitive guidance, but we cannot recognize or trust it because of our attachments.

With this painfully clear understanding of why success was not evident in my own life, and because I never wanted to go through that pain again (and I certainly didn't want that for any of my clients), I determined that I would "work" to create a process we all could use to consciously create unlimited success in every area of our lives.

For approximately two months I spent anywhere from thirty minutes to an hour a day in stillness. I could feel the power and the energy of inspiration and surety. I was actually receiving guidance literally one step at a time for myself. I knew that if I could just find the courage to follow through with everything I was sensing, the previous pain of financial ruin I had endured would be a thing of the past.

So often, we don't want to do what we've been told. We don't want to follow through with our intuition. We're scared of looking foolish, we're in fear of what others will think or do if we change, and we find it so hard to trust ourselves; but I did.

Exactly ninety days later, I had manifested over $575,000! I also had the inspiration that created my tremendously successful coaching certification programs that continue to prosper me today—all from adding this one discipline of connecting to intuitive source and inspiration to my life.

WRIGHT

So what is this intuitive source you talk about?

COFFEY

The intuitive source that I refer to is the life force in all things. People throughout the world know it as many different things; it's the same energy that sustains all of nature without a thought. What makes our heart beat? What makes us breathe? It is this life force—this energy some call God or Spirit. Whatever you call it, it's the same thing. People just use different words to express or define this force. It is greater than ourselves and, as finite beings, we can't quite wrap our minds around it.

In my experience, this intuitive source is a powerful force that is the core, the light, and the wellspring of information, intuition, and inspiration. We are all born with this force within us and the ability to feel, sense, and know intuitively our paths. Somewhere along the line we simply forgot that we are able to tap into it. We somehow allowed our minds to take over, to control our direction, and we don't tap into our soul—into our intuition. My life now

3

is all about bringing people back to this powerful inspiration of intuitive source. When we discipline ourselves to connect at this level, that's where we find all of the answers that bring us joy, happiness, wealth and good health. We just have to tap into it.

WRIGHT

So help me understand how you obtained this connection and, more importantly, can anyone get these kinds of results from connecting to their intuitive source?

COFFEY

The good news is Yes!

I was working in sales and marketing. Like so many other people today, I was working sixty hours a week, burning the candle at both ends. In the end, I became violently ill with chest pains and numbness down my left arm, certain that I was having a heart attack. I went to a hospital and got tested, yet nothing wrong was found. I went home, numb on so many levels, out of breath, and still having chest pains. I finally knelt down in the living room and said, "God, Universe, whatever is out there, I don't know anymore, but I am in pain and I need you now, more than I've ever needed you in my life."

In that moment, I experienced something so strange and foreign to me that I didn't quite grasp what it was. It was as if I heard a voice or very loud thought saying "Go write" as in go write something down. I could barely comprehend what was being said as though there was too much interference in the broadcast. I had to intently listen to make out the words once more telling me to "Go write". I thought I was going crazy! But I continued praying and crying for help, healing, and guidance.

Through the tears and sadness, I heard it again: "Go write something down." This time it was a little clearer, almost as though I was tuning in a little bit more. I continued to ignore it because I thought I was about to have a breakthrough.

Isn't it funny when you think you know what's going on and you really have no idea? I heard it yet a third time, so loud and clear that I stood up. I wondered what in the world was that?

I kept an old notebook by my nightstand and I began writing what ended up being 134 letters. I called it "my letters from God" in the beginning and it became my first book, *Hearing the Voice of Our Spirit*. They were the most beautiful words I had ever heard.

So my experience—my connection—began with a physical illness. What I didn't know then was that everyone has the ability to create this connection with their source or intuition. Over the last eight years since that happened I have been given process after process of how to connect, and I've taught thousands of people to connect to that source and use it to create highly successful businesses and relationships. Not one person has walked away not knowing how to connect. I have a huge smile on my face right now because it is amazing for me to see the results.

WRIGHT

Are there other instances where you used this intuitive source for successful results in your life?

COFFEY

Oh gosh, yes! There are so many. You and I understand that success is defined in different ways, but I know the majority of people look at money and finances as a way to gauge their success.

For me, in this next example, success was both in the listening and the outcome. A couple of years ago, my friend had a beachfront condo in Florida where I wanted to stay. I loved hearing the ocean every night, having the doors open, and being able to go down to the beach and sit in my chair. It fed my soul.

One morning, as I was enjoying my stillness and connection, I got the guidance, "Buy a beach condo." I had to laugh because everybody wants to hear that, right?

"Okay, how am I going to do that?" I asked.

"Find a realtor today and go look."

I didn't have the money to buy a beach condo, but I followed through with my guidance, found a realtor and found the most beautiful beach condo on the ninth floor of a high-rise directly on the Ocean.

"Great! How will I afford this?"

So back into the stillness I went.

I had a small safety net in my IRA of $16,000. As I connected to this intuition I heard exactly, one step at a time, what to do, and I followed it. So often, if we are told the entire plan, we jump into fear and refuse to do what we're guided to do. I have found that it is better to ask only one step at a time. I always use the phrase "what is my next Inspired step in regards to this situation?" I don't look for more; I'm just looking for one. At the end of a week, I have seven solid steps to follow through with. When I follow through, it always leads to massive results and massive results lead to freedom.

So, I was told, "Take the $16,000 out of your IRA as a down payment." Well, in our society we just don't do things like that. That was supposed to be for my retirement. I shouldn't touch it and I would be penalized; but I followed my guidance and I purchased that beachfront condo.

Fast forward six months later, I again heard a voice. Now, I enjoyed the condo, it was wonderful and our family had a great time. This time, however, I heard, "Sell the beachfront condo." I couldn't believe what I was hearing and I didn't want to hear it. I thought, "No! You just told me to buy it and now you're telling me to sell it; this is crazy. No, no, no!"

But I had learned the pain of not following through with my guidance and so I did what I was told. I called the agent in Florida and said, "I'm getting the impression that I need to sell this."

"Well," said the realtor, "prices have absolutely skyrocketed in the last six months and we should have no problem selling it." I was blown away. In two weeks time I had sold it for $160,000 more than what I had paid for it just six months earlier, and exactly ten times the $16,000 I had taken out of my IRA.

I was so grateful. I couldn't believe it. In that moment, what I sensed from my intuition was, "I will be guided to prosper in retirement just as I am now. I don't have to follow societal rules. Follow my inspiration and I will prosper."

This is just one of the many incredible experiences in my life where I was so financially blessed by inspiration I tapped into.

WRIGHT

Now, most people today aren't experiencing this kind of success. I know that you train, coach, and certify others around the world. Will you share with our readers some steps that they can take right away to become successful in their own lives?

COFFEY

Absolutely. My first piece of advice is to begin a daily discipline of connecting with this intuitive source. I call it "Fifteen Minutes to Success."

What that means is to dedicate fifteen minutes minimum everyday to getting still at the beginning of your day.

The first part of this process to make it successful is to have a strong desire to connect to this intuitive source and a belief that you can. So many people believe they can't do it

There are various ways in which you can learn to connect. Lifting our physical vibration is one important aspect of connection. If we can clear ourselves of stress, negative thoughts and emotions, as well as negative things that affect our lives then it's easy to get inspired. My Fifteen Minutes to Success deals with just that, but there's more we can do. We can evaluate our environment and remove those things that are cluttering our lives, remove distractions and noise such as the television, then the lighter and clearer you are and the easier it is to connect. Play some soft music, drink more water, and eat lighter foods so we don't feel as heavy. Add activities and hobbies that you enjoy back into your life. We all let that slide. Buy flowers, enjoy nature, hold your shoulders back and smile at others.

Another key to hearing this intuitive source is to get out in the sunshine and get out in nature. Just take your shoes off, let your feet walk in the sand, or actually walk barefoot through the woods.

Then take fifteen minutes a day to be still, to breathe, and be in the presence of this source. Become as relaxed as you possibly can. Relax your body and close your eyes. Set an intention for your time, to connect with your inspiration and source of intuition. The process I use after I'm relaxed is I imagine that a doorway is in front of me and from around this doorway I can see light emanating. It feels to me like the energy and the light of what I imagine to be God light and it's waiting for me to open the door.

For me it's like being a kid at Christmas. Remember how excited you'd be to open your Christmas gifts? That feeling of anticipation? Well, this doorway is no different. I cannot wait to open that door and feel the immense warmth and power of the light. It's just incredible. And when you're basking in the light just let go of your mind and all your thoughts and concerns. For these fifteen minutes you don't need to worry about anything. It's all handled.

When you connect to this light every day, even if it's only for fifteen minutes, it naturally serves to bring you to your center of balance—your core—allowing you to make clear decisions and glean successful guidance with an amazing amount of clarity, wisdom, and understanding. I urge everyone to stay in this presence for as long as you can to bring more clarity, guidance, success, and happiness into your lives and businesses. Who doesn't want more of that?

The second step in this process is to journal. When I say "journal," I mean write a two-way gratitude letter to the universe—to God source or whatever you want to call it. Begin by writing everything you are grateful for—things you appreciate in your life, what's right in your life, and what's right about you.

Once again you're lifting into a positive mindset. Then simply ask one question and one question only. "Is there any inspiration or next step that you would like to share with me today?" Write down the first thing that comes to mind. This intuition speaks in a way that is very subtle and very soft. There is no booming voice or loud instructions. It's just very simple. So write down the first thing that enters into your mind, whether you think it's true or not, don't sensor, just begin writing. Don't think, write. Don't judge or edit the thoughts, be a scribe only and write.

The third step is to find your passion, find your purpose, and then have fun making money doing it. So many of us have been taught to get a job, stay there, and then we'll have security. Our current economic times have shown us that there is no security in the workplace and in searching for security we've perhaps lost our passion and joy. What I have found is that we can have both! If you're not living a passionate life, one that excites you to be a part of everyday, then your connection will be weak.

Here's another fun process. Think back to a time when it seemed as though you were on top of the world and everything was just clicking. Your decisions were clear and life was fun. Now, reverse engineer your life and start with the fun. That will open up your heart and your mind wide to clear inspiration and success.

WRIGHT

How do you feel about the things that stand in the way of success for most people?

COFFEY

We create blocks culturally and personally. We often do this unconsciously. First and foremost, many people are doing work they dislike in a desperate search for security. How can they give their heart and create a successful income for themselves if they are doing work they don't enjoy—

work that no longer serves them or feeds their sense of excitement and achievement? It's difficult to be happy when your soul wants more out of life. It's difficult to make a greater contribution.

Secondly, what blocks many people from success is not taking a chance and listening to their intuition because of fear. A culture of fear steps in the way. We want to do things our own way because it feels good or feels safe, not allowing the natural progression in our lives. Many people think what they want is the most important thing. However, they often do not realize that what they want is based solely on emotions and judgment, feelings of "I'm not getting enough, this is good, this is bad, this is acceptable, this is not", and their ego, keeping up with the Jones', etc. Based on these feelings they're always pushing and pushing to make things happen to get to their destination. So often, they see their destination, but don't know how to get there. They think, "If I go up here and I take a right, I'll get there, but their intuition says "no take a left," but they're hearing only their own thoughts, not the thoughts of their soul, or intuitive source. They may still get to the destination, but it takes them twenty years vs. one or two. They have yet to learn how to truly hear, so they remain stuck in their perceived path.

If you desire to be successful in relationships, in business, in family matters, in your life purpose, then you must learn to listen to your gut, take a chance, and move away from fear. We fear that we're not going to be able to support our families; we fear that people will judge us and say we're crazy to leave a stable job to do something that seems quite questionable.

To say "That, is what I love—that's what I want to do no matter what others think". That's freedom. People will always find a reason to look at you as though you are crazy. Give them a good reason. Have courage to move through that fear and know that when you live from that place of inspiration you will get where you want to go. If you are living your purpose and passion, then nothing can stop you—nothing. It's when we are trying to do it our own way that we run into brick walls repeatedly. Not connecting, not being clear, and living and acting out of fear are the things that block people the most in truly reaching their success.

WRIGHT

Are there processes you have personally used in partnership with intuitive source that direct your clients and audiences forward to success in their own lives?

COFFEY

Absolutely.

One of the processes I really enjoy doing with audiences around the country is what I call the "Funnel of Life Experiences." Picture a funnel. Everything you've ever done goes into the top of this funnel—every skill that you have, everything that you've ever enjoyed, and the things that absolutely light you up and that you love doing. This is a process of finding your life direction and your life purpose. We all know that our purpose here is to contribute to the world in a loving way and to bring more joy, but life direction is an entirely different animal. So, how do we find that? Well, after adding all the good things, we look at all the difficult experiences we've overcome in our lives—the things that may have been absolute hell to go through—and we accept that we went through them for a reason, perhaps that we now have the ability to help others going through the same thing. So we put in the funnel all of the difficulties we've overcome and all the things we absolutely love about life—what we enjoy and brings us pleasure.

The next step is to ask yourself, "If I had to go on stage and give a presentation in five minutes, with no warning, what could I talk about and what do I love talking about?"

For me, my greatest joy is seeing people succeed financially doing work that they love—I can talk all day about that. I love assisting them one-on-one and in audiences. What comes out of the bottom of my funnel of life experiences is what I love doing more than anything and it's being a Million Dollar Success Coach—it's what inspires me and what jazzes me in the morning when I wake up. It's what keeps me up till three and four in the morning working because I am so excited.

That's just a simple process, and we go more in-depth in our intensives. It's a phenomenal experience for people to walk away knowing exactly what direction they should take and how to prosper from it.

WRIGHT

You love what you do, don't you?

COFFEY

I do. To be able to inspire others and guide them into successful lives and financially thriving businesses and giving them the tools to succeed on their own is extremely rewarding to me. For me, there is nothing better than to see others on fire about the work they're doing in the world and being supported by it through their own connection to that source greater than themselves, guiding them step-by-step to success.

One of the disciplines taught to me by a friend that I do each and every day is to wake up in the morning and say, "Today is an amazing day. I am here and I am ready. How may I be of service and contribute to others today?" It completely changes my mindset and the flavor of my day. Even when I don't feel 100 percent up to it, it still has a great affect on the successful results I attract into my life; and yes, I love what I do.

WRIGHT

One more question for clarification before we go on. How does connecting with intuitive source differ from what I would define as praying? Praying seems to be a one-sided conversation.

COFFEY

Yes, there is an absolute distinction between intuitive connection and prayer. In connection, you go into the experience with the intention of listening. Prayer is most often the intention of speaking and asking for assistance of God. You are asking for help or thanking Him. Often, though, people do not know how to hear the guidance. They are so focused on the requests that they miss the subtle responses.

I believe that's why we've seen a shift over the past few years, instead of saying, "I will pray about this," people are beginning to say, "I will take this into prayer and meditation." They realized that prayer was more focused on speaking than listening. In connection, we get still, with the intention of connecting with all that is—this universal wisdom, intuition,—and we're saying, "Guide Me. I surrender what I think and want and I listen for inspirational guidance only. I allow you to guide my every move because I know therein lies my success."

WRIGHT

So what message would you like to leave with our readers and listeners today?

COFFEY

I would like to leave them with this - Our success in life depends solely on the degree in which we are connecting to this source—this intuitive, inspirational source. We're either allowing the expression of this connection in our life through our prosperity and our loving relationships or we're blocking it with our own agenda. We're either in spirit, which is inspired, or we are without spirit, which is expired or dead. So, from that true source connection comes all of our inspired actions—the very truth of our path, our direction, and expression in life—a blending of physical and spiritual, which is true success.

WRIGHT

What a great conversation. I appreciate all this time you've taken with me to discuss this very interesting subject.

COFFEY

Thank you so much for having me; it's been a pleasure.

WRIGHT

Today we've been talking with Karen Coffey who is the Founder of The Million Dollar Success Circle Programs, the first and only conscious approach to creating six and seven figure business success. In her quest and passion for meaning in her own life she lost everything (her story is fantastic) but she kept her connection to what she calls her intuitive source. This is very easy to understand for her. Perhaps we should try to listen more. Maybe then we could talk about some of the same results she talks about, at least I'm going to try doing this, Karen.

COFFEY

That's wonderful. Make sure you share with me the success stories.

WRIGHT

Thank you so much, Karen Coffey, for being with us today on *Stepping Stones to Success*.

About the Author

Karen Coffey is the Founder and Facilitator of The Million Dollar Success Circle Programs, the first and only conscious approach to creating six and seven figure business success. She is also an internationally sought-after speaker, the author of two books, and the CEO of The Hope of Humanity Foundation. In her quest for passion and meaning in her own life, Karen lost everything but kept her connection to what she calls her intuitive source. In little over a year she went from losing everything she owned to making over a half a million dollars following the guidance and direction of this intuitive connection.

Those desiring to explore this type of connection and experience more success in their lives are invited to contact Karen.

Karen Coffey

13470 Providence Lake Dr
Suite 100
Atlanta, GA 30004
800.240.5602
info@karencoffey.com
www.karencoffey.com

CHAPTER TWO

Leadership is an Inside Job

An Interview with . . . **Ken Jacobsen**

DAVID WRIGHT (WRIGHT)

Today we're talking today with Ken Jacobsen, Founder and President of *CourageWorks, Inc.* Ken is a leadership consultant, executive coach and cultural change facilitator, helping leaders create innovative and high-performing organizations that are magnets for key talent, loyal customers and sustained profitability.

Ken, welcome to *Stepping Stones to Success*. We're asking our guests for their insights and experiences about how to be better, live better, and be more fulfilled in our lives—in business, relationships, indeed, in general. Will you share something that helps evolve this conversation?

KEN JACOBSEN (JACOBSEN)

Well, I'm finally getting clear on something pretty basic—life is one thing: life! We tend to compartmentalize it as if there are different me's. Some examples: me at work, me at home, me bustling down a crowded street, and me away from it all and hitting a crisp nine iron in the Florida sunshine. But they're all aspects of my one life, wherever I am. And the quality of each experience is sourced inside *me*, not by the circumstances or actions of others around me. *I* interpret whether a moment with my friend or spouse is a good one. *I* choose whether work is drudgery or a joyful expression of my gifts and talents. A chilly hailstorm in a Utah canyon can be a rich, soulful experience for me or a miserable day in the elements. It's all how I choose to see it.

Personal mastery is about getting to know that inner source. This is our primary life task. The further we evolve it, the more effortless and fulfilling every situation becomes.

WRIGHT

You make that sound easy, but situations vary widely. When a customer is angry or a reckless driver cuts us off, those are different moments than receiving a child's infectious smile or taking a Saturday hike along the river.

JACOBSEN

Correct. Every circumstance is different, and some are far more challenging than others. We can't escape that, short of dropping out of modern society, which some people actually do. But most of us live in the thick of it—freeways, deadlines, budgets, family matters, and all the rest. So the question becomes, how do we steady the inner waters? And how does doing so influence the outcome of each event, or even bigger, influence the world around us?

WRIGHT

You're using a language we haven't grown up with—each situation's experience is based not on the event itself but according to the inner experience.

JACOBSEN

True, however, it is not new language. It is a re-emerging wisdom, gone dormant perhaps in a fast era of commercialism, technology, and derivatives. This deeper human discussion is returning with increasing force. Just look at the self-discovery aisles in the bookstore, at the number of people going on spiritual retreats and vision quests, and at the growing popularity of meditation and yoga and holistic modalities. More of us are going green, taking volunteer vacations, and finding ways to simplify our lives. All of this reflects a larger shift and is guiding an inner journey people are enjoying again, for the first time in years.

WRIGHT

And the inner journey does what for us, exactly, when a client fires us or the boss is angry because we missed our numbers?

JACOBSEN

Great question. For starters, if we don't mirror the negative energy coming at us in the moment, that allows us to infuse positive energy and constructive dialogue into the situation right when it is needed the most. Every business has its screw-ups and unpleasant situations. We've all been on both ends of that many times. The same is true in our personal relationships. Have you noticed, though, that nothing settles a situation down like calm and genuine truthfulness? Owning our part and exploring what really happened as an effort to be in service goes much further than to blame, alibi, or avoid accountability. As straightforward as that sounds, it isn't easy for most of us. It's challenging to be that way, and it is what I call an "inside job," meaning it's mine and mine only to figure out.

WRIGHT

How do we get there?

JACOBSEN

Everything begins with intention. If we truly intend to embrace this principle in our lives, we can get there . . . with a lot of work, as I'm sure you know. But without that intention, we stay right where we are, repeating our patterns no matter what we might otherwise declare with our words. The critical question is: what's my intention?

WRIGHT

What do you mean by "intention"?

JACOBSEN

Wayne Dyer and others have provided some great insights on this. Let's go with Dyer's primary definition in *The Power of Intention*: "A strong purpose or aim, accompanied by a determination to produce a desired result."

WRIGHT

How important is intention in our lives?

JACOBSEN

Intention is vital to living better, being more fulfilled, and to making a difference in the world. Everyone determines his or her own intentions, in his or her own time. We choose our journey freely, and at different points we make different choices. Some choices move our lives forward, others backward, which is all part of life, really. The more courageous choices are the ones that contradict strong aspects of the life we've lived so far. Giving up an old belief, pattern, or story is no easy task. It takes both humility and resolute intention. As Dyer indicates, it requires strong purpose and determination.

WRIGHT

What moves a person into having a new intention?

JACOBSEN

Sometimes it's a cathartic moment or a life event such as a death or divorce or illness. Other times it's a matter of our natural growth—a shift in our center of gravity from first to second half of life thinking. I've seen people attend a workshop, a retreat, read a book, see a film, and be so inspired that they choose to set a new intention for themselves right then and there. Almost anything can stimulate it. What I am certain of is nobody else can set an intention for us.

WRIGHT

You keep mentioning "choose" and "choice."

JACOBSEN

Yes, if we don't choose to change our lives or any aspect of it, we won't.

WRIGHT

It's that simple? Just choose?

JACOBSEN

On the surface it is, but we're much more complicated beings than that. For starters, we're seldom in a state of true awareness, which means seldom in choice. We're just reacting all the time, almost machine-like, and we don't even know we're doing it. Mention the Yankees, put a certain news station on, bring up a family holiday conversation from 1993, and bam! we're responding the same way we always have. There's virtually no chance in that moment that we'll see life differently. And whaddya know? Most of life is an endless stream of those moments. The stimulus-response game is all we're playing, repeating the same patterns and getting the same outcomes over and over again. We aren't even aware that we aren't even aware of this.

No awareness, no choice. No choice, no intention. No intention, no change. In that pickle, we always get what we always got, and that's only the basic quandary. The larger one is that when we stay in our old story, we usually miss out on discovering our life purpose. Now that's big. Most of us want to make a meaningful difference in life, yet how can we if we aren't living in self-awareness, choice, and intention? The ramifications go beyond our own lives. So many of us are unconsciously darting in and out of the fast lane that the world isn't receiving our deeper gifts. And on a collective level, the planet is struggling for it.

WRIGHT

How do you translate this into your work with leaders?

JACOBSEN

The work we do with leaders relates to anyone's life. We dedicate ourselves to those in positions of influence and authority because they mean so much to so many people and to the overall human story.

We guide leaders to live and serve with greater purpose. The likelihood of success in an organization is enhanced when the leaders are in a more conscious and purposeful state of mind—living in greater awareness of who they are and what they are up to *in action*. This sounds abstract at first, but it's far from that.

The first step is for leaders to explore their core values so they know what matters deeply to them. Then we engage them in an authentic contemplation: how consistently do you actually live your values? Usually this reveals a life of compromise. Does that sound familiar to you and your own life?

The next thing is to identify principles that when practiced not only solidify your values but guide you in every situation, *if you so choose*.

I like to introduce the CASTLE Principles here, from Lance Secretan's book, *ONE: The Art and Practice of Conscious Leadership*. Beware, they sound like motherhood and apple pie, or "everything I need to know I learned in kindergarten" (remember Robert Fulghum's book?). At first glance, these principles can lull us into a false sense of contentment because they sound simple.

Here they are and I encourage you to read Secretan's book to appreciate them fully:

Courage
Authenticity
Service
Truthfulness
Love
Effectiveness

Elementary, right? Well, that's the illusion, or the false sense of it. We impulsively think we already know and live these principles. However, I assure you that any time we compromise our values, which rarely produces a deeply satisfying outcome, one or more of the CASTLE principles is being compromised.

For example, let's say one of your top values is integrity but in order to get through a situation you silently give in to something that doesn't feel right in your gut. Going along may create a "successful" outcome, but not a satisfying one from an integrity standpoint. There are two things to ponder there:

1. Which CASTLE principle did we compromise in that moment? Generalizing for the example, we probably weren't being authentic or truthful, which probably means we weren't being courageous either. That's information we can really use if we're working on being intentional in our lives.
2. Why do we believe we can't achieve the "successful" outcome *without* compromising? Let's reframe that picture and go for what we want by applying our core values and practicing principles that lead to a win-win, meaning success *and* satisfaction.

So in our work, we tie the two together for people: values and principles. The exploration is essentially one of self-awareness. What do I stand for, and more importantly, what am I actually up to about that?

Once we increase our awareness it's a matter of choice: what do I want to do differently to become a stronger and more influential leader? Am I willing to go there? Remember, giving up an old belief or pattern takes humility as well as intention. These are courageous acts—it is easier to choose not to change than to change, which often looks like this: we're too busy, we're in crisis, it's the economy, it's the competition, it's the board of directors, it's other people's actions that are the problem. This is how we avoid change. Stay busy. Stay innocent. It's them, not me. We all do this, and it's all fine, except that it doesn't challenge us with respect to your question: how can we live better and be more fulfilled in our lives?

WRIGHT

How do people respond to all this? It sounds like you push some buttons.

JACOBSEN

They respond with passion! We are all yearning to live more authentically. Once we give each other permission to explore our truth, a burden is lifted. That inspires us to make new choices and change the game together.

WRIGHT

What's next then, after values and principles? It sounds exciting.

JACOBSEN

It's an evolutionary process. Again, what's next relates to each of our lives even though we happen to focus on leaders.

In the values and principles exploration, we get to see the true inner place we've been living and leading from. In that contemplation we can see where we might like that to be, if we reached for something more. There's your gap, where we are versus where we might be. That awareness allows us to make different choices—small or large—and declare our intentions about them. This is where the real work begins. New intentions are motivating and exciting, but as Dyer said they need to be "accompanied by a determination to produce a desired result." To make that easier we draw an even bigger picture. At this point we delve into the north star of our lives: our dreams, passions and life purpose. We help leaders explore the question, why am I here?

By getting above the immediate challenge of the gap and discovering our life purpose, we power the intention by giving it a grander perspective. Indeed, it often helps refine the intention itself. The larger context also releases the feeling that the intention requires yet another act of rigid discipline that we must carry out in our lives. Quite the opposite. This is about inspiration, not obligation. It is remarkably freeing.

WRIGHT

I can see this all takes time to unfold. Do leaders find this exploration a valuable use of their time amid their urgent deadlines and fiscal responsibilities?

JACOBSEN

There's no single answer there. Adopters find it highly valuable, yes. Leaders who take this on and incorporate values, principles, life purpose, and intention into their work lead stronger operations and more fulfilled lives personally. But to answer your question, often this type of leadership exploration doesn't make it onto the corporate calendar. And it is not only a matter of schedule—it isn't given a permission space.

WRIGHT

Doesn't that make sense, though? I mean, the legal and moral responsibility of a corporation is to make a profit for its owners, not bring joy and purpose to its employees.

JACOBSEN

What you are saying is true. What it implies, though, is that being "conscious" while running our businesses will negatively affect the bottom line. Where did we get that idea? We aren't suggesting leaders take even one eye off the financials in this work; we look to reawaken our values, principles, and purpose in service to an *enhanced* bottom line. This occurs through a reawakened culture guided by more conscious leaders.

WRIGHT

Perhaps it's the terms you are using, like "conscious leadership" as an example. Does language like that come across as soft to CEOs?

JACOBSEN

To some CEOs, yes; to others, no. This is new thinking but it is far from odd or impractical. Leaders are professionally and technically proficient; what separates the great ones is how they engage and inspire people.

Plus, we're in transition. The world is changing rapidly. Markets and industries are being reinvented overnight. The economy is on a long road back. We've exhausted accounting techniques like downsizing, outsourcing, and write-offs as a sustaining solution. Demographics and social attitudes are much different than they were even at the turn of the millennium. The old leadership model doesn't work for Gen Y'ers, for example, and Boomers are moving out. All these shifts invite a new brand of leaders.

If you Google topics like Conscious Leadership, Authentic Leadership, Corporate Soul and other similar terms they produce millions of hits. That tells us a lot about what is emerging in the Western leadership conversation.

WRIGHT

Are you saying leaders need to change?

JACOBSEN

Our leaders are smart, hard working, and, except for a few outliers, they have the common good in mind. The question is what will inspire our people next? In every sense the question is new: can we create wealth in a more holistic way? Will people give the hard business response necessary to what initially sounds like a soft invitation? Putting the question into balance, can we build a great organization that integrates meaning and purpose with profitable operations? These are challenging questions for anyone in a leadership position. But they sure are timely, don't you think?

WRIGHT

Yes, they're quite provocative and inspiring. What is your personal dream about all this?

JACOBSEN

What I hope for is to help leaders see the value of an expanded style of leadership and present them with a viable context for making it practical. I also hope to create a permission space for leaders to explore this in what is a compelling time for all of us, business or otherwise.

Jean Houston provides a simple image when she says that we're living in the parenthesis—a *between time* where the old is moving out and a new era is arriving but hasn't settled in yet. This shift is visible all around us.

The question for our times and for us as leaders is what will we do with the moment? We can all feel the shift. What we do next is not only our choice but our responsibility. The idea of the parenthesis might have been viewed with more cynicism a few years ago, but it's presenting a larger conversation for us now. We are alive in a time when the universe has opened an exciting new field of possibility. And in that field we have also been given sobering messages to frame the discussion. September 11, global warming, Madoff, Lay, Kozlowski, Wall Street's serious blow in September 2008, an unhealthy red-blue divisiveness, the BP disaster in the Gulf of Mexico, the extinction of ten thousand species each year, and health care costs bankrupting earnest people. Seriously, what are we doing?

WRIGHT

You seem focused on business leaders in all this.

JACOBSEN

That's my passion. I believe that business and the media are the two institutions that most influence the human story today. My energy, at least in the moment, is directed toward business.

You asked about my dream. Let's paint a big one. Imagine if the CEOs of five of Fortune's top ten multinationals banded together to change the world. Their companies operate in one hundred and fifty countries—their people, products, and services touch millions of communities and billions of human souls every day. While local cultures and conditions vary, their corporate messages are consistent and their business and social practices have tremendous influence on worldwide attitudes, lifestyles, and politics. What if those five giants awakened to the possibility of significantly changing the world for the better?

I believe it's entirely possible that 5 out of 6.7 billion people have the unique opportunity in their roles to create a new human story.

WRIGHT

Isn't that pure idealism? The pressures, complications, politics, and lack of real control these leaders deal with would make your dream more whimsical than viable.

JACOBSEN

Is that really so, or is it that it's never been tried? What we learned on September 11, 2001, is that nineteen people with no clout or position whatsoever can wake up on a Tuesday morning and change the world. In their case it certainly was not in the direction we're pondering here, but the fact remains they did it. Couldn't five CEOs, or nineteen for that matter, create an amazing movement with their tremendous sphere of influence? As Margaret Mead told us, "Never doubt that a small group of thoughtful, committed citizens can change the world. Indeed it is the only thing that ever has."

We become whatever story we tell ourselves. Right now, in the parenthesis, there's a cosmic opportunity to create a new story. And mega-corporations have the reach to hugely influence that if they are so inspired. The story must include profitability and create a healthy global economy, which only makes sense. The question is, can we earn satisfactory profits on a sustaining basis while serving the world with powerful intention?

WRIGHT

That's dreaming big all right. Wouldn't it be amazing if your idea took wind!

Let's bring this back around to this moment though, I'm curious about how can we relate this conversation to the 6.7 billion of us who are trying to live better, be better, and have more success in our lives?

JACOBSEN

Wonderful association. And indeed, it is *the* question. We're all seeking an essential joy and satisfaction in life. That begins with understanding that it's one me—my one life—and wherever I go I am in charge of the inner experience. For most of us, that's a new perspective so we need to both unlearn and learn in order to come to peace with it.

There are endless ways to gain insights and guidance on this, with books, CDs, teachers, coaches, retreats, workshops, quests, and so forth just about everywhere. There is no one way or one guru who knows all, so the wise thing is to learn through as many guides and modalities as possible. Every method and message enters through a different pore, each going to the same inner place through a series of interconnected receptors. The mind hears one thing, the heart another. The body and soul and spirit each listen in their own ways.

Through all of them, find your truth and you will find the joy you seek and deserve.

Once grounded in your truth, if you are driven by a passion to make a difference, go for it! Move toward your life purpose. And for this intention here's a better use of the old adage: size does not matter. Being who you were meant to be, and serving the world in your space by any measure is what absolutely matters. You may be passionate about ending poverty or violence or social injustice. Maybe your desire is to help someone you know gain self-esteem or guide people to financial security or career success. Perhaps your have a deep passion about children, animals, or the environment. Whatever your purpose, it is uniquely yours and has most likely has lived inside you for many years. The world needs it. Your bringing it will fulfill you and those you touch. To quote the Hopi elders, "We are the ones we've been waiting for."

WRIGHT

You paint an inspiring picture for our lives, which we truly appreciate. Will you give us a closing insight, perhaps tying it into the question we're exploring for our readers: how to live better, be better, and live more successful lives?

JACOBSEN

At the core is that life is an inside job. Most of us have bigger dreams and passions within us than we actually go out and live. For whatever reasons, we're waiting for someone else to create the opening or stop doing something we believe is in our way. While we can usually justify and defend that story, it's the very thing that keeps us stuck. We are all free to make new choices. Self-awareness and personal mastery with respect to our values and principles are what lead to us a successful and satisfying life. And from that state of being, every dream is possible.

WRIGHT

Thanks, Ken. This has been an enjoyable and enriching conversation. I appreciate the time you've taken to answer these questions. I believe our readers will learn a lot from what you've had to say.

Thank you for being with us in *Stepping Stones to Success*.

ABOUT THE AUTHOR

KEN JACOBSEN, President of CourageWorks, Inc., helps create high-performing organizations through powerful leadership practices that shape an innovative, collaborative, and highly committed culture, establishing a distinct competitive advantage for your company. He brings more than twenty years of executive experience as president of a health care coalition, senior vice president of an actuarial and human resources consulting firm, executive vice president of a national health insurance administrator, and owner-operator of a consulting company.

Ken is a leadership consultant, executive coach, and cultural change facilitator. His work is dedicated to helping leaders cultivate a climate of innovation, collaboration, and committed action in service to high stakeholder satisfaction and a healthy bottom line.

Ken serves on the faculty of The Secretan Center, a worldwide leadership consulting firm whose cause is to reawaken spirit and values in the workplace. He is a longtime instructor of self-discovery workshops including *Freedom to Be*, and *Discovering Your Life Purpose*. The accumulation of these executive, consulting, and teaching experiences presents a successful business leader who is skillfully practiced at developing and executing visionary strategies, strengthening relationships in service to the bottom line, exploring a deeper purpose to our work, and building cooperative, highly effective organizations.

Ken obtained a degree in Sociology from Merrimack College in Andover, Massachusetts, and completed the acclaimed Executive Program at the University of Michigan in Ann Arbor. In addition to serving as a senior executive for three different companies, he earned a faculty designation at The Secretan Center and has studied at numerous alternative learning organizations, including Your Infinite Life Teaching and Coaching Organization in St. Louis, Missouri; the Center for Inner Knowing in Atlanta, Georgia; and the Animas Valley Institute in Durango, Colorado.

Ken Jacobsen

President & Founder
CourageWorks, Inc.
116 Fish Fever Lane,
St. Simons Island, GA 31522
770-851-3425
ken@courageworks.biz
www.courageworks.biz

CHAPTER THREE

Deliberate Well-being

An Interview with . . . **Fritz Petree**

DAVID WRIGHT (WRIGHT)

Today we're talking with Fritz Petree. Fritz is regarded by the learning and talent management industry as both a thought leader and strategist. He has spent nearly twenty-five years building personal learning and development programs for his employers and clients. During the course of his career, companies such as RadioShack and Southwest Airlines have looked to Fritz for help. He has evaluated, designed, and implemented personal development learning programs and maps that have served as a foundation for strategic plans ranging from changing corporate culture to boosting customer satisfaction.

As the Founder of DeliberateMind®, Fritz serves as an advisor and architect for individuals who want to take control of their learning and their life. He has been a guest speaker at The American Society of Training and Development, Chief Learning Officer Magazine's Annual Symposium, The Human Resource Management Association, and the Training Directors' Forum.

Fritz, welcome to *Stepping Stones to Success.*

FRITZ PETREE (PETREE)

Thanks, David; I am very happy to be with you today.

WRIGHT

So what do you consider the most important component of success?

PETREE

Being deliberate and intentional about one's direction is what leads to success, thus, my company is called, DeliberateMind. It's all about achieving consistent success by taking the initiative and being intentional about your learning process. That is what I do and that is what I teach.

WRIGHT

Would you tell our readers what it means to be an "intentional learner"? How can someone become a more intentional learner?

PETREE

There are two primary components: desire and initiative. Before I discovered that, though, I had worked for many years with two assumptions about learning. The first assumption was that people really wanted to learn, and the other was that they knew how. After several years, I found out that both of those were probably not as true as I believed them to be. So I made a shift in direction and I began asking two questions: "What can we do to help someone be an intentional learner?" and "What are the attributes that make someone intentional?"

An intentional learner is an individual who has a desire to learn. Intentional learners apply their learning to their goals and they're going to take initiative to determine whatever their requirements are. They're going to set motivating and specific goals, they'll identify and assess the resources that are going to be most useful in reaching their goals, and they'll implement and measure their own progress.

That's the process framework of what it takes to be intentional. But over the years we found, more specifically, that there are characteristics or attributes that describe someone who is intentional. These include initiative, inquisitiveness (not just curiosity but really finding information to help you reach your goals), perseverance, ambition, having a learning plan, and engaging others in the learning. Engaging others means that the learner wants to discuss with others about his or her learning.

Intentional learners also desire a sense of completion—they'll want to reach for their learning goal. In addition, we found that they're traditionally more positive and optimistic about the learning outcome, and their life in general.

WRIGHT

So having more than twenty-five years of experience helping people and organizations, what experiences or people have influenced you?

PETREE

My parents were a major influence; they both supported my inquisitiveness and my desire to learn. I was blessed, at fifteen years old, when we moved to Dallas next door to the coach of the Dallas Cowboys, Tom Landry. We had many conversations over the years. I interviewed him for school newspapers and I really learned what it meant to be a coach and, more importantly, the difference between being a coach and a mentor.

Landry was a fabulous coach; he was a coach's coach. He taught me that a mentor is somebody you would want as a role model. Among the things that I learned from him was that people come first, and you play to people's strengths. You provide good, solid, and specific feedback and, without judgment, you encourage and acknowledge successes. He also provided learning tools, and went out of his way to make sure that the players had all the tools they needed to have the edge that made them so successful.

There are a couple of other people who have influenced me. Malcolm Knowles is one. Knowles is considered the father (or by some the grandfather) of adult learning. He separated the notion of what distinguishes how an adult learns from how a child learns. Adults want to contribute to the learning environment; they want to be participants. But most importantly, they need relevance to their lives. Adults want learning activities that are relevant to themselves, their personal growth, interests, and their job.

Ned Herrmann is another person who's influenced me. I worked with him in his organization in the 1990's, he is the creator of the Herrmann Brain Dominance Instrument. That instrument helped me understand the connection between the mind, brain, and learning and how all those pieces work together.

And, most recently, Frederic Hudson also had a significant impact on me. He founded the Hudson Institute of Santa Barbara, California, and he's also a preeminent coach. He's one of the finest coaches that you'll ever find. I went through a year-long master's level program with him to find out what it really means to be a coach.

What I learned from Tom Landry, Malcolm Knowles, Ned Herrmann, and Frederic Hudson became the foundation that got me started. From that starting point, I have honed and refined my skills, leaping several paradigms forward into new dimensions of optimal learning. The brain science of neuroplasticity did not exist until recently. Today, we know so much more about learning, behavior, and the brain.

WRIGHT

Your experience includes almost ten years with Southwest Airlines. Southwest is known for having a positive culture and a focus on employees. How did working for Southwest change the way you think about learning?

PETREE

Southwest is an incredible company. I've worked with Motorola Communications, Microsoft, RadioShack and a lot of other organizations as both a contractor and employee. But at Southwest Airlines, their learning environment is completely connected to the culture of the company. It's an optimistic culture that encourages authenticity. When people are positive and light-hearted in their work environment, this attribute of being yourself really comes out. And that's what people really love about working for Southwest. It's a very altruistic culture that modeled for me the benefits of really playing "team." My years at Southwest Airlines proved to me that contributing and being of service is the most beneficial thing you can do at any level in an organization.

There is a story about Herb Kelleher (former CEO and President of Southwest Airlines) going to the parking lot and seeing someone needing a tire changed; He immediately started helping out. Even during busy times, Herb will help load bags on the airplanes. Service is really a key component to the success of Southwest. I was fortunate in my learning to be the designer of their career development program. For almost a decade, I coached hundreds of people every year. It was amazing. The real benefit and lesson for me was how the organization let us coach people without a tight focus on the ROI or what they're going to give back to the company. They just allowed us to coach and help people the best we possibly could because they wanted to do the right thing to support the employee.

WRIGHT

You believe that real success is achieved from intentional learning and deliberate actions, but it's getting more difficult to stay focused with so many distractions and changes in our lives. What can help us manage this overwhelming overload of demands and conflicting priorities?

PETREE

To help people prevent and manage the information overload of today, DeliberateMind developed a special version of the mind map—a concept popularized in the 1980s. Our methodology quickly brings to life a multi-dimensional map of your business strategy, your projects, or your life. It is graphic, it is clear, and it is very holistic in its nature to inspire and deliver solutions. These maps are sophisticated tools to create different layers and action items. We use the maps to help organize and group, not only all of the demands that you have, but also the goals and the directions that you want to go.

People can be so cluttered with so many distractions and things on their mind. We use the DeliberateMind map to help filter out the noise. Our minds create thoughts that we desire to manifest in the real world. We map individual, team member, or family members' interest as a way to collect and unify their thoughts to clarify what they want to accomplish.

Mind maps are the most effective way I've found to coach people by getting all their thoughts on a page and quickly be able to realize what's clutter and what's really helping them reach their goals.

WRIGHT

So what are the steps to creating a deliberate mind map?

PETREE

The first step is to just collect what's on your mind. The first session we do is typically an hour to an hour and a half; it's just inquiry. The first question is: "What's on your mind?" We pay a lot of attention to what shows up first because it's many times the most important.

Next, we sort these thoughts into major branches or themes. The person we're working with might mention family, relationships, spiritual growth, and educational growth as well as career, work goals, or specific projects. As we start to organize the thoughts into each of these categories, we can draw a map that is very specific to the individual.

Then we'll group all the thoughts over time and create a technical map on the computer. Using the map, we begin to organize and prioritize life themes. Each of the sections of the map will reveal what's most important and specific steps to achieve these priorities. When priorities are ranked by importance, the focus becomes clear and builds momentum to foster successful completion.

The end product is a map that clearly displays the goals with their major categories and branches of related activities and ideas. The final touches are specific action items to help reach the most important goals. At the end of each branch of the map are action items with designated dates and deadlines to keep the project or life goal moving forward.

WRIGHT

Can we use these maps to manage all the activities in our lives?

PETREE

Yes! Maps are helpful in reaching any goal or destination that is significant. For routine activities such as household chores or shopping lists, these detailed maps are not necessary. Any activity that would contribute to your goals and to your vision would be appropriate to map. Capturing them on the map keeps you focused. They're similar to a blueprint that provides a clear vision on how to build your house. It includes components of your desires, as well as the path to get you there.

WRIGHT

That's interesting.

Sometimes people seem to give up on goals and resolutions easily. How can people stay committed when they get discouraged because they don't have the ability or the activity doesn't motivate them?

PETREE

That problem quickly melts away. Our learning and change-management tools help people look at each task and immediately determine whether or not they're going to take action. When your personal ability meets a challenge and the level of your ability meets that level of challenge, then you're in the flow and you're likely to take action. It's easier to get engaged in activities where this sense of flow and energy is carrying you to your goal.

To help get people engaged with their goals, we teach them how to reformat their map when the challenge seems greater than their ability. To ignore this problem is to invite failure by putting off actions because they seem too overwhelming. To overcome this, we include strategies for developing resources and lifelines that can overcome any potential delay, before it happens. Our clients stay deliberately on task and learn to meet their deadlines with ease.

At the other end of the spectrum is where someone's ability is much higher than the challenge. That is when complacency can set in. In those instances, one can develop an apathetic view of the activity and lose the "energy" associated with "flow." Thus, you're not going to feel that it's something you really want to engage in and the task may never happen. So on those activities, we can either increase the likelihood of success by setting deadlines or increase the level of complexity for the task.

We can also realign the work to more clearly match the vision so that there is more of an intrinsic motivation to get the activity done. When you manage individual activities in this way, you can easily make a determination as to whether the ability is high enough to meet the challenge of the activity and, if not, go back to the map—back to the drawing board, so to speak.

I need to get personal for a moment. When hard-working, intelligent people start making their goals consistently, something wonderful happens in their family. The family gets their mother or father back. No longer distracted and stressed about office matters, they become more present and available to the needs of their family at home. Great family life further enhances productivity and creativity at work. That is why I do what I do. It is good for you and your family to have a deliberate mind.

WRIGHT

Absolutely.

You have worked extensively within organizations to create learning cultures, so what is the benefit to organizations for employees to develop maps and be deliberate about their learning?

PETREE

When employees start to have a better life at home and at work, their heightened sense of achievement and insight builds their self-esteem. Thus, the return on this investment for organizations is unending and ever-expanding.

Today, the corporate culture places a high value on employee retention, engagement, and productivity. My clients want to insure that their company can compete in that environment as well. The whole DeliberateMind program not only increases productivity but also customer service and engagement. Employees feel more confident when they're learning; they have a competent confidence. If an employee is engaged in his or her job, then performance and flow is going to be much higher. That is measurable and there are studies demonstrating the importance and business return of engagement. But engagement also implies a sense of loyalty associated with it, so turnover will decrease as your employee engagement increases. Families, of course, love this as well.

The Gallup Q12 survey verifies the importance of this kind of engagement with employee comments such as, "I have an opportunity to learn and grow; my leader encourages my development; my natural ability and skills align to the job position I have."

WRIGHT

I can sense that you are really passionate about being deliberate and intentional, so what drives your passion?

PETREE

What drives my passion is seeing people taking initiative and being deliberate, not only about their own development and their own lives, but in being able to help in their communities and to help with issues we are facing on our planet right now.

What drives me is seeing people who might not have otherwise taken initiative, stepping up and taking action because we're providing them the tools; we're providing them insight and encouragement to be deliberate about the things that are important in their life. My favorite quote from Gandhi is that you must be the change you wish to see in the world. We want to support that with very solid tools, methodologies, and action. As far as I know, the tools we provide are the only person-centered, activity-specific ones that exist for a program like ours.

WRIGHT

You quoted Gandhi who said that you must be the change you wish to see in the world. What change do you wish to see in the world?

PETREE

I asked my eleven-year-old daughter, Lydia, and fifteen-year-old daughter, Hana, this very question. Hana wants to rid the world of hatred. She wants to rid hatred and tension because of the discord it creates for families and cultures, for me that was incredibly inspiring. Then I asked Lydia, and she said, "I want to see peace in my world," and I was touched.

My passion is to provide the tools to fuel people's passion, to reveal that passion, and to help them achieve their goals in life.

But there is much more. There are issues with our planet's natural resources and there are healthcare challenges related to nutrition and obesity, healthy lifestyles and sustainable solutions. DeliberateMind is helping a wide range of organizations with finding solutions to these vital problems.

WRIGHT

This interview will be featured prominently in our book *Stepping Stones to Success*. What are your final thoughts about helping others achieve success?

PETREE

First, no matter what the scope is of what you want to do, you are the change that you wish to see in the world. Recently, President Barack Obama said, "Change will not come if we wait for some other person, or some other time. We're the ones we've been waiting for. We are the change that we seek."

This is the time to take initiative and not just talk about the things we want to see change in the world. Take action, create a map, and know where you're going. Have a clear direction of what drives your passion and have action steps so that you can know you are making progress. Be fully present, be fully alive, and care deeply for the life that you have.

WRIGHT

Well, I really have enjoyed this conversation. I have really learned a lot. You have opened my mind to some things I haven't thought about in a while. I really do appreciate it, and I know our readers will.

PETREE

You're very welcome.

WRIGHT

Today we've been talking with Fritz Petree. Fritz is the Founder of DeliberateMind. He serves as an advisor and architect for individuals who want to take control of their learning and their life. He has evaluated, designed, and implemented personal development and learning programs that serve as the foundation for strategic plans ranging from changing corporate culture to boosting customer satisfaction.

Fritz, thank you so much for taking this time with me to answer all these questions. I'm really glad that you are with us in *Stepping Stones to Success*.

PETREE

Thank you so much; it's been an absolute pleasure. I am honored to share the vision and unlimited possibilities of DeliberateMind.com with your audience.

About the Author

FRITZ PETREE, regarded by the learning and talent-management industry as both a thought leader and strategist, has spent nearly twenty-five years building top-flight training and development programs for his employers and customers. During the course of his career, companies such as RadioShack and Southwest Airlines have looked to Fritz for help. Fritz has evaluated, designed, and implemented learning technology that served as the foundation for strategic plans ranging from changing corporate culture to boosting customer satisfaction.

As founder of Petree & Associates LLC, Fritz serves as an advisor and architect for clients of all sizes wanting to build and promote a learning culture across their organizations. As someone who is keenly aware of the major shifts as well as the nuances affecting workers today, Fritz has counseled senior-level executives on ways learning and development affects technology, culture and business.

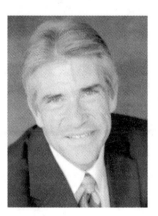

FRITZ PETREE

DeliberateMind
3358 St Cloud Circle
Dallas, TX 75229
214.366.3664
fritz@deliberatemind.com
www.deliberatemind.com

CHAPTER FOUR

Drop and Give me 20 . . . Pounds!

An Interview with . . . **Jay Kerwin**

DAVID WRIGHT (WRIGHT)

Today we are talking with Jay Kerwin. Jay is the owner and lead drill instructor at Boot Camp L.A. in Los Angeles, California, which has been recognized as one of the most successful fitness programs in the United States. Jay and Boot Camp L.A. have been featured on Discovery Channel's *FitTV*, ABC's *Extreme Makeover*, The Fine Living Channel, *Good Day LA*, *CBS News*, *ABC News*, and most recently recognized by Associated Press TV. Jay has been a leader in the fitness and personal training arena for more than twelve years. He proudly lives what he teaches and has become a champion in natural bodybuilding competitions.

Jay Kerwin, welcome to *Stepping Stones to Success*.

JAY KERWIN (KERWIN)

Thanks for having me, David.

WRIGHT

Jay let's start with a question I know a lot of people have and that's the stomach. I do a lot of sit-ups, but it doesn't seem to make the fat on my stomach go away. What is that all about?

KERWIN

Well, I can appreciate what you're saying and it's so common for men as well as women to ask me this question. The answer is if you want to lose fat in any particular area, you can't hone in and focus on that one area by using the muscle that happens to be underneath the fat. You have to lose fat all over your body and that is all related to changing your diet. The fat will leave from that particular area when it's ready to, but basically our bodies have different areas that it likes to store fat in. It's very common for men to store fat in their midsections and for women to store fat in their hips and their thighs.

When you gain fat, you can't really tell the fat where to go to and it's the same when you lose fat—you can't tell it where to leave from. Simply put, when your body has too much food to process, it turns that excess food into fat; it puts it wherever it likes to put it, and basically stores it somewhere for the future. Some people have no fat on their thighs but they have a lot of fat on their bellies, and some people have exactly the opposite. Looking at ourselves in the mirror is the easiest way to tell where our bodies seem to like to store our fat.

When it comes to "spot reducing" fat, think of it this way: If I put clay on top of your stomach muscles and you do a bunch of sit-ups, the "clay" is not going to just melt away because the muscles underneath are being used. Another way to think about it is if you're doing push-ups and I sit on your back, I'm really just along for the ride going up and down with you as you do all the work—I'm not going to be affected by the push-ups you are doing.

Your body will only get rid of stored fat if it really knows that you're going to be eating more consistently and using the calories in the stored fat to get you through your workouts.

You'll often see people working out on machines that are obviously meant to reduce the size of the area that they are working, like their hips or especially their midsections. It's just not going to happen. In the same way, doing side twists or side bends does absolutely nothing to get rid of the fat in your "love handle" area. You can twist and shake all you want, the same way you could twist and shake a jar of mayonnaise, but unfortunately, it will do nothing to reduce the amount of mayonnaise in the jar.

WRIGHT

Those abs machines that I see on television look like they are really effective. Do they work?

KERWIN

I know; I find myself watching those infomercials and I can see why people would fall into the trap of thinking "Wow, maybe that *does* work." So the ads are doing their job effectively. It is said that most people will buy three weight loss items in their lives—whether they are meant to electrify, shake, or melt the fat away.

I often test people in my fitness program by saying that I discovered the secret to losing weight—you have to jump up and down twenty-two times right before you go to bed and this will speed up your metabolism because it makes your adrenal glands work while you are sleeping. Some participants will say, "Really?" Then I let them know that I was just kidding. It's a way for me to prove how easy it is to convince people there is a magic way to lose weight, but there isn't. You can actually stop doing sit-ups altogether and still lose fat from your stomach area. It's all about changing your diet to speed up your metabolism to turn your body into a fat-burning machine.

WRIGHT

Is it true that you should use light weights with high repetitions to tone up, and heavy weights with low repetitions to bulk up?

KERWIN

That's another common myth people believe and basically, unless you are taking anabolic steroids, you're never going to rapidly gain ten or fifteen pounds of muscle—a person would be lucky to gain four or five pounds of muscle in a whole year.

I am a natural bodybuilder, which means I don't take steroids or human growth hormone. So you can imagine that it's much harder for me to gain muscle. Last year I was able to gain four pounds of muscle and it was a result of lifting up to three or four hundred pounds of weight on some exercises.

When it comes to lifting weights, I believe that unless you are warming up or are injured, it's pretty much a waste of time to use light weights because there is no reason for your body to change. Why? Because your muscles are not being challenged. Now, of course, the word "heavy" is a relative term. What may seem heavy to you may not seem heavy to me. I always say that the only weightlifting sets that are going to change the way you look are the ones where you have a "Struggly" face. If you can easily lift the weight that you're making your muscles lift, why would your muscles have any need to get stronger?

When it comes to the question about toning up, it's important to understand that you can't tone fat. Fat is fat and muscle is muscle. You can't turn fat into muscle; they are two totally different materials. You can, however, be toning or strengthening the muscle underneath with exercise, but you'll never see the results you're getting until you get rid of the fat on top of the muscle, which, of course, is a result of changing your diet. Additionally, if you just use light weights and do high repetitions during your workouts, it's not really going to cause that much of a change because your body is already able to do what you are asking it to do—your body only changes as a survival mechanism.

Let me explain this further. When it comes to working out, what usually happens is people fall into the rut of doing the same exercises over and over. They become efficient at doing these exercises and there is no reason for their body to change because it has already adapted to the movement. In the end, you have to keep challenging your muscles and keep doing different movements in order for your body to keep changing and progressing, which should be the goal of all people when they exercise, don't you think? You don't want to go to the gym every day and workout really hard and not see any changes for your effort, do you?

I teach people that they should look different week after week and if they are not, then something is wrong and they need to assess and change their workout and eating plan. That's also why it's important to weigh, measure, and body fat test yourself every few weeks. If you don't feel like doing that, then take a picture of yourself and again, after a few weeks, the results of your efforts should be pretty easy to see. Don't just step on the scale and look at how much you weigh; you want to make sure you are losing fat instead of muscle. A lot of times people say to me that their bodies are changing but they haven't lost any weight and maybe it is because they are gaining muscle, which is why they weigh the same. No, if you are losing fat, you should be weighing less. There is no way to lose fat and replace it with the same amount of muscle. It's practically impossible.

I think the whole idea of toning up muscles was invented because back in the day, when mostly men went to gyms, the owners of these gyms would say, "How can we get more women to come to the gym? They don't want to become big and bulky like male bodybuilders, so we'll tell them that if they lift light weights, it won't make them bulky—it will give them long, lean muscles." I still hear that information on fitness infomercials, "These exercises won't bulk you up—they will give you long, lean muscles like a swimmer."

The truth is, there aren't really any exercises designed to give you long, lean or short, bulky muscles. When you lift weights you are either sending a signal to your muscles that they need to change and become stronger or you are just telling them that they need to stay alive or maintain, which is what happens when you lift light weights—you send a signal for the muscle to stay the same. When you really use a muscle and "beat it up" as I say, then you are telling your muscles that they are not strong enough and you need them to recover and come back stronger than before.

I often see people doing small, intricate movements with weights that seem to hone in on one very small muscle group. These are called "finishing movements." It is almost like they are thinking that they need to do these small movements to achieve cuts or definition in those areas. I tell them that if they do big, heavy movements like the bench press, squats, or pull-ups, it will all be taken care of. You don't have to focus so much on the little stuff.

WRIGHT

So how many times a day should I be eating and what should I be eating?

KERWIN

That's a great question; let me answer that with an analogy. If you went camping and you made a campfire, you would want to get it going as soon as possible with some sticks and some newspaper. But if you overload it with two or three big logs, it takes a while for it to get going and will not burn as quickly.

I want people to avoid putting one huge "log" (meal) on the fire and then adding on another one later in the day. A lot of people will only eat one or two big meals a day. What I want to teach people to do is to eat more often throughout the day. First things first—get the fire going by adding a small load of kindling made up of some sticks, and some newspaper. Then, once the fire starts dwindling down, you have to be prepared to add to it another small load of kindling. Your goal is to have a nice hot fire, burning all day long. You don't want it to burn out and you also don't want to smother it. In this analogy, the sticks would be protein and the newspaper would be carbohydrates.

A lot of times people will only eat carbohydrates, which is like throwing newspaper on a fire—it just goes up into a big flame and then it rapidly goes back down. The sticks—the protein—help you to equalize the fire and this will make it last longer. Every two or three hours, you should be eating small, nutritious meals consisting of protein and good carbohydrates. Think about the campfire analogy—you want to get it going as soon as you wake up and you want to keep that fire burning hot all day long.

Once your body's metabolism (fire) gets going, you have to keep feeding it to keep it burning. So the goal is to never let the fire go out and never overload it.

It is all too common for people to believe that the way to lose weight is to skip meals and learn to live with hunger pangs. You'll see a friend and say, "Hey, do you want to get some lunch?" He or she will say, "No, that's okay. I'm on a diet. I need to lose weight." But, not eating is like holding your breath underwater. When you finally do come up for air, you are going to be taking in a lot of it.

Studies have shown that in one day of not eating enough food, you can lose one pound of muscle or more. To get back that pound of muscle, it can take almost two months of proper diet and rigorous weight training and proper rest. So the odds are really against you if you do any type of crazy diet or fasting to try and lose weight. You're only setting yourself up for a long road ahead, and that's just to catch up to where you were before, not to get better.

If I had figured this out years ago, I could have saved myself so much time and effort. I wrestled my whole life and I grew up thinking that if you want to lose weight you've got to work out like crazy and sweat the weight off and not eat too much. Sadly it was not uncommon for me to work out at wrestling practice for two hours and lose ten pounds and go home and only eat an orange for dinner!

People have the tendency of looking at the scale too much. When they see results, they think, "Hey, I lost ten pounds in two weeks!" I would question this by asking, "Ten pounds of what?" You've really got to keep track of whether you are losing fat or muscle.

Recently, a female participant at Boot Camp L.A. told me that she had lost sixteen pounds by dieting. After testing her body fat, I had to inform her that she had not been eating enough and that she had actually lost a lot of her hard-earned muscle. I explained to her that she should not try and beat the system. I told her that she had to eat smaller meals every two or three hours and that she would still lose weight, maybe not as fast, but she would be losing fat and not muscle. She did what I suggested and she eventually lost over fifty pounds in about seven months! When people lose only fat from their body instead of fat *and* muscle, they end up looking and feeling so much healthier.

WRIGHT

Let's say we have some readers who are injured and can't run, what else can they do to help themselves lose weight?

KERWIN

Anything you do that gets your heart rate going is going to help you burn calories, even if you have to sit down and do it. If you broke both of your legs, you could still sit and move your arms up and down in different directions and get your heart rate up. So there is always something you can do to burn calories.

One of the best things you can do to burn calories without running at all would be swimming, because it burns a lot of calories and there is very little, if any, impact on the joints and bones. But be prepared—swimming is very challenging when done properly. Of course, you could just float around in the pool and wonder why you are not losing weight or you could change your body by challenging yourself and swimming from one end of the pool to the other repeatedly.

What I have clients who come to me with injuries do, if their injuries allow, is walk and do little spurts of jogging for fifteen seconds, just to get them back in the swing of moving again. I have found that it's is not always an injury that keeps people from running; the reason can often be psychological. Believe me, if you were crossing the street and a bus was coming at you, you'd run (or at least I hope you would)!

A lot of people don't think they can run because they are afraid they're going to get out of breath. Everyone who runs gets out of breath. If you just get out there and challenge yourself and try a little harder each time, you'd be surprised at how fast you will see improvements in your breathing and changes in the way you look and feel.

Walking does have many benefits, but I see people all the time in the gym walking too slow on the treadmill. I really feel like asking them to speed up a little bit and challenge themselves. Their heart rate is approximately ninety beats per minute, which is really not going to make them get in better shape. Granted, they are burning calories and it is better than sitting on the couch. But if you're going to drive to the gym or if you're going to get your workout clothes on and go outside and work out, why not challenge yourself a little bit? You'll feel good about what you're accomplishing instead of just doing the minimum, such as walking two miles an hour and not even getting out of breath.

I have an eighty-year-old client who walks three and a half miles an hour for two miles—and that is *before* we lift weights in the gym together! That gives us all something to compare ourselves with. She is inspiring many by her strength and determination.

WRIGHT

Are there any diet pills out there that actually work?

KERWIN

I believe that if a diet pill came out on the market that *really* worked, Oprah Winfrey would feature it on her show. Currently, there really is no magic pill or magic fat-melting exercise machine. Marketing executives know that many people are looking for the easy way out and that is why they are always advertising miracle diet pills and potions.

Changing your body takes some dedication and work. If people would pay attention to what time they ate last and when they are going to eat again, and make good decisions when they do, they would start seeing changes in their bodies right away. You can't expect full-time results from part-time work. And you can't expect to eat whatever you want and just take a pill and think you are going to lose weight.

Once I start eating my first meal, I note the time on my watch. I then know how long it will be until I eat again. So if you asked me, "Do you want to get some lunch?" I would say something like, "Well, I ate an hour and forty-three minutes ago and I ate a two-hour portion of food, so yes, in seventeen minutes I'll be hungry; let's go eat." This is the way I always keep track of when I'm going to be hungry next. People don't usually stop to think, "I ate this much food this many hours ago, and in this amount of time I should be hungry." It's more common for them to be hungry for hours on end with no real thought of when they are going to eat again until they feel like they are starving.

The body only asks you for food for a certain amount of time before it goes into survival mode, which means it will get food from within (your muscles) and start storing fat because it doesn't know how long it will be until you feed it again. If somebody tells you, "I'll pick you up at 10:00 in the morning, be in front of your house," when the time comes and no one comes by to pick you up, and then 11:00 rolls around and still no one has come, you're pretty much going to figure out that the person is not coming and you've got to figure out some other way to get a ride. Your body has to do the same thing.

Your muscles are like steaks and your fat is like the fat on the end of a steak. When your body has to live off itself because you didn't feed it, it's going to eat away at the steak (muscles) because steaks are full of proteins, vitamins, and nutrients. The fat is just energy and your body will burn a little bit of that, but mostly it's going to eat away at your muscles. So when you don't eat, you will weigh less, but, as I mentioned before, it will come from a loss of both muscle and fat.

WRIGHT

I have friends who use trainers and they speak very highly of them. I've considered doing that a few times, but I've always thought my form was pretty good. Do you think I should hire a trainer?

KERWIN

Having a good trainer is a great way to go, but to be honest, the hard work is up to you during the hours of the day when you are left to make your own decisions (i.e., choosing what to eat and what not to eat). You have to discipline yourself to make the right decisions all day long—your trainer can only guide you. Your trainer isn't going to cook for you and force you to eat all the correct portions and selections. Thinking you will see magic results from one hour of exercise, when you have the whole rest of the day to eat high calorie food is not realistic at all, no matter how hard the workout is or how expensive the trainer is. Seventy percent of changing your body is going to be the result of your food choices and the timing of your meals.

That being said, if possible, I usually recommend that people hire a trainer at least a couple of sessions to learn proper form when lifting weights and to get a workout plan written out for them. Then it's a good idea to revisit the trainer after a few weeks to change up your workout routine. You have to consistently change the way you use your muscles, which means you can't do the same workout over and over again.

I believe that having proper form when exercising can greatly affect the results you get. When I really started to get into learning about personal training, fitness, and exercise, I learned the importance of how each exercise works and how it's designed to improve various muscles.

In addition to good form, you should know what the exercise is going to accomplish before you set the amount of weight you are going to use on that movement. When I lift a particular weight up and down, I know which muscles are working and how they are being used. You should have a good idea about what is happening when you are lifting weights. It doesn't mean that you have to have a doctorate in physiology, but you should know where you are going to feel the movement before you start doing the exercise.

Before you hire a trainer it would be best to go to your gym, do your workout, and watch the trainers; it's almost like you are auditioning them. Are they sitting around on the phone texting people or are they really paying attention? A really good trainer is always watching, always following the form, isn't afraid to stop the client and say something like, "Wait a minute. This is wrong. I want you to do it like this. This is where you should feel it. Here is what you're doing, but this is how I want you to do it."

If you cannot afford a trainer, there are many books and videos out there that can help you. Also, I tend to notice that when I am training people at the gym, there is usually someone on the machine next to us listening and giving the "Now I understand" expression. This is one of the main reasons my wife, Marcella, and I started Boot Camp L.A. It was a great way for us to teach proper form and good nutrition to a large group of people all at the same time.

WRIGHT

What do you think about my cutting calories way down to help me lose weight?

KERWIN

That's a common myth that a lot of people believe.

Everyone always thinks more is better, meaning that if cutting calories a little helps you lose weight, then cutting calories a lot will make you lose even more weight. What you should really do is figure out how many calories you burn on a daily basis by taking your body weight and multiplying it times thirteen for men and eleven for women. Of course it would be higher if you worked in a job that required a lot of use of your muscles, such as construction work, compared to someone who is sedentary. The number you get from using this formula is about how many calories you need a day in order to lose weight. Going any lower than that would not be healthy for you.

A good way to understand the whole calorie concept is to imagine you have a hot air balloon floating across the sky and it takes two thousand pounds of hot air to keep it up in the air. Now, if you cut the hot air pressure by a thousand pounds, then basically that hot air balloon is going to be sinking fast and the pilot is going to do what he has to do to keep it aloft. He will take all of the heavy items out of the basket including the heavy sandbags and start throwing them over the side so that the balloon won't crash to the ground.

This is what your body would do if you cut your calories too much. It would get rid of the heavy stuff, which in this case would be your muscles.

I can't stress enough the importance of maintaining your hard-earned muscles. The more muscle you have, the more calories you can afford to eat. This is a great way to understand why two different people who weigh about the same can eat the same amount of food and one of them will gain weight and the other will stay the same or even lose weight. The reason is because one has built up muscle mass and the other person has a higher percentage of body fat.

It is a good idea for you to be knowledgeable about the amount of calories there are in the meals you commonly eat. You may be surprised to learn how many calories are in that portion of food you find yourself eating on a regular basis. Also, many times when I talk to people about portion sizes, they are way off on their thinking of what a good portion is. I usually say that whatever you think is a good portion size, cut that in half and that is more like the correct portion. I am not saying you have to walk around with a calculator and a food scale, but you should have a good idea of how many calories you should have at each small meal and how many you are actually having. Remember that you take your total allowable calories and cut them up into small one- to three-hundred-calorie portions made up of protein and good carbohydrates, depending on how many times a day you eat.

Also, be careful when it comes to soft drinks because they do nothing to take away your hunger and they pack a lot of calories. This also includes coffee drinks and at the top of the list is "alcohol!" If you go out drinking, you can set yourself back a few days with only a couple of drinks. On the other hand, small, positive changes can add up to a lot over a week. For example, order your salad with dressing on the side, choose chicken or fish instead of steak, and have water as your drink of choice—yes, only water!

WRIGHT

Will you teach me some basic rules to follow when I exercise?

KERWIN

Yes. The first basic rule I teach is that you should have confidence when you are working out—you should look like you know what you're doing. You should be standing up tall or sitting up straight, your chest should be out, your feet and legs should be well placed, and every movement you do should have a slow part and a fast part.

The slow part would be considered the easier part of the exercise. For example, for bicep curls: if you hold the weights down by your thighs and you curl them up toward your shoulders, that's the hard part. The easy part is lowering them back down to your thighs. So if lowering the weights back down is the easy part, then what you want to do is to let them fall back down slowly—twice as slow as you brought them up. This will make it equally difficult on the way up as on the way down.

As I mentioned earlier, there should be a fast part and a slow part to every weightlifting exercise. But "fast" is a relative term. Every weightlifting exercise you do should be done at a pace where if I said, "Stop right there!" you would be able to stop—you should use slow, controlled movements. You want to use challenging weights, however, if you are not able to have good control and keep good form, then the weight you are using may be a bit too heavy. In the future you can go back to that weight as you get stronger.

When you are lifting weights you should understand the machine settings. For example, you should know where a certain bar should line up and how you should be sitting so that your knee is lined up with the pivot point of the machine. That's another good reason to hire a trainer—to show you some basics such as where you should be sitting, what setting the weight should be on and how high or low the bar should be. But if it is not possible to hire a trainer, there are usually diagrams on the machines that explain and guide you where to sit and where to line up your moving parts.

Maintaining a good breathing pattern while you're weightlifting is also important. The breathing pattern is to "exhale on the exertion," which means blow out at the end of the hard part of the movement. On bicep curls, for example, the hard part is lifting the weight up from your thighs because you are pulling up against gravity. So you would blow out at the top of the movement and then come down slower as you breathe in.

Try to do each exercise as if you're teaching someone how to do it. Pretend that someone is standing next to you and you're saying, "Lift the bar up like this and lower it down slow like this." So always do your exercises slow enough to teach someone else how to do them. But don't forget you're there to challenge yourself; you didn't go into the gym to waste time moving weights around willy-nilly. Get in there and work hard!

WRIGHT

So what would you say are the top five things I should work on to change my body?

KERWIN

If I had to put them in order, I'd say the most important thing would be proper nutrition, eating small, nutritious meals more often with a portion of protein and good carbohydrates with every meal. Remember, the more often you feed your body, the faster your metabolism will be. So in reality you are in charge of how fast the weight comes off your body.

Next would be adding some serious weight training into your regimen. People are sometimes intimidated by weight training, but if you do it properly and challenge yourself, you will do fine. I think the minimum weight training that a person should do is thirty to forty-five minutes, two or three times a week. You'd be surprised how much your body can change in a small amount of time. Remember that when you are lifting weights, your goal is to send a signal to your muscles that they need to change by challenging them. Then your muscles will heal and come back stronger than they were before.

Exercise your body in different sections. For example, work out your legs, shoulders, and calves on Monday, then on Wednesday, exercise a different section, like your chest, biceps and abdominals. On Friday exercise the third section, which would be your back muscles, your hamstrings (back of the legs), and your triceps (the back of your arms). By the end of the week you will have worked out your entire body.

If you haven't been working out for a while, you may need to put in a couple of easy weeks to get started. Going to the gym and working out like crazy on your first day is not a good idea. Just as you wouldn't start training for a marathon by going out and running twelve miles on the first day. You might start out with running two or three miles and then gradually adding on distance throughout your training. The key is to get started and to challenge yourself to do a bit more than you normally would each time you work out.

Behavior modification is another important part of the transformation process. Changing behavior patterns, the way that you do things on a daily basis, can make a huge difference in the way you change your body. Getting enough sleep and planning your meals ahead of time will help you to make good food choices. This will result in eating out less often, which can be a great way to save on both calories and money. When you eat at a restaurant, you may not realize that everything is so high in calories. Even if you order egg whites for breakfast, there's a good chance they were cooked with oil or butter. Instead of probably twenty calories per egg white, you're now looking at fifty calories per egg white because of all the oil and butter. If you made them yourself you can use a little non-stick spray on the pan and you would know that you're only getting twenty calories per egg white.

Your mindset should be to think differently about yourself so that you're really making an effort to get back into shape. At Boot Camp L.A., I tell the participants that they can always push a little more than they think they can, and they usually do. When it comes to nutrition, they know that they have to be doing the right thing to accomplish the changes they want to see. When it comes to dessert, I encourage the "no thanks, but I'll have a bite of yours" approach. Also, I reiterate the importance of limiting alcohol consumption because it can easily lead to a lot of late-night over-eating.

When I say that you should eat every two or three hours, that may seem like a lot of work. That is why I recommend adding a protein shake or a protein bar to your diet. There are many types of protein shakes and protein bars you can have to supplement your intake of small meals. Find one that you like, then always have one with you, so that two or three hours after you've eaten half of your lunch, you can either have the other half or you can have half of a protein bar or shake. Half of a protein bar or shake will usually last people about one or two hours.

Vitamins are also important. I highly recommend taking a multi-vitamin on a daily basis to help you get all the vitamins and minerals your body needs.

The last thing would be cardiovascular activity. You want to try and burn as many calories as you can throughout the whole day, not just when you are at the gym. For example, select a parking spot that's farther away than you normally would, or take the stairs whenever possible instead of the elevator. Get together with a friend from work and walk for half an hour during your lunch break. You'll be burning calories and getting a break from your normal work routine. Including others in your mission is a great way to get and stay motivated!

WRIGHT

Do you have any secrets you will share with our readers that you save for your celebrity clients?

KERWIN

Well, that's a good one. My celebrity clients use what I call the "Secret-Secret" to prepare for an upcoming role or a walk on the red carpet. It is something I came up with to help me when I started competing in natural bodybuilding competitions.

To prepare for these events or competitions, you have to reduce fat while keeping all of your hard-earned muscle naturally. What I found is that eating every two or three hours helped to keep me very lean, however, for me, the competitions required that I become even leaner. The Secret-Secret is eating even smaller meals consisting of nice, clean proteins and good carbohydrates almost every hour!

I take what would be considered a normal meal—basically a plate of food made up of clean protein such as chicken, turkey breast, or fish and good healthy carbohydrates such as vegetables or brown rice—and cut it into thirds. I have a third of a meal one hour, then another third in another hour, and the final third an hour after that. Then, an hour later, I either repeat this or I might have half of a protein bar or shake and then the other half an hour later. I continue this throughout the entire day.

The Secret-Secret is a way of speeding up your metabolism to an incredibly fast rate. Eating every hour, compared to every two or three hours, is going to give you a lot of energy. It will take some timing and some effort, but it doesn't take long to drink half of a protein shake. So stop for a minute or two and drink half of a protein shake, and mark the time. Let's say you started eating (or drinking) your last meal at 1:15 PM. An hour later, you're going to be hungry, so you'll need to be prepared to eat again at 2:15 PM.

Many people don't understand or think about the fact that when you put food into your body it's like putting food on an assembly line. When the assembly line starts working, bells and whistles go off and the digestion machine comes to life. Your body has to take the food you eat apart and separate the protein, carbohydrates, vitamins, and minerals. Your blood pressure goes up, your body temperature goes up, and a lot of calories are being burned. So by making your body metabolize little nutritious meals all day, you are burning a lot more calories than usual.

Imagine you have a delivery guy waiting at your front door. Every time you say, "Here, take this small package and deliver it," he goes out and delivers the package. Then he comes back and is ready to go again. So instead of giving him three or four packages at once (a large portion size), you give him one small box to deliver every hour. He now has to make ten, eleven, or twelve deliveries throughout the whole day as compared to just three deliveries. To do all of these extra deliveries, your body will need a lot more energy. This energy will come from stored body fat.

A few weeks prior to my bodybuilding competitions, I do the Secret-Secret, eating every hour to make my delivery guy work, twelve, thirteen, or even fourteen times a day.

In my first competition I didn't win, I earned fifth place, but I sure changed my body a lot. I lowered my body fat to 4 percent and was really surprised when I looked at the pictures from the competition. My "Secret-Secret" had worked! A few years later, with a little more experience, I went on to win first place, not only in my weight class, but in the overall category as well. While I am very proud of winning, I was really most excited about the fact that I had changed my body. Now I have that personal experience to share with others on how to change their bodies.

For day-to-day living, I recommend eating every two to three hours. Eating every hour is something that is usually for a special occasion or, in my case, a competition and done for a short period of time like two to three weeks.

WRIGHT

So what can I do right now to start on the road to losing weight?

KERWIN

The most important thing you can do is figure out your eating patterns. Start by assessing what you've eaten so far today and when you ate it. Did you start your day with breakfast? If you didn't, you're not alone; it is very common for people to not eat breakfast. When they do, it is usually not the best of food choices (a scone, muffin, doughnut, bagel or in some cases just coffee). It is important to start your day with a healthy breakfast, such as egg whites and a piece of wheat toast or a piece of fruit. This will provide balanced fuel for your body to start the day. Then you should continue to eat small, healthy meals throughout the rest of the day.

Being prepared ahead of time with your meals or plans of where and when you are going to eat next is important. We all get busy and sometimes plans change. This is why protein bars and shakes are good to keep on hand. They are very convenient when you don't know what you are going to eat or don't have time to eat because of your busy schedule.

 Also, be careful about eating carbohydrates at night; they are important for your body throughout the day but not at night. Eating carbohydrates in the evening is a sure way to sabotage your weight-loss efforts. You should be eating at night, but you should be shooting for protein-based meals only and staying away from bread, rice, cereal, and pasta.

At the end of the day, you'll never regret being able to say to yourself, "I worked out today. I made good decisions in my eating, I drank plenty of water, and I did great at timing my meals so that I ate every two or three hours." After that, it is about being consistent and keeping up the good work. Before you know it, you'll look in the mirror and realize, "This really works; it is possible to change the way I feel and look!"

WRIGHT

Well, what a great conversation, Jay. I have really learned a lot here today. Of course, I also learned that almost everything I'm doing is wrong.

KERWIN

Don't feel bad—I was doing the wrong things for a long time myself. There is so much to be gained from learning and trying new ways to improve our health and our bodies. It requires putting yourself first, but you won't regret it because of how you will feel and the difference it can make in the quality of your life.

WRIGHT

This has been great. I'm sure our readers are going to have a lot to think about, just as I have.

KERWIN

Thanks, I really want to help people to realize that it's never too late to change their bodies. It takes a little effort, but it is all worth it!

WRIGHT

Today we've been talking with Jay Kerwin who is the owner and lead drill instructor at Boot Camp L.A. in Los Angeles. He has been a leader in the fitness and personal training arena for more than twelve years, and he is a champion in natural bodybuilding competitions.

Jay Kerwin, thank you so much for being with us today on *Stepping Stones to Success*.

KERWIN

It's been my pleasure!

ABOUT THE AUTHOR

JAY KERWIN is a world renowned personal trainer to celebrities and individual clients in Los Angeles and he is the owner of Boot Camp L.A., which is one of the most successful outdoor fitness programs in the country. He has been featured in magazines and newspapers including *Shape* magazine, *Vanity Fair, Los Angeles Magazine, Los Angeles Times* and *The New York Times*. He has also appeared on numerous television shows including *Extreme Makeover* on ABC, *FitTV*, HGTV's *Smart Solutions,* The Style Network, The Associated Press TV, ABC News, and CBS News. He is a leader in the fitness industry and is responsible for thousands of people getting in better shape and having fun doing it. He is a champion natural bodybuilder, and dedicates his life to helping others accomplish living healthy lives.

JAY KERWIN

6423 Moore Dr.
Los Angeles, CA 90048
323-938-6179
major@bootcampla.com
www.bootcampla.com

CHAPTER FIVE

Find a Mentor and Believe in Your Dreams

An Interview with . . . **Jack Canfield**

DAVID WRIGHT (WRIGHT)

Today we are talking with Jack Canfield. You probably know him as the founder and co-creator of the *New York Times* number one bestselling *Chicken Soup for the Soul* book series. As of 2006 there are sixty-five titles and eighty million copies in print in over thirty-seven languages.

Jack's background includes a BA from Harvard, a master's from the University of Massachusetts, and an Honorary Doctorate from the University of Santa Monica. He has been a high school and university teacher, a workshop facilitator, a psychotherapist, and a leading authority in the area of self-esteem and personal development.

Jack Canfield, welcome to *Stepping Stones to Success*.

JACK CANFIELD (CANFIELD)

Thank you, David. It's great to be with you.

WRIGHT

When I talked with Mark Victor Hansen, he gave you full credit for coming up with the idea of the *Chicken Soup* series. Obviously it's made you an internationally known personality. Other than recognition, has the series changed you personally and if so, how?

CANFIELD

I would say that it has and I think in a couple of ways. Number one, I read stories all day long of people who've overcome what would feel like insurmountable obstacles. For example, we just did a book *Chicken Soup for the Unsinkable Soul*. There's a story in there about a single mother with three daughters. She contracted a disease and she had to have both of her hands and both of her feet amputated. She got prosthetic devices and was able to learn how to use them. She could cook, drive the car, brush her daughters' hair, get a job, etc. I read that and I thought, "God, what would I ever have to complain and whine and moan about?"

At one level it's just given me a great sense of gratitude and appreciation for everything I have and it has made me less irritable about the little things.

I think the other thing that's happened for me personally is my sphere of influence has changed. By that I mean I was asked, for example, some years ago to be the keynote speaker to the Women's Congressional Caucus. The Caucus is a group that includes all women in America who are members of Congress and who are state senators, governors, and lieutenant governors. I asked what they wanted me to talk about—what topic.

"Whatever you think we need to know to be better legislators," was the reply.

I thought, "Wow, they want me to tell them about what laws they should be making and what would make a better culture." Well, that wouldn't have happened if our books hadn't come out and I hadn't become famous. I think I get to play with people at a higher level and have more influence in the world. That's important to me because my life purpose is inspiring and empowering people to live their highest vision so the world works for everybody. I get to do that on a much bigger level than when I was just a high school teacher back in Chicago.

WRIGHT

I think one of the powerful components of that book series is that you can read a positive story in just a few minutes and come back and revisit it. I know my daughter has three of the books and she just reads them interchangeably. Sometimes I go in her bedroom and she'll be crying and reading one of them. Other times she'll be laughing, so they really are "chicken soup for the soul," aren't they?

CANFIELD

They really are. In fact we have four books in the *Teenage Soul* series now and a new one coming out at the end of this year. I have a son who's eleven and he has a twelve-year-old friend who's a girl. We have a new book called *Chicken Soup for the Teenage Soul and the Tough Stuff*. It's all about dealing with parents' divorces, teachers who don't understand you, boyfriends who drink and drive, and other issues pertinent to that age group.

I asked my son's friend, "Why do you like this book?" (It's our most popular book among teens right now.) She said, "You know, whenever I'm feeling down I read it and it makes me cry and I feel better. Some of the stories make me laugh and some of the stories make me feel more responsible for my life. But basically I just feel like I'm not alone."

One of the people I work with recently said that the books are like a support group between the covers of a book—you can read about other peoples' experiences and realize you're not the only one going through something.

WRIGHT

Jack, we're trying to encourage people in our audience to be better, to live better, and be more fulfilled by reading about the experiences of our writers. Is there anyone or anything in your life that has made a difference for you and helped you to become a better person?

CANFIELD

Yes, and we could do ten books just on that. I'm influenced by people all the time. If I were to go way back I'd have to say one of the key influences in my life was Jesse Jackson when he was still a minister in Chicago. I was teaching in an all black high school there and I went to Jesse Jackson's church with a friend one time. What happened for me was that I saw somebody with a vision. (This was before Martin Luther King was killed and Jesse was of the lieutenants in his organization.) I just saw people trying to make the world work better for a certain segment of the population. I was inspired by that kind of visionary belief that it's possible to make change.

Later on, John F. Kennedy was a hero of mine. I was very much inspired by him.

Another is a therapist by the name of Robert Resnick. He was my therapist for two years. He taught me a little formula: E + R = O. It stands for Events + Response = Outcome. He said, "If you don't like your outcomes quit blaming the events and start changing your responses." One of his favorite phrases was, "If the grass on the other side of the fence looks greener, start watering your own lawn more."

I think he helped me get off any kind of self-pity I might have had because I had parents who were alcoholics. It would have been very easy to blame them for problems I might have had. They weren't very successful or rich; I was surrounded by people who were and I felt like, "God, what if I'd had parents like they had? I could have been a lot better." He just got me off that whole notion and made me realize that the hand you were dealt is the hand you've got to play. Take responsibility for who you are and quit complaining and blaming others and get on with your life. That was a turning point for me.

I'd say the last person who really affected me big-time was a guy named W. Clement Stone who was a self-made multi-millionaire in Chicago. He taught me that success is not a four-letter word—it's nothing to be ashamed of—and you ought to go for it. He said, "The best thing you can do for the poor is not be one of them." Be a model for what it is to live a successful life. So I learned from him the principles of success and that's what I've been teaching now for more than thirty years.

WRIGHT

He was an entrepreneur in the insurance industry, wasn't he?

CANFIELD

He was. He had combined insurance. When I worked for him he was worth 600 million dollars and that was before the dot.com millionaires came along in Silicon Valley. He just knew more about success. He was a good friend of Napoleon Hill (author of *Think and Grow Rich)* and he was a fabulous mentor. I really learned a lot from him.

WRIGHT

I miss some of the men I listened to when I was a young salesman coming up and he was one of them. Napoleon Hill was another one as was Dr. Peale. All of their writings made me who I am today. I'm glad I had that opportunity.

CANFIELD

One speaker whose name you probably will remember, Charlie "Tremendous" Jones, says, "Who we are is a result of the books we read and the people we hang out with." I think that's so true and that's why I tell people, "If you want to have high self-esteem, hang out with people who have high self-esteem. If you want to be more spiritual, hang out with spiritual people." We're always telling our children, "Don't hang out with those kids." The reason we don't want them to is because we know how influential people are with each other. I think we need to give ourselves the same advice. Who are we hanging out with? We can hang out with them in books, cassette tapes, CDs, radio shows, and in person.

WRIGHT

One of my favorites was a fellow named Bill Gove from Florida. I talked with him about three or four years ago. He's retired now. His mind is still as quick as it ever was. I thought he was one of the greatest speakers I had ever heard.

What do you think makes up a great mentor? In other words, are there characteristics that mentors seem to have in common?

CANFIELD

I think there are two obvious ones. I think mentors have to have the time to do it and the willingness to do it. I also think they need to be people who are doing something you want to do. W. Clement Stone used to tell me, "If you want to be rich, hang out with rich people. Watch what they do, eat what they eat, dress the way they dress—try it on." He wasn't suggesting that you give up your authentic self, but he was pointing out that rich people probably have habits that you don't have and you should study them.

I always ask salespeople in an organization, "Who are the top two or three in your organization?" I tell them to start taking them out to lunch and dinner and for a drink and finding out what they do. Ask them, "What's your secret?" Nine times out of ten they'll be willing to tell you.

This goes back to what we said earlier about asking. I'll go into corporations and I'll say, "Who are the top ten people?" They'll all tell me and I'll say, "Did you ever ask them what they do different than you?"

"No," they'll reply.

"Why not?"

"Well, they might not want to tell me."

"How do you know? Did you ever ask them? All they can do is say no. You'll be no worse off than you are now."

So I think with mentors you just look at people who seem to be living the life you want to live and achieving the results you want to achieve.

What we say in our book is when that you approach a mentor they're probably busy and successful and so they haven't got a lot of time. Just ask, "Can I talk to you for ten minutes every month?" If I know it's only going to be ten minutes I'll probably say yes. The neat thing is if I like you I'll always give you more than ten minutes, but that ten minutes gets you in the door.

WRIGHT

In the future are there any more Jack Canfield books authored singularly?

CANFIELD

One of my books includes the formula I mentioned earlier: E + R = O. I just felt I wanted to get that out there because every time I give a speech and I talk about that the whole room gets so quiet you could hear a pin drop—I can tell people are really getting value.

Then I'm going to do a series of books on the principles of success. I've got about 150 of them that I've identified over the years. I have a book down the road I want to do that's called *No More Put-Downs*, which is a book probably aimed mostly at parents, teachers, and managers. There's a culture we have now of put-down humor. Whether it's *Married...with Children* or *All in the Family*, there's that characteristic of macho put-down humor. There's research now showing how bad it is for kids' self-esteem when the coaches do it, so I want to get that message out there as well.

WRIGHT

It's really not that funny, is it?

CANFIELD

No, we'll laugh it off because we don't want to look like we're a wimp but underneath we're hurt. The research now shows that you're better off breaking a child's bones than you are breaking his or her spirit. A bone will heal much more quickly than their emotional spirit will.

WRIGHT

I remember recently reading a survey where people listed the top five people who had influenced them. I've tried it on a couple of groups at church and in other places. In my case, and in the survey, approximately three out of the top five are always teachers. I wonder if that's going to be the same in the next decade.

CANFIELD

I think that's probably because as children we're at our most formative years. We actually spend more time with our teachers than we do with our parents. Research shows that the average parent only interacts verbally with each of their children only about eight and a half minutes a day. Yet at school they're interacting with their teachers for anywhere from six to eight hours depending on how long the school day is, including coaches, chorus directors, etc.

I think that in almost everybody's life there's been that one teacher who loved him or her as a human being—an individual—not just one of the many students the teacher was supposed to fill full of History and English. That teacher believed in you and inspired you.

Les Brown is one of the great motivational speakers in the world. If it hadn't been for one teacher who said, "I think you can do more than be in a special education class. I think you're the one," he'd probably still be cutting grass in the median strip of the highways in Florida instead of being a $35,000-a-talk speaker.

WRIGHT

I had a conversation one time with Les. He told me about this wonderful teacher who discovered Les was dyslexic. Everybody else called him dumb and this one lady just took him under her wing and had him tested. His entire life changed because of her interest in him.

CANFIELD

I'm on the board of advisors of the Dyslexic Awareness Resource Center here in Santa Barbara. The reason is because I taught high school and had a lot of kids who were called "at-risk"—kids who would end up in gangs and so forth.

What we found over and over was that about 78 percent of all the kids in the juvenile detention centers in Chicago were kids who had learning disabilities—primarily dyslexia—but there were others as well. They were never diagnosed and they weren't doing well in school so they'd drop out. As soon as a student drops out of school he or she becomes subject to the influence of gangs and other kinds of criminal and drug linked activities. If these kids had been diagnosed earlier we'd have been able to get rid of a large amount of the juvenile crime in America because there are a lot of really good programs that can teach dyslexics to read and excel in school.

WRIGHT

My wife is a teacher and she brings home stories that are heartbreaking about parents not being as concerned with their children as they used to be, or at least not as helpful as they used to be. Did you find that to be a problem when you were teaching?

CANFIELD

It depends on what kind of district you're in. If it's a poor district the parents could be on drugs, alcoholics, and basically just not available. If you're in a really high rent district the parents are not available because they're both working, coming home tired, they're jet-setters, or they're working late at the office because they're workaholics. Sometimes it just legitimately takes two paychecks to pay the rent anymore.

I find that the majority of parents care but often they don't know what to do. They don't know how to discipline their children. They don't know how to help them with their homework. They can't pass on skills that they never acquired themselves.

Unfortunately, the trend tends to be like a chain letter. The people with the least amount of skills tend to have the most number of children. The other thing is that you get crack babies (infants born addicted to crack cocaine because of the mother's addiction). As of this writing, in Los Angeles one out of every ten babies born is a crack baby.

WRIGHT

That's unbelievable.

CANFIELD

Yes, and another statistic is that by the time 50 percent of the kids are twelve years old they have started experimenting with alcohol. I see a lot of that in the Bible belt. The problem is not the big city, urban designer drugs, but alcoholism.

Another thing you get, unfortunately, is a lot of let's call it "familial violence"—kids getting beat up, parents who drink and then explode, child abuse, and sexual abuse. You see a lot of that.

Wright

Most people are fascinated by these television shows about being a survivor. What has been the greatest comeback that you have made from adversity in your career or in your life?

CANFIELD

You know, it's funny, I don't think I've had a lot of major failures and setbacks where I had to start over. My life's been on an intentional curve. But I do have a lot of challenges. Mark and I are always setting goals that challenge us. We always say, "The purpose of setting a really big goal is not so that you can achieve it so much, but it's who you become in the process of achieving it." A friend of mine, Jim Rohn, says, "You want to set goals big enough so that in the process of achieving them you become someone worth being."

I think that to be a millionaire is nice but so what? People make the money and then they lose it. People get the big houses and then they burn down or Silicon Valley goes belly up and all of a sudden they don't have a big house anymore. But who you became in the process of learning how to be successful can never be taken away from you. So what we do is constantly put big challenges in front of us.

We have a book called *Chicken Soup for the Teacher's Soul*. (You'll have to make sure to get a copy for your wife.) I was a teacher and a teacher trainer for years. But because of the success of the *Chicken Soup* books I haven't been in the education world that much. I've got to go out and relearn how I market to that world. I met with a Superintendent of Schools. I met with a guy named Jason Dorsey who's one of the number one consultants in the world in that area. I found out who has the bestselling book in that area. I sat down with his wife for a day and talked about her marketing approaches.

I believe that if you face any kind of adversity, whether it's losing your job, your spouse dies, you get divorced, you're in an accident like Christopher Reeve and become paralyzed, or whatever, you simply do what you have to do. You find out who's already handled the problem and how did they've handled it. Then you get the support you need to get through it by their example. Whether it's a counselor in your church or you go on a retreat or you read the Bible, you do something that gives you the support you need to get to the other end.

You also have to know what the end is that you want to have. Do you want to be remarried? Do you just want to have a job and be a single mom? What is it? If you reach out and ask for support I think you'll get help. People really like to help other people. They're not always available because sometimes they're going through problems also; but there's always someone with a helping hand.

Often I think we let our pride get in the way. We let our stubbornness get in the way. We let our belief in how the world should be interfere and get in our way instead of dealing with how the world is. When we get that out of that way then we can start doing that which we need to do to get where we need to go.

WRIGHT

If you could have a platform and tell our audience something you feel that would help or encourage them, what would you say?

CANFIELD

I'd say number one is to believe in yourself, believe in your dreams, and trust your feelings. I think too many people are trained wrong when they're little kids. For example, when kids are mad at their daddy they're told, "You're not mad at your Daddy."

They say, "Gee, I thought I was."

Or the kid says, "That's going to hurt," and the doctor says, "No it's not." Then they give you the shot and it hurts. They say, "See that didn't hurt, did it?" When that happened to you as a kid, you started to not trust yourself.

You may have asked your mom, "Are you upset?" and she says, "No," but she really was. So you stop learning to trust your perception.

I tell this story over and over. There are hundreds of people I've met who've come from upper class families where they make big incomes and the dad's a doctor. The kid wants to be a mechanic and work in an auto shop because that's what he loves. The family says, "That's beneath us. You can't do that." So the kid ends up being an anesthesiologist killing three people because he's not paying attention. What he really wants to do is tinker with cars.

I tell people you've got to trust your own feelings, your own motivations, what turns you on, what you want to do, what makes you feel good, and quit worrying about what other people say, think, and want for you. Decide what you want for yourself and then do what you need to do to go about getting it. It takes work.

I read a book a week minimum and at the end of the year I've read fifty-two books. We're talking about professional books—books on self-help, finances, psychology, parenting, and so forth. At the end of ten years I've read 520 books. That puts me in the top 1 percent of people knowing important information in this country. But most people are spending their time watching television.

When I went to work for W. Clement Stone, he told me, "I want you to cut out one hour a day of television."

"Okay," I said, "what do I do with it?"

"Read," he said.

He told me what kind of books to read. He said, "At the end of a year you'll have spent 365 hours reading. Divide that by a forty-hour work week and that's nine and a half weeks of education every year."

I thought, "Wow, that's two months." It was like going back to summer school.

As a result of his advice I have close to 8,000 books in my library. The reason I'm involved in this book project instead of someone else is that people like me, Jim Rohn, Les Brown, and you read a lot. We listen to tapes and we go to seminars. That's why we're the people with the information.

I always say that your raise becomes effective when you do. You'll become more effective as you gain more skills, more insight, and more knowledge.

WRIGHT

Jack, I have watched your career for a long time and your accomplishments are just outstanding. But your humanitarian efforts are really what impress me. I think that you're doing great things not only in California, but all over the country.

CANFIELD

It's true. In addition to all of the work we do, we pick one to three charities and we've given away over six million dollars in the last eight years, along with our publisher who matches every penny we give away. We've planted over a million trees in Yosemite National Park. We've bought hundreds of thousands of cataract operations in third world countries. We've contributed to the Red Cross, the Humane Society, and on it goes. It feels like a real blessing to be able to make that kind of a contribution to the world.

WRIGHT

Today we have been talking with Jack Canfield, founder and co-creator of the *Chicken Soup for the Soul* book series. Chicken Soup for the Soul reaches people well beyond the bookstore, with CD and DVD collections, company-sponsored samplers, greeting cards, children's entertainment products, pet food, flowers, and many other products in line with Chicken Soup for the Soul's purpose. Chicken Soup for the Soul is currently implementing a plan to expand into all media by working with television networks on several shows and developing a major Internet presence dedicated to life improvement, emotional support, and inspiration.

CANFIELD

Another book I've written is *The Success Principles*. In it I share sixty-four principles that other people and I have utilized to achieve great levels of success.

WRIGHT

I will stand in line to get one of those. Thank you so much being with us.

ABOUT THE AUTHOR

JACK CANFIELD is one of America's leading experts on developing self-esteem and peak performance. A dynamic and entertaining speaker, as well as a highly sought-after trainer, he has a wonderful ability to inform and inspire audiences toward developing their own human potential and personal effectiveness.

Jack Canfield is most well-known for the *Chicken Soup for the Soul* series, which he co-authored with Mark Victor Hansen, and for his audio programs about building high self-esteem. Jack is the founder of Self-Esteem Seminars, located in Santa Barbara, California, which trains entrepreneurs, educators, corporate leaders, and employees how to accelerate the achievement of their personal and professional goals. Jack is also founder of The Foundation for Self Esteem, located in Culver City, California, which provides self-esteem resources and training to social workers, welfare recipients, and human resource professionals.

Jack graduated from Harvard in 1966, received his ME degree at the University of Massachusetts in 1973, and earned an Honorary Doctorate from the University of Santa Monica. He has been a high school and university teacher, a workshop facilitator, a psychotherapist, and a leading authority in the area of self-esteem and personal development.

As a result of his work with prisoners, welfare recipients, and inner-city youth, Jack was appointed by the State Legislature to the California Task Force to Promote Self-Esteem and Personal and Social Responsibility. He also served on the Board of Trustees of the National Council for Self-Esteem.

JACK CANFIELD

The Jack Canfield Companies
P.O. Box 30880
Santa Barbara, CA 93130
Phone: 805.563.2935
Fax: 805.563.2945
www.jackcanfield.com

CHAPTER SIX

Crossing Bridges to International Assignments

An Interview with . . . **Myriam-Rose Kohn**

DAVID WRIGHT (WRIGHT)

Today we're talking with Myriam-Rose. She is known as "Your Passport to International Career Success." Having an unmatched blend of career credentials, experience, language, and cross-cultural skills, it is easy to see why. With the ability to work with any professional in the world who has Internet and telephone access, and speak with him or her in English, French, Dutch, German, or Italian, Myriam-Rose is passionate about providing her clients with a personalized combination of exactly what they need to be successful in their international career. Having faced challenges and major transitions herself, Myriam-Rose is supportive while also straightforward. She has found joy in a rewarding career that fits her unique interests and talents, and that is exactly what she wants for her clients. She is the only international career expert to have completed all of the following certification programs: she was among the first fifty worldwide Certified Personal Branding Strategists, she possesses certifications in 360 Degree Reach and Personal Brand Assessment, she is an

Authorized DISC Administrator, a Credentialed Career Master, a Certified Career Management Coach, an International Job Career and Transition Coach, a Certified Professional Résumé Writer, a Certified Employment Interview Professional, an Accredited Translator, and a Registered Interpreter (the last with the Judicial Council in the State of California).

Myriam-Rose, welcome to *Stepping Stones to Success*.

MYRIAM-ROSE KOHN (KOHN)

Thank you very much, David.

WRIGHT

So how did you get involved in the international career service business?

KOHN

Well, I fell into it because when I first started out, I thought that I was going to provide tutoring in foreign languages and translations because of the languages I speak and the training I had had at the university. But as it turned out, I was becoming more and more an administrative assistant—a profession for which I had studied while I was in Belgium, and I did that in several languages. Four languages are the minimum requirement for this profession in Belgium. So I started to provide administrative support services and after a while, my clients said, "Well, before, the jobs always came to me, but now I have to go and find a job." They wanted me to help them with their résumé writing, which only gets your foot in the door. So, as you mentioned, I became a Certified Employment Interview Professional in order to help my clients ace their interviews and negotiate their salaries. Then I went into job searching techniques because the market was changing so much.

What happened, David, was that my business made a full circle because as my clients moved around and they started working internationally, the administrative part and the translations came back into the picture again because my clients and I were working on the transition to first getting their foot in the door of these foreign companies; in other words, putting their best foot forward. Then they could switch back to English, but at least my clients had made the effort of approaching the companies in their own languages.

WRIGHT

Are there many differences between the different cultures?

KOHN

Oh, there are, and it makes a big difference whether you're going to work in Western Europe, Eastern Europe, Southern or Northern Europe, or Asia. I don't have too many people who go to Africa. The people who go there do so mostly on a volunteer basis. Business for profit happens mostly in Europe, South America, sometimes Central America, and Asia.

WRIGHT

Will you give us an example of something that I need to know to conduct business?

KOHN

Oh, absolutely. For instance, let's take two extremes: if you go to China, the best thing to have is contacts there. People tend to clan together and there is a greater intimacy among business relationships.

I'll take Belgium as another example because it's a country I know very well. It doesn't take much to start a business. You just go to the chamber of commerce, request a license, pay your fees, and you can just do it; but then how do you conduct the actual business? Well, you have to know that, of course, as in any business, the more contacts you have, the better it is, but you also have to be aware of how people conduct business.

In China, a lot of business is accomplished over meals—business and family gatherings are very intertwined. You can bring the hostess baskets of food or wine or hard liquor, but neither beer nor flowers, and definitely not daisies, because daisies are the flower for funerals in China.

In Belgium, if you can't drink alcohol, you had better let your hosts know or they will be offended that you are not drinking. You will also conduct some business over a meal, although it's beginning to happen more often. While it is not as big as it is in the United States yet, business is more often being conducted in restaurants. In Belgium, chrysanthemums are the flower for funerals. You can see that it is important to learn about cultural differences.

You also need to learn about the holidays. For instance, in China, obviously businesses close down for the Chinese New Year, but they close down for an entire week, so if you're used to doing business the American way, and you forget that, you're going to have to wait to conduct business until after the holidays. Businesses shut down on May 1 and on October 1 (National Days).

These are also extended holidays in China, so right there, you have three times during the year when you're not going to progress as fast as you want to.

When in northern Belgium, you have to contend with June 11, which is a Flemish holiday. Then, of course, July 21, which is the Independence Day of Belgium, and while they don't slow down an entire week for it, they do take those days off. If they fall on weekends, they try to combine it like we do here. August is always the month where not a lot gets accomplished because most people go out of town. August is the month for vacation in Western Europe.

You also have to learn, for example, to really make a good impression. If you're in China and someone toasts you, wait a couple of minutes, and then toast back. It is expected that you know how to drink. If you have an allergy to alcohol, request to use tea instead and let the host know ahead of time so that he or she is not offended. They don't want you to get sick, but if they don't know the reason why you're not drinking, they're going to take offense. You never pour for yourself first; this applies to tea as well. You start with the elders and you work your way down; the elders are very important to business in China. You watch others and see how they behave. You want to fight for the bill, it's expected that you fight for the bill in China, although they won't let you pay for it; but you have to make the attempt. Eventually, they will let you pay, but in the beginning, at least make the effort. You don't want to wear white in China because the color white is for funerals in that country. It is acceptable for a man to wear a white shirt in business, but generally, you don't want to wear white as a color for business clothes.

WRIGHT

So is doing business in China much different than in Europe?

KOHN

Yes, because if we go back to Europe, it's a different thing. You're also expected to drink, so let them know if you have an allergy or if you cannot drink alcohol. They won't force you to drink, but you need to let them know ahead of time because otherwise they, too, will be offended.

Taking the example of toasting again: if someone toasts you, it is not necessary to toast back if you are dealing with the nouveau riche, but if you deal with old money, then it is expected etiquette. This means you have to do a little homework and see how long whomever you're dealing with has been in business and what their renown is; it doesn't matter whether it's a company or a family business.

The one who invites you is the one who pays in Belgium, and he or she will be offended if you try to pay your share. Just say thank you very graciously and go on from there. Business casual is best in Belgium.

So you see there are, right off the bat, a few things that are vastly different.

WRIGHT

So where do I start the training to work internationally?

KOHN

Well, I don't think there is anything specific that you can do to start training. What it requires first of all, is that you need to start with a clear picture of what kind of work you want to do, and you have to stay the course no matter how many obstacles come along the way—and there will be many. So a clear focus of what you want to do and where you want to work, a willingness to do your homework, and keeping the end goal in mind, no matter how many obstacles pop up are all important.

There are really no rules about how to secure international employment. Unlimited ways exist to find an international job that is right for you. It is not a position in itself, but rather a counterpart to a position that you might find in the United States, so if you want to find an international position, it requires determination, a belief in your ability to succeed. It requires discipline and perseverance because the work might be the same, but what will be different is where and how the work is done.

For example, the further south you go in the country (and you can compare this if you want with Italy in Europe or with Southeast Asia), where the climate is a lot warmer, people don't work as fast. It's not that they do not work well, it's just that they work at a slower pace, and you don't want to get on their bad side because they can do all kinds of things to you so you can't get your work accomplished. So the ideal situation is, if you're really sure that you want to start on an international adventure, if at all possible, take a vacation for a few days or stay a few days after a business trip to explore the area in which you think you might like to work.

Then even though they say it is not necessary, I strongly recommend to my clients that they learn the language of the country in which they're going to be working. As a matter of fact, I can tell you that in Belgium, they are trying to pass a law that would state that if you have lived in the area for six months, you need to know how to say a few basic things in Dutch (if you are in the northern part) or French (if you are in the southern part). In other words, they want to make it so that even when you rent an apartment or a place to stay, if you cannot answer basic questions like what is your name, what is your address, what country are you from, and what is your position in the language of the country, then they will not allow you to rent, which means you cannot stay and work. So just learn a few words to show your goodwill. They don't expect you to speak the language fluently, but they do expect you to have some basic knowledge of the language.

WRIGHT

What are some of the items that would be necessary to have before applying for a job, such as a passport, resume, salary, and perhaps negotiations?

KOHN

When it comes to passports, visas, and all of that, I am not an attorney or a paralegal, and the rules and regulations vary so widely from country to country that I recommend that my clients check with an attorney or the consulate for the necessary paperwork.

Salary negotiations come under contract negotiations to which there are three parts. You negotiate before, during, and after the assignment. I don't know how many details you want, but if you want to start working internationally, you really should find a mentor and people who have worked where you want to go. Prepare questions for an informational interview. Your mentors will know what they are because they will have gone through it themselves or they would not have been successful. Prepare a list of things that you would like to know so you take only a few minutes, fifteen minutes, or half an hour of their time, rather than taking up hours of their time. So this is a good way to start as well.

The organizations that employ workers abroad include the federal government, educational institutions, international public organizations, international consulting firms, U.S. multinationals, foreign-owned companies, nonprofit, and volunteer agencies.

Before we move on, I would like to point out that international résumés are very different than U.S. résumés because in the United States, résumés use a lot of action verbs and they are "right in your face." That is very offensive to people of other countries. You know, the Donald Trump style—you're fired—is not going to fly in other countries. So what you want to do is use a lot of substantives instead of action verbs when you write your résumé. Most countries also require personal information such as your age, whether you are married, single, divorced, whether you have children, and the state of your health (you can say good or excellent). I would avoid bad unless it's really, really bad. Some sections come before and after, it all varies from country to country.

As far as salary requirements are concerned, during the informational interview, when you have done your research and have prepared your specific questions, you want to learn about how you extend culturally appropriate greetings, and you want to find what the salary ranges are like over there. The easiest way, of course, is to go with an American company overseas if you're an American; that is really the easiest way to get into it. When people come over here, it's a little bit different. You have to keep in mind that it costs more than $50,000 on average to move an expatriate family. So you want to make sure that you really want to work overseas, not go over there for two weeks and tell the company that it is not working out. A failed overseas assignment can cost the company as much as $350,000 or more. So be very sure that it is something you want to do.

Let's look at what is open for negotiation in an international contract. Well, there is always room for negotiation when a company believes that you are the right candidate. Compensation levels vary widely among voluntary, government, and corporate organizations. So you definitely want to talk about salary before you go, but while you're on the international assignment, the subject can come up again for re-evaluation.

Another thing (and a lot of people forget about this part) is that you want to think about the return as well—what are you going to do after the international assignment? You have return shipping costs and interim housing to consider until you find your own place back in the United States again. Your completion bonus needs to be discussed, and you have to prepare for your repatriation.

Many people neglect to think about what they will be doing when they come back. Usually, when you come back, everything is a blur. So to soften the cultural blow, you have to involve your family—if you have one. You want to talk with other expatriates once you're back, you want to stay connected to your host in the country where you stayed, you certainly want to keep a journal if you can, you want to seek out the international community once you're back, and seek out your favorite activities to get some sense of normalcy. People don't think about that, but you are never the same once you come back.

WRIGHT

So there are differences in coaching Americans as opposed to Asians or Europeans?

KOHN

Definitely yes, because when we coach American people for a job in the United States, they already know they have to put their best foot forward, that this is the time to toot their horn, and not be shy about their accomplishments. When you talk with Asian people or European people, however, it's a little different. European people also know they have to present themselves and they are not as subdued as Asian people, but there is still an adjustment to be made.

I will use myself as an example, David. Where I come from, if you address clients by their first name, you would never see them again; you always say Mr. X or Mrs. X, or Ms. X, or the equivalent. But here, if you do that, you get a completely different result. I thought I was being polite, but it turned out that people thought I didn't know what I was doing because I wasn't putting myself on an equal footing with them. I had to learn that once people come to me, they look upon me as the expert. It was very hard for me to start calling my clients by their first names, but once I did, the dynamics changed and it was very interesting. Of course now, I have no more problems with it, but just think, for an Asian person, it is that much more difficult to do. So you have to teach them first to be assertive—not aggressive, assertive—and then go from there, so yes it is very different. You have to have an understanding of their culture so that you can show them and tell them what they have to do to adapt to American culture if they want to work here.

WRIGHT

I've often wondered about the language barriers. How important is it to be fluent in the language?

KOHN

To come here or to go over there?

WRIGHT

To go over there.

KOHN

Well, a lot of people don't tend to learn the language of the country and it is a real shame. I think people are much more willing to help you if they see you making an effort to learn their language and to adapt to their culture. You never, ever, want to make a comparison between this is what we do in the United States, or say, "Where I come from, we do it this way or that way." Always be respectful and really want to learn.

If you are in an area where they serve monkey brains and you don't want to eat it, just very respectfully decline or leave it on your plate and don't eat it, but don't say, "Oh, yuck!" If you learn some of the language and the people around you see that you are trying to adapt to their culture in other ways, they won't take offense to it as much. They'll be more willing to see you succeed and they'll help you be more successful than if you refuse or just won't learn the language. I think it's a big plus. Yes, English is spoken in most of the world, but what if they ship you to an area where it's not as prevalent? So just making the effort, even where they do speak English, speaks volumes about the person you are.

WRIGHT

How important is networking to the international job market?

KOHN

It's crucial, just like it is for finding a job here. You see, the United States lost a lot of power on the world market a few years ago—between 1978 and 1988—when foreign languages were not required in the schools and universities. For example, when you take someone to lunch here, it is not because you want to have an enjoyable lunch with that person, but to find out what makes this other person tick, how they behave, how they eat their food—all very important aspects of the hiring process. The United States has lost a lot of business because people from other countries did not see any forthcoming effort from the American people in even trying to get to know them. Mistrust emerged as a result of that. And who wants to do business with someone whom you feel you cannot trust?

Another aspect of this is that a big part of what I do is educate my clients on etiquette—whom to introduce to whom when they walk into a room. Somebody else walks into a room when you're already talking with someone, what do you do? It is different from a social setting to a business setting. It even involves how to hold your utensils. All that makes a very big difference.

In the networking community, once they get to know you, it spreads very fast what kind of a person you are. Networking is somewhat the same thing it's not whom you know, it's who knows you. So if you become known for something, then you develop a worldwide reputation.

I have an article on my blog about Philippe Lescornez who is a manager for Masterfoods, a division of Mars, in Brussels. Because of Philippe's managerial style, he developed a worldwide reputation (he continuously scores among the top 20 percent of supervisors worldwide). So it is very interesting to see what you can do today with your network as a global community. It definitely increases your chances for success and learning about the opportunities coming up. This may or may not interest you, but at least you know about them because they're not all going to be publicized.

When we talked about the cultures at the beginning, I mentioned a lot of business is being done within a family, over meals, and that is where you will learn a lot about the opportunities as well. So if you attend various networking groups, not necessarily dealing with what you're doing, but other experiences as well, you will be a lot more successful.

WRIGHT

You talked about a career activist. Would you tell our readers what a career activist is?

KOHN

Absolutely. A career activist is defined as someone who sets the direction for his or her career by identifying longer term goals that are interesting, challenging, and meaningful to him or her. It is someone who initiates the specific actions; for instance, finding a mentor, acquiring a certain kind of experience, learning a new skill or new skills that will enable him or her to make steady progress toward those goals and actually accomplishing them. So career activists are in charge of the change in their careers rather than being victims of the environment of what happens to them.

Job seekers are under the control of those who hire them while career activists take charge of and control their own career destiny. They make the decisions and do so to meet their own goals.

So the best way for me to give an example of that to which anyone can relate is that of filmmaking. When they make a film, once the project is over, the actors, producers, directors, cameramen, the boom people, and everyone involved in the project has to find another job. Well, how do they find another job? They accomplish this by being known for what they've done.

Usually you can become known by a group of people around you who know who you are. They let you know what's happening in the job market and you let them know you're available, and you move on. So it's not about being stagnant—it's really about always finding and setting your goals and moving forward.

The selection of one course of action over another is always based on a single guiding tenant and it is to do that which will advance you toward being the best that you can be at your profession, craft, or trade. Career activism is essentially a pair of commitments you make to yourself, being the best you can be at work each day, and improving your personal best every day. Those promises provide the only real security that there is in today's volatile and perilous workplace because you are relying on yourself, not on somebody else. In other words, as a colleague of mine was said, you become the architect of your life, not the victim of your career. When you consider that the average tenure of a CEO is now less than four years, there is reason for concern. Add to that the CEO fiascos like Enron, WorldCom, and Hewlett-Packard. Loyal employees were left without a job and companies had to cut their budgets or file bankruptcy after paying out big severance packages, which resulted in hundreds of innocent employees being left in financial distress.

Another very famous career activist whose name is Peter Wells says that in 2006, 14 percent of the world's largest companies fired their CEOs for lousy performance. What this means to employees is that no matter how much they work, or how hard they work, and how much education they put in their work, there is no job security. And that's why you have to become a career activist, in other words, take charge of your career.

What are some of the questions that career activists can ask? Here are some good questions you can ask yourself: Am I doing my best work in my current job or am I just coasting? Are my skills and knowledge at the state of the art in my career field or am I growing obsolete? What job should I be doing in the next twelve to eighteen months in order to upgrade my performance and my satisfaction at work? What do I need to do now to prepare myself so that I can compete successfully for that job at that time? Asking questions like these is what a career activist does.

WRIGHT

What do you think is the most positive benefit I might derive from working overseas?

KOHN

You can uncover new opportunities for using your talents and expertise while gaining additional knowledge and skills. You can also expand into an international environment. You learn how to cope, adapt, and succeed in a foreign country, and that will raise your self-confidence and enable you to better meet other difficult situations that life may throw your way in the future. You will also develop an international network that you can tap into, not only for future professional opportunities, but also for your personal fulfillment. When you work abroad, you have the potential for personal and professional growth. You gain an entirely new perspective on life.

WRIGHT

Well, what a great conversation! Working overseas is a really interesting subject and I appreciate all this time you've taken with me today to answer these questions. I've learned a lot and I'm positive that our readers will do the same.

KOHN

Thank you very much for having me, David.

WRIGHT

Today we've been talking with Myriam-Rose Kohn who is known as "Your Passport to International Career Success." She is passionate about providing her clients with a personalized combination of exactly what they need to be successful in their international career.

Myriam-Rose, thank you so much for being with us today on *Stepping Stones to Success.*

KOHN

You're welcome, David, thank you.

ABOUT THE AUTHOR

MYRIAM-ROSE is known as "Your Passport to International Career Success." Having an unmatched blend of career credentials, experience, language, and cross-cultural skills, it is easy to see why. With the ability to work with any professional in the world who has Internet and telephone access, and speak with him or her in English, French, Dutch, German, or Italian, Myriam-Rose is passionate about providing her clients with a personalized combination of exactly what they need to be successful in their international career. Having faced challenges and major transitions herself, Myriam-Rose is supportive while also straightforward. She has found joy in a rewarding career that fits her unique interests and talents, and that is exactly what she wants for her clients. She is the only international career expert to have completed all of the following certification programs: she was among the first fifty worldwide Certified Personal Branding Strategists, she possesses certifications in 360 Degree Reach and Personal Brand Assessment, she is an Authorized DISC Administrator, a Credentialed Career Master, a Certified Career Management Coach, an International Job Career and Transition Coach, a Certified Job Search Strategist, a Certified Professional Résumé Writer, a Certified Employment Interview Professional, an Accredited Translator, and a Registered Interpreter (the last with the Judicial Council in the State of California).

MYRIAM-ROSE KOHN
JEDA Enterprises
27201 Tourney Road, Suite 201M
Valencia, CA 91355
661-253-0801
myriam-rose@jedaenterprises.com
www.jedaenterprises.com

CHAPTER SEVEN

Philosophy of a Battle Axe

An Interview with . . . **Karen Baetzel**

DAVID WRIGHT (WRIGHT)

Today we're talking with Karen Baetzel. Karen is a sought-after national consultant, trainer, writer, and award-winning public speaker. After a thirty-year career in the United States Navy, Captain Baetzel retired as one of its most senior female aviators, having qualified to fly seven aircraft types, including jets, helicopters, and propeller aircraft, and she served aboard six ships. While serving in the Navy Reserve, Karen transitioned to successful engagements in the corporate, academic, and nonprofit world before founding Battleaxe Consulting Services. (What a great name!) She currently serves a nationwide client base in inspirational and motivational speaking, corporate and government leadership, development and homeland defense education, and consulting.

Karen, welcome to *Stepping Stones to Success*.

KAREN BAETZEL (BAETZEL)

Good morning, I'm glad to be here.

WRIGHT

So what did military service teach you about success?

BAETZEL

It is really hard to find a better human development and leadership laboratory in the entire world than in the United States military. From your first day to your last day, you are constantly reminded of the importance of standards and the importance of training, and they're never separated. There is a standard for everything you do and you train to it. The military does a great job clearly identifying and communicating standards and then exhaustively training to it.

You are a lifelong learner in the military and you have constant challenges, constant training, and constant change. It is a competence-based organization and it is a meritocracy, so you can't ever comfortably plateau. You are always pushed to do something new, something different, something challenging. This taught me that success is all an inside job. You have to keep the mind and body open to the fact that you are never finished learning. When you go to this leadership laboratory, you learn the fundamentals and then you push yourself to the next step. That is the most valuable takeaway for any pursuit of success in any field.

WRIGHT

Your military operational specialty was aviation. As a Navy pilot, what practical leadership lessons did you learn that helped you succeed outside the cockpit and the military?

BAETZEL

The first lesson I learned was never underestimate human potential. I gradually came to understand that with sufficient training and preparation, the world has far fewer limits to achievement than most people believe.

Naval aviation is an amazing, complex organizational system and it is operated by an incredibly young population. The flight deck of a ship—a dangerous and demanding work environment—is run by a very well trained and supervised team of professionals, and a large percentage of them are teenagers. They are performing at an incredible level of achievement in a very demanding and unforgiving occupation.

The lesson of human potential is accentuated in aviation. The stakes are always high. If you make mistakes, somebody can get killed, and there is just no way to fake it. This profession will push you to your full potential. You have to always do your homework. Many people are surprised to know what a significant amount of sheer technical memory work is required to be a proficient pilot. You just have to have things memorized cold, and you have to have immediate recall of procedure every time you strap in because you may be forced to use them. You can't learn it once and then file it away in a file cabinet—it has to be right there every day. That intensity toward professionalism is an excellent habit for any endeavor.

Another valuable lesson I learned in the cockpit was the necessity and power of precision in communication. In aviation, communication is never careless, and words are used in disciplined and unambiguous ways. Messages must mean exactly the same thing to everybody on the frequency. Emergency fuel state or routing directions are two examples.

I found that insistence on precision in communication is a very powerful and effective style and habit in corporate America, too. It definitively marks a superior leader and prevents many problems.

I also learned the value of compartmentalization, long before the multitasking became popular and then discredited. Because flying takes more than a little focus, pilots are schooled in intense concentration techniques. It's impossible to manage all the inputs in the cockpit if your mind is elsewhere, such as trying to resolve an argument from yesterday or planning tomorrow's agenda. Long before multitasking became a popular way to do business, the military was teaching its aviators just the opposite. Aviators are taught to focus and put everything aside. If you can't set aside thoughts, problems, or emotions while flying, stay out of the cockpit. This form of discipline is a learned skill set—a mastery of self that anyone can do with sufficient training and motivation. I learned the value of compartmentalizing, and for me (and I think for many people), find it a much more efficient way to work.

And lastly, the ultimate teamwork experience is flying, especially around the ship. Because there is such a small margin for error, everybody has to work together and do exactly what they're trained to do. If the team isn't working, you are not going to be able to successfully complete the mission, or even worse, somebody is going to get hurt. I really value the beauty of teamwork and those are things that come directly out of aviation experiences.

WRIGHT

You went to military flight training and served aboard ships when women were very few and far between. What success strategies did you learn from that pioneering experience?

BAETZEL

For one thing, I hate being called a pioneer. One of the things I have found about being a middle-aged woman is I hate to brag about having done anything for thirty years! When you're called a pioneer it really makes you feel like you're over the hill. That's the first thing—you've got to have a sense of humor about yourself and you cannot take anything personally.

The time I was serving aboard ship was before the repeal of the combat exclusion laws, so there were no female sailors as permanent ship's company on the ships I was deployed aboard. They were aboard other classes of ships, but not those carrying an aviation detachment. As an aside, that was an interesting paradoxical policy situation, but the wheels of progress were somewhat uneven. Nevertheless, I was either the only woman on the ship or one of two. The squadron would send us to sea in pairs if possible so we could share a stateroom. The ratio was often five hundred men to one or two women, so a pretty thick skin and a good sense of humor were essential. I learned, first and foremost, to never take anything personally. If you're going to take things personally, you'd better pick another line of work than Uncle Sam's military.

I also learned that my fellow female pilots and I were going to be conspicuous. You could not hide or keep a comfortable low profile. You couldn't slink back against the wall and keep your head down, do your job, and hope no one would notice. Back in that time, female pilots were simply too much of a novelty. So, I made up my mind if I was going to be conspicuous, I might as well be conspicuously excellent; if people are going to be watching me, I was going to give it a 110 percent. I know that sounds cliché, but if every day someone is forming a seminal opinion about women's suitability in the military aviation (and you particularly), you might as well make it a good one.

At that time, every day we were on display for the whole program in general, not just for ourselves. I wouldn't call it a burden, but it was a responsibility. Many times I was the first woman who had been on the ship and many times I was the first woman my male colleagues had flown with. Fair or not, many were making their initial assessment about whether this was a good idea based on how we behaved and how competent we were as individuals.

The first thing they assessed was not really competence in aviation, because we are all learning. They were assessing the attitude—why are you here, what's your point, do you have a chip on your shoulder? So I learned very early on to always work on the attitude first. After that, you'd better be competent at what you're doing and conspicuously so, because you're going to be watched. So, it's important to rally the attitude and be bold. Don't strive for anonymity—strive for conspicuous excellence.

Would I trade that pressure and those memories for anything world? Absolutely not. Would I want to go through them again? I'm not so sure about that, but it was a great experience. I'll work the rest of my life and still never repay the debt I owe to the Navy for the opportunities. I say that not as a woman, but as a working class kid from a blue collar home. I had doors kicked open and I was pushed through them by the Navy. That would have never happened had I not joined.

WRIGHT

Do you believe women have any special leadership challenges or advantages?

BAETZEL

That's all about the context, David. You can find yourself in situations where you're leading those who might have reluctance, for whatever reason, to follow your leadership. That may be because of gender issues, it may be because of an age issue, it may be because of an experience issue. It doesn't really matter what constitutes the credibility gap, you simply have to address it and you may have to work harder to establish credibility.

My solution is simple and unfashionable—get over it and get to work! Don't whine because another leader's resume or background is more immediately resonant. People desperately want to be lead. Establish yourself as worthy of being followed and don't rely on the fact that somewhere there's an organizational chart that says you are in charge. Lines on a piece of paper do not constitute genuine leadership.

It's important to ask yourself "why would people want to follow me in the first place?" If you can't answer that yourself, how can you expect your followers to respond? If you're in a situation where you have a leadership advantage and where you have an immediate connection with those you're leading, all the better. Leverage that connection and excel. It's all about the attitude and context.

The other thing I would also tell women and all people I work with in leadership development is this: choose your role models and your mentors very, very carefully. Just because somebody claims to be an expert doesn't mean he or she is one. I would ask very hard questions about what qualifies an individual to be an expert. Also, you should have many role models. Even history's greatest leaders had shortcomings and faults. Seek and study multiple role models and mentors and take only the best of what they have.

You also don't have to occupy the same time and space to have a role model. Be a lifelong reader and student, especially of biographies. Find the great leaders in your library from whom you can learn. That's the "poor man's university." Enroll in "the University of Car." Use drive time to listen and learn in the car instead mind numbing radio or music. The car is a great, quiet place to discover role models, understand their context, and get some insight into your own life. It will help you figure out if your leadership situation has advantages or challenges or both.

WRIGHT

With the advent of the all volunteer force, the demographic of those serving in the military is shrinking. Do you see any potential consequences or reduction of military leadership qualities being transferred to the civilian world?

BAETZEL

I do, and I'll tell you I think there are two. First, any loss of leadership/followership training and experience hurts our country. The military offers such an intense experience. This is true for lifers like me and for those who only spend one hitch of a few years. Veterans return to the civilian world with such a wealth of knowledge about human development. They have been taught critical thinking and planning skills that are hard to match. So they come back to civilian world with great leadership and followership momentum.

A young veteran who is twenty-five or twenty-six years old has skill sets and habits, discipline and ethos that employers would die for. When I was hiring people I wanted to make sure they knew how to get to work on time. I wanted to make sure they knew the rudiments of working on a team. I wanted to make sure they weren't so self-possessed or self-centered that they didn't understand that there is give and take in a work situation. Whether you're working for a cable company or in an office setting or teaching school, you have to know how to lead, how to follow, and occasionally how to get out of the way. I think the military does a great job teaching these things for people to take back to the civilian world.

The second thing I see is a loss of a "reality compass." Veterans serve as interpreters for popular culture myths and misinformation about the military, most of which is perpetuated by Hollywood and the media. Having many veterans in the civilian population helps those who never served in uniform to understand what they're seeing in movies and television and give it a reality check. Every veteran's experience is different and that's good too, because they can offer multiple points of view. This shrinking body of experience is a loss for our nation and our culture.

The military is always a servant of the larger civilian population. We need to make sure our "customers" understand what it is we're about. This is especially critical in wartime when the average citizen needs informed insight into the military (not entertainment interpretations) to make the vital decisions that citizens in a democracy need to make. You don't really get that from popular culture; instead, you get some sort of exaggerated view of things that is often just flat out wrong. I think that having fewer veterans going back into the civilian world, either as retirees or single enlistment veterans, diminishes that understanding.

WRIGHT

You're also extremely successful as a nonprofit and corporate leader. Is civilian leadership fundamentally different than military leadership?

BAETZEL

I don't think so. I think good leadership is good leadership, whether it comes from a twenty-two-year old civilian shift manager down at McDonald's or it comes from a four-star General in a theater of war.

I think good leadership speaks to one's ethical basis and it's about standards and training. The military does not have a monopoly on that idea. Many corporations and civilian organizations have high standards and they have excellent training programs. If they're good, they are obsessed with the idea of clarity of the standards. They are obsessed with making sure that the detail is communicated.

Lastly, a good leader, whether he or she is civilian or military, is willing to underwrite the honest mistakes of those they lead, up to and including their own job. That idea comes from my Naval tradition. When you hear about the rare occasion when a Navy ship goes aground, the Captain is responsible—period. Although one of his young ship handlers might have made the actual mistake, it's the Captain who is ultimately accountable. That's part of the burden of being a leader—you're responsible for your mistakes and every mistake your people make. If they make the mistake because you failed to communicate standards or train them to the standards, then that's your hit to take. I believe in that.

The military has a triad of responsibility, authority, and accountability, and good civilian leadership has exactly the same thing. There is really no difference in my mind.

WRIGHT

Now you do speaking in leadership development through your own consulting firm, Battleaxe Consulting Service, and please tell me your husband did not name that company! Why choose the name Battleaxe and what is the philosophy behind it?

BAETZEL

Did I mention that having a good sense of humor is important in life? Any good Navy pilot likes to work hard and play hard and while taking the work seriously, doesn't take himself or herself too seriously at all.

It was not my husband who came up with that name, it was my son. When most mothers were opening their Christmas presents and getting things like bottles of perfume or bathrobes, I got an exact, authentic replica of a medieval battle axe. At the same time, my Navy peers had started calling me that, sometimes to my face, sometimes behind my back. I thought "Well, if you've got a recognizable brand you might as well go for it."

After doing some research, I found that the battle axe was really nothing more than a specialized utility axe—a ubiquitous domestic tool. It cut firewood to warm the home and cook the food and when necessary, was appropriated into military service. I thought, I'm rather a "ubiquitous domestic" myself, who also saw military service.

I then researched the slang definitions. I found that a battle axe was a fierce, protective, sharp-tongued woman. Heck, what's so wrong with that? So I decided to go for it for my company name and I liked it. It suits my business direction, my personality, and it appeals to my wacky sense of humor.

WRIGHT

What personal characteristics do you see as necessary to make a successful leader?

BAETZEL

I think a true leader—a leader I want to follow—is one who has an attitude of servant leadership. It's hard for people to understand, but even in the military we lead others by their consent. The days of Frederick the Great, when leaders would stab somebody with a sword or a spear to get them to comply and go into battle, are over. We have an all volunteer force. Every young man and woman in Iraq and Afghanistan right now is there by their own consent. So servant leadership is the model that I think is at the heart of the personal characteristics of a great leader. A great leader is someone who understands the covenant between the leader and those whom he or she leads. This leader says, "I will do my part to take care of you if you do your part to follow me." It is sacrificial, it is multidimensional, and it has to be devoid of narcissism—it can't be about the leader. A good leader has to be willing to hurt. There is going to be some suffering involved if you're doing it right.

Back when I was a young mother, I had somebody tell me the most profound thing about parenting. It was this: "If they don't hate you once in a while, you're not doing your job." That's the same way with a leader—"If they don't hate you once in a while, you're not doing your job." You're doing the easy stuff and letting the hard stuff and the dirty work be done by somebody else or not at all.

Those are the things that I see at the heart of the personal characteristics that describe servant leadership.

WRIGHT

So what role does one's ethics play in success?

BAETZEL

I love talking about this; it's one of my favorite topics. No truly successful person is without a well-developed sense of ethics. Successful people have to have an ethos—an inner sense of beliefs—that speaks and informs others about the fundamental values of their character. The trouble is, especially now regrettably, you can be rich and famous, and you can be a celebrity, and you can have absolutely no respectable standard of ethics whatsoever. Interestingly and paradoxically, ethics education is in vogue now. Nearly every college and business organization has some sort of ethics training. But ethics education that is "about" ethics should not be mistaken for having and practicing ethics. I liken it to studying about pregnancy compared to actually having a baby.

You can't be a successful person, in the true and complete definition of the word, without underlying character based on rock solid, not situational, ethics. You can get rich without ethics. Criminals make money all the time without any sense of ethics. But the truth of the matter is you have to have them and it has to be a set of core values that makes your character. Some people will say, "Well, I have ethics, they're just different." If you're not making the planet a better place to live, then you're not an ethical person and you're not a successful person. You may be rich, you may be famous, but you're not successful. It goes down to that precise definition.

WRIGHT

So what in your view are the special responsibilities of a leader?

BAETZEL

After thirty years of learning it the hard way, as a leader you are often going to know more than you want to know. You will find yourself burdened with information or responsibilities or knowledge, so as a leader you have to be prepared for that. You also have to be prepared to make decisions that ultimately will disappoint or anger or hurt someone.

I took part in a survey some years ago where the members of the organization were asked to judge organizational ethics at three levels—the lowest level workers, the mid level managers, and the high level leadership of the corporation. Not surprisingly (to me), the highest level leaders were the ones judged as having the lowest set of ethics; but I don't really think that was true at all. The higher level members of leadership were called to make much tougher decisions than anybody in the middle or the lower levels of management. They often had to make difficult decisions that angered and hurt and disappointed people, so their ethics were called into question. The ethical base of those folks was not any worse (in fact, there was ample evidence they were actually better), but they just had to make harder calls. That's exactly what a leader is called to do. The further up the chain you go, the harder calls you're going to make and the more pain you are potentially going to have to deal with, both in the decisions that you make and how those decisions are going to play out for others.

Many years ago, I had a Navy Master Chief mentor me. As a young officer, you pray for a wise Chief to guide you along. He was from North Carolina, an old southern boy, and he had a way of putting things that were unforgettable. One day, he said to me, "Miss Stottlemyer (my maiden name), the further up the flag pole you go, the more your fanny shows." What he meant, of course, was the stuff of many professional and leadership development training efforts. That little folksy homespun leadership lesson was priceless. The more responsibility and power you have, the more people are going to look at you and make value judgments about the decisions that you make; if you don't want that scrutiny, don't be a leader.

The third special responsibility of a leader is expressed by a metaphor that I really like: The distance between your mouth and your feet better be pretty darn close. You should walk your talk, and talk your walk. If you are saying one thing and doing another thing, you're not going to survive as a leader. You have too much scrutiny, you're too conspicuous and too many people are depending on you to give tone and context to their decisions, ethics, and behavior. Those are three things that make for great leader and leadership. I have found if you do all of those things, and do them well, that's a life's work.

WRIGHT

Are successful people (and I'm borrowing a little here from the words of Shakespeare), born, made, or have success thrust upon them?

BAETZEL

You know, I think it's all three. Some folks are blessed with the natural gifts that help make a leader. They might have a strong and compelling voice or they may have a powerful physical presence. It's no coincidence that all our American presidents are statistically taller than average. Some leaders have a natural quick wit or confidence that can be effectively leveraged to be a great leader.

I had the pleasure of serving with one such leader who had none of those natural gifts. He was a leader by sheer force of hard work. He was quiet, he was taciturn, and did not have what I would call a powerful or impressive physical presence. But, when he led, you wanted to follow. He had done so much homework, cared so deeply and professionally, and had worked so hard that you couldn't help but to follow him. He convinced me that you can "make" yourself a successful leader.

Lastly, I do think there are circumstances where people have success "thrust upon them" by fate. Now, usually those people were unaware of how well they had prepared themselves. Most of the time those "success circumstances" gel around people who are groomed, primed, and available to life. I believe in the adage "fate is infatuated with the well prepared." That is how people get leadership and success "thrust upon them."—they are ready. So I think success can be all three: born, made, and thrust upon them or usually some combination thereof.

WRIGHT

One of your personal interests is the study of military history. How does that apply to personal leadership development?

BAETZEL

There is a treasure trove in the study of history about personal leadership development for today. Even if you don't have an interest in it for the historical value, the personal leadership value of is immense. For one thing you have to learn about the theories of history. If you remember your social studies in high school, you probably looked at theories such as "history is geography," or "the great man theory of history" or that technology or war is the "engine of history." All of those conceptual frameworks can help us learn lessons about personal leadership today.

I don't believe that history repeats itself, but I do think that people repeat themselves. You only have to go as far as Aesop's Fables and Greek mythology, the Old and New Testament, and any of the great writings of spiritual and theological leaders of any denomination or any culture. We're predictable pack animals, often irrational, and we can always learn something from the study of these things.

One of the things that you learn when you study military history is a pattern of critical thinking. When you study human conflict and ask "who has the bigger stake here?" or "whose side does time favor?" you discover that these are valuable questions to ask when solving all sorts of problems. When looking at a military campaign, ask, "Were these things good ideas, were they bad ideas, or were they good ideas badly executed?" Those are excellent questions to ask as you approach a leadership situation and assess your success in your own personal development and in reaching your goals.

I walked away from the study of military history thinking there is a whole lot for me to learn about myself and my own personal development by using these same sorts of principles.

WRIGHT

This is very interesting. I really appreciate all this time you've taken with me today to answer these questions. It's been fascinating for me, and you've brought out some leadership points here that I really need to think about myself. I really do appreciate the information and I know that our readers will, too. Spending this time with you has been pleasurable and I thank you for it.

BAETZEL

Well, thanks very much, David. I love the opportunity to discuss these ideas, as this is a passion for me. I could have talked for hours about any one of these questions, but I know time does not permit. I would love to sit and talk about these stories any time you want.

WRIGHT

Today we've been talking with Karen Baetzel. Karen is a consultant, trainer, writer, and award-winning public speaker. Through her company Battleaxe Consulting Services, she serves a nationwide client base in inspirational and motivational speaking in corporate and government leadership development and homeland defense, education, and consulting.

Karen, thank you so much for being with us today on *Stepping Stones to Success.*

BAETZEL

Thank you David, see you next time.

ABOUT THE AUTHOR

KAREN BAETZEL is a sought-after national consultant, trainer, writer, and award-winning public speaker. After a thirty-year career in the United States Navy, Captain Baetzel retired as one of its most senior female aviators, having qualified to fly seven aircraft types, including jets, helicopters, and propeller aircraft, and she served aboard six ships. While serving in the Navy Reserve, Karen transitioned to successful engagements in the corporate, academic, and nonprofit world before founding Battleaxe Consulting Services. (What a great name!) She currently serves a nationwide client base in inspirational and motivational speaking, corporate and government leadership, development and homeland defense education, and consulting.

KAREN BAETZEL
BattleAxe Consulting Services
Effective. Sharp. Results.
603.553.1483
truebattleaxe@mac.com
www.truebattleaxe.com

CHAPTER EIGHT

How to Confidently Sell with Compassion
An Interview with . . . **Heather Dominick**

DAVID WRIGHT (WRIGHT)

Today we're talking to Heather Dominick. Heather is the creator of the EnergyRICH® Entrepreneur Success System™ and EnergyRICHCoach.com, a company devoted to teaching healers, coaches, and heart-centered entrepreneurs around the world how to partner universal energetic principles with practical step-by-step how-to's to joyfully make more money in their businesses so they can better serve the world. Through her EnergyRICH® Business Boot Camp™, private mentoring coaching programs, and products, she teaches her students how to transcend lower level energies like fear and doubt to be able to build their businesses from a place of serving, joy, and abundance.

Heather, welcome to *Stepping Stones to Success*.

HEATHER DOMINICK (DOMINICK)

Thank you so much. I'm so happy to be here today.

WRIGHT

So tell us about EnergyRICH®. Where did that name brand come from and what does it mean to you, the Founder of EnergyRICH® Coaching?

DOMINICK

Well, that's a great question. Actually, the name came to me in a dream. I literally woke up one morning and it was just emblazoned across my mind— EnergyRICH®. What was shown to me was that EnergyRICH® is about when your personal life force is just emanating from you in such a strong, powerful way, it cannot help but create riches on the outside! That's where the essence of success comes from, that's where the power comes from, and it's really where the magic comes from, especially for those who are entrepreneurs and self-employed. The key is to allow that rich energy to just stream forth from you and support you in making connections with those with whom you are meant to serve through your business and your marketing. Then just allow those outer results to show up! It's just a sense of effortlessness and ease.

WRIGHT

So how did you become the EnergyRICH® Entrepreneur Success and Master Coach?

DOMINICK

It's so interesting because everything that I teach and coach in EnergyRICH® Coaching, and everything I train my EnergyRICH® coaches to teach and coach on as well in all of our programs, comes from my own experience.

Before I became self-employed I was working in a job where I was faced with what I like to refer to as the three O's: I was overwhelmed, I was overworked, and I also happened to be twenty-five pounds overweight. I knew this was not my destiny. I couldn't imagine the rest of my life being like that. At that time I wasn't even thirty yet and I really felt ready to retire! I just kept thinking, "Please, somebody take me out of this!" I couldn't maintain a romantic relationship to save my life; it was just a real state of misery.

So, as I entered into the world of being self-employed what did I bring with me? Well, I brought everything from my old life! And when I realized that this was the situation, I just literally fell down on my knees in front of my couch, hands together praying, "Please Universe, Spirit, Source, God, Buddha, whatever is there, please just take this monkey off my back—I know that I am meant to be living in a different way."

From that point I was shown the power of what is now the philosophy and foundation of EnergyRICH® Coaching, which is the partnering of the energetical with the practical. See, I've always really been, what I like to say, a get-it-done gal. Tell me what to do and I'll do it. I understand that it's about being in action, but I knew that the *way* that I was in action previously in my life had left me with those three O's. So that was no longer an option. I needed a new way.

From there I started on a whole new way of activating universal energetic principles and partnering them with some easy step-by-step business-building techniques. That's when everything in my business took off—everything just lit up and exploded. That was when I knew that what I had to offer was not just of value to myself but it was making a difference in my client's lives. From there it just spread to all of the people we are blessed to be connected with and to coach with in EnergyRICH® Coaching around the world, literally.

WRIGHT

So what makes the EnergyRICH® Entrepreneur Success System™ unique?

DOMINICK

I would say the difference is in the partnering of the inner and the outer. It is in the partnering of what I like to say "the energetical with the practical." Please understand, when I first started in business I was absolutely taking in a lot of very valuable and useful information when it came to business building—ways to increase my success and to build my wealth.

At the very same time, there was a lot that I was learning and studying and reading in terms of spiritual principles and mastering of mindset, but there wasn't really anything that showed me how to bring them together in a way that was feasible, easy to put in place—a side-by-side, step-by-step process. I understood that this was what I needed—it was the Golden Key or the giant steppingstone to success. It truly is what made such a difference then and continues to fuel my success as well as the success of EnergyRICH® Entrepreneurs everywhere. You can't just have one or the other. See, you can't just be hanging out all the way in the outer focuses. That's what had me struggling with those three O's. I could make things happen and I made some pretty great things happen, but at a very high price. You also can't just be dwelling over in the inner world. The Universe is waiting for you to partner with it. That's what we teach in EnergyRICH®, that's the actual step-by-step system of the EnergyRICH® Entrepreneur Success System™. It is a partnering of the inner and the outer—the energetical with the practical every step of the way.

WRIGHT

So what kind of person would benefit from using your system?

DOMINICK

I would say pretty much anyone can benefit from using this system. But primarily the person who is open, the person who is ready to release what hasn't worked up until now. If you're completely done with struggling, you're done with feeling like you have to push your business and your life forward, this system is for you. If you're done with just being able to get by, with just living paycheck-to-paycheck, or client-to-client, you're done with those fifteen-hour workdays, and you're ready to say, "Okay. I'm open to a new way!" you're willing to actually move into action in this new way. You are the person who is really truly ready to change your business; you are a person who is really truly ready to change your life. You are the person who is ready to transcend. You are the person who recognizes that what you've done up until now isn't working. Even though it might feel comfortable to hold onto it, you are willing and ready to release so that you can step into the success that you truly say you want and you truly do desire. If you are that person, you will benefit from the EnergyRICH® Entrepreneur Success System™.

We've had so many people come into our program, the EnergyRICH® Business Boot Camp, as well as my private mentor programs, and they say they have tried everything. Now they're ready to step into their brilliance, to allow themselves to move into the magnificence that we are all coded for. This requires, again, a release of the need to hold on to the old way and the need to believe that only you can make it happen. It requires being ready to step into receiving guidance and support from a much larger energetic source.

WRIGHT

You talk about the magic key to entrepreneurial success being the partnering of the energetical with the practical. Will you tell our readers what you mean by that?

DOMINICK

Sure, absolutely. When I talk about partnering the energetical with the practical, the real key word there is "partnering." It doesn't work as well if you're just hanging out in one or the other—if you're just hanging out in the practical or if you're just hanging out in the energetical. The key is partnering, which can be misunderstood. Often, what happens for entrepreneurs or people just looking to make a change for themselves in their life, is they might gather all of this energy oriented knowledge and information and then they say, "Okay, I've got it. So now I have to move into action." Once they move into action, everything they have gathered from the energetical just gets lost.

Or the other way, which is that they say, "Okay yeah, I understand, energy. Okay, I understand 'spiritual principles,' but really, when it comes down to my core beliefs, there isn't room for that in my business. My business is a little bit too important so I need to take over from here."

Either way by itself is a mistake. So the partnering isn't about just a little bit of one or just a little bit of the other, it's truly an integration—a consistent weaving—so that energy management becomes a consistent part of your day, a consistent part of your tasks, your daily to-do's, and a consistent part of your marketing. As you fuse the energetic in with the practical and allow the practical to not be so difficult, then this is when things really take off. Then the marketing that you're putting out there is infused with a very dynamic energy—an energy that is authentic from you, an energy that is a match for you *and* your ideal clients. You can already begin to feel what a difference that makes. There is just such a difference between when you really step out in a powerful way, versus "Well, I'd better play it safe. I'd better just do what everybody else is doing. I'd better just do what so and so told me to do because I don't want to risk being myself or being powerful when it comes to business."

It's the partnering that is the real magic. It does require being ready and willing, but boy, when you step into it, you'd better be ready to just stand out and to receive accolades and awesome, successful results.

WRIGHT

What step in your system is the most important step?

DOMINICK

Oh boy, it's a nine-step system. Every step is so very, very important and they're all integrated together. But I will tell you that probably one of the steps

I've seen that has made a major difference for entrepreneurs is the step where we focus on shifting from selling to serving. This is an energetic shift that makes such a difference for so many entrepreneurs. I've found that there is a block when it comes to being in business, especially for those who tend to be more in the healing arts professions, or they're helpers, teachers, coaches, or they care deeply about their business and those they serve.

When it comes to selling there is an energetic block; it tends to show itself in a few different ways. There is such a fear among many entrepreneurs of being perceived as pushy or manipulative. That doesn't feel good; we can all recognize that. Who wakes up in the morning and says, "Hmm, today I really feel like being pushy. I really feel like manipulating people today." I think there are very few of us who actually wake up and desire that.

We might believe that we don't have any other choice but, when it comes to the desire, we are all coming from an original base of the desire to serve and to serve through love. So when it comes to the idea of pushing and selling and being manipulative, because we don't want to do that, often entrepreneurs don't do anything, so they just stop. You sabotage your business. Your marketing doesn't get executed and you don't take the steps you know you need to take. You might spend a lot of time sitting behind your computer answering e-mail or surfing the Internet or looking at the Web sites of others who are doing things similar to what you want to do and you are feeling bad because you're not. You're doing anything to avoid connecting with a potential client! You just don't want to be perceived as being pushy or manipulative. So that's one mistake.

The second mistake is to have a block against selling so you go out there and you do it anyway because you know that you have to take action, but you just don't have the energy behind it—you have so much fear that your efforts fall short. Then you don't get the results you want and it just starts to spiral downward.

I'll add one more in here as well. You don't want to be perceived as being pushy or manipulative, so you just give everything away. You want to be able to help people because that's the area of service you're in, but because you don't want to be pushy, you just give it away—you discount your services, you give longer amounts of time on your sessions, and then you end up feeling resentful. You also don't have enough income to take care of paying the bills and making sure that you as a service professional are cared for.

If you make the above mistakes, you will believe that you're not good at this or you just flip into servitude and end up feeling resentful. Obviously you can begin to understand that this doesn't create what you want.

What we do in EnergyRICH® is we literally create an energetic shift from selling into serving. I would say the most powerful key of that belief transformation—of that energetic shift—is the recognition that you as an entrepreneur are here to serve the highest good of everyone through your business. Your business is a vehicle of service and your business is a business of healing. Because part of your purpose is to serve the highest good of all and the key in that shift is that the highest good of all includes you and your business.

As you create that shift, begin to embrace this and recognize that when customers come to you—when they are drawn to your business—there is something in them that wants to change. If you're not available because you're so afraid of selling or coming across as pushy and aggressive because that's all you can believe you can do or you're discounting your services and feeling resentful, you really aren't able to be in a place of higher service. Therefore, the customers who have been drawn to your business are not able to receive what you have to offer to its fullest capacity. It is a disservice to them as well as a disservice to you.

If you're here to serve the highest good of all, and as you shift into that, and you go back to partnering the energetical with the practical, showing up in a way that's big, bold, strong, beautiful, and magnificent, then everyone moves forward. This is what you're coded for, just like an acorn is coded to turn into a magnificent oak tree. That is the power of shifting from selling to serving. Then from there, everything, in terms of the results you desire to create in your business, is able to actually take place.

WRIGHT

I know you have a unique approach to selling that has helped so many become successful in their businesses. Will you tell our readers about that?

DOMINICK

Sure, absolutely. This is what is lovingly known in EnergyRICH® Coaching as selling confidently with compassion. It's a process that was shown to me that has a very unique step-by-step approach. It and allows your customer or client to be guided to choice. It's literally you as the expert, as the practitioner, as the business owner stepping into the position where you support the people who want their lives to change to be guided to choice. You do what I like to refer to as "activating the inner decision guide."

So again, you can see how this partners with shifting from selling to serving. This is what we call confidently selling with compassion or moving potential clients into paying clients, known in EnergyRICH® coaching circles as the P2P™ process. This is where you, as you're coming from a place of service (because you've already shifted from selling to serving), are able to show up and through a very special step-by-step process literally guide your potential clients through the process of choice. That does not mean that you have to convince and "tap-dance," and sell because when you're in that energy it is about serving the highest good of all.

What we want is everything to become client centered. You partner with your potential client, heart-to-heart, energy-to-energy. You will get a real sense of what it is they need. You will sense how your business or service is a match to what they need. You literally engage them in a process of being guided to choice from a place of energy, and as they come to the decision, they feel called to be a part of you and your business and your service. Though you haven't yet begun to work together or partner together, in whatever your business or service is. However, you are already in a high-energy place because you've joined together through the decision process. You haven't felt that you've had to push or convince or manipulate, and make your potential customer/client do something.

No one likes to be made to do anything. I think we can all remember back to a time of being young and being told we had to do something, and what did you do? You dug your heals in and gave that famous two- or three-year-old battle cry, "No! No!" We recognize that this is scattered, fragmented, and disjointed energy. Through the EnergyRICH® "confidently selling with compassion" process—the P2P™ process—you partner with your potential client and that client is guided to choice. It's a beautiful experience and it's changed the life of so many entrepreneurs.

WRIGHT

What are some of the biggest mistakes that you see entrepreneurs make when trying to build and grow their business?

DOMINICK

That's a great question. One area I see is people's mismatch with money. This is what I refer to as your "money belief" or your "money story." You have to be very clear about what you as the entrepreneur are bringing to the table in terms of your beliefs about money. There are a couple of keys to this that I'll share with you today.

The first is if you have any beliefs that being in business is hard, you need to stop and examine what is happening. What is the story that you are telling yourself about the fact that being in business and building business is hard?

From there you also want to clarify that whatever you believe you may know about people and their money, you do not know. You may understand what they've told you based on your money story. I often hear from entrepreneurs, "Oh, I need to tap into a market where they have the money to pay," or "Oh, I can't connect with that person because he [or she] will never be able to afford my services." If you find yourself making statements like that you need to become, what I like to call, energetically responsible and really be honest with yourself: Do you know that to be true 110 percent true? Often the answer is no. Again, you only know what you're bringing to the situation based on your own money story.

When you come from a powerful place of serving, as we were talking about earlier, it's none of your business what is going on with others and their money—you are there to serve. The minute you engage with someone's supposed money story, it only has to do with you and yours. So it truly is your responsibility—your energetic responsibility—to discover what your money beliefs are and then to redirect that energy to change your story so that you are fully available to serve. That is definitely a major mistake I see entrepreneurs make.

Other mistakes are not activating the inner decision guide, not guiding a person to choice, believing that it is up to you to convince someone, or believing that if you don't convince someone then you're being inactive. Neither of those are 110 percent true with a capital T.

Another big mistake I see entrepreneurs make is that they just do what everybody else is doing. They aren't willing to create their own shatter-the-myth marketing, to claim what their business is here to serve and provide to the world. It doesn't matter if there are a million other people who are doing the same business you are. No one can be in business the way that you can be in business, because you are a unique individual and the more you give permission and allow that uniqueness to come forth and shine, and then take that uniqueness and put it in a process, because people really enjoy and like to buy processes, so as you take your uniqueness and put it into a process, this is what we refer to in EnergyRICH® as your Unique Serving System, then you are in a place of power, you are in a place to powerfully serve, versus believing that you're better off if you just fit in.

WRIGHT

If an entrepreneur could only start with three things, what would you recommend those be?

DOMINICK

The first thing that I would recommend is to get very clear where there are energy mismatches in your business. How can you tell if there is an energy mismatch? This is very simple—you want one thing, but you're experiencing something else, and that is an energy mismatch. Here is the key: whatever you say that you want to have happen on the outside, and it isn't happening, nine times out of ten it has to do with what's happening on the inside. So you want to be very, very clear about where your energy mismatches are.

From there you want to be clear with yourself—how willing are you for that to change? How willing are you to receive support in order to create that change? Get support on an energetic level from a source of energy that is available to each and every one of us, and get support on a practical level from a group of like-minded folks who are there to support you, to celebrate you, to cheerlead you on, or from a high level mentor whose been there, who's done what it is that you say you want to do. How willing are you to receive support? No one is meant to do most things alone, specifically when it comes to building a business. To believe that you can do this or that you should be able to do this all on your own is a major energetic mismatch right there. It will keep you very limited, it will keep you stuck, and it's going to keep you very, very small.

Again, you want to check where the energy mismatch is and then become energetically responsible. Are you willing for this to change? Are you willing to receive support, both energetically and practically so that change can truly take place? To believe that you should do this all by yourself is really just another way of playing small.

WRIGHT

Would you tell us why your work is important to you?

DOMINICK

I really feel so extremely blessed with what I am able to offer and how I can serve through all of our programs and products at EnergyRICHCoach.com. I recognize that I am truly in my purpose. Being truly in my purpose is the recognition that I am here to support others and being on a self-healing journey, to step out of a place of fear and a place of unworthiness into a place that truly does activate that service of the highest good of all, to recognize that when we come from a place of collaboration versus competition, that is a place where accelerated success takes place for everyone, there is no separation, there is no only you, or there is no only me.

I really believe that entrepreneurs are here to shift and change the world from its old view of success that says you have to grab the bull by the horns. (If you stop and think about it this is a very scary, bloody, dangerous thing to do.) Entrepreneurs are here to bring a new dynamic of success—success is not just about one person being at the top. We will shift from a pyramid into a circle, and with that circle we are able to expand and move, all of us—the entire planet—into a place that is filled with purpose, high level creative productivity, and with profit and prosperity for all. And I truly feel I am playing my part through my EnergyRICH® programs, which is why it's so very important to me.

WRIGHT

Well, what a great conversation. I have really learned a lot here today. Your EnergyRICH® Success System™ is interesting. One of these days you can tell me all nine steps.

I really do appreciate all this time you've taken to answer these questions. I am sure our readers are going to get tremendous value from this chapter in our book.

DOMINICK

Thank you so very much. It's a real joy and an honor to be a part of this project.

WRIGHT

Today we've been talking with Heather Dominick. She is the creator of the EnergyRICH® Entrepreneur Success System™ and www.energrichcoach.com. She teaches her clients how to partner universal energetic principles with practical step-by-step how-to's. Heather shows her students how to transcend lower level energies like fear and doubt to be able to profitably build their business from a place of serving, not selling, to discover joy and abundance.

Heather, thank you so much for being with us today on *Stepping Stones to Success.*

DOMINICK

Thank you.

ABOUT THE AUTHOR

HEATHER DOMINICK is the creator of the EnergyRICH® Success System for Entrepreneurs™, the essence of her years of education, intuitive studies, marketing training, and sales tools. Heather uses this proven step-by-step system to coach entrepreneurs by creating an energetic map to harness their energy once and for all. Her coaching philosophy is that an individual cannot "do" business, but needs to BE business at a holistic level that integrates thoughts, feelings, words, and actions. She calls this "managing your energy". It's important that an entrepreneur do the inner and outer work necessary to activate this skill and belief in them. Only when you have activated this in you, can you fully and confidently present yourself and your business to others. That is what is at the heart of assisting individuals in making any outer changes in their businesses.

Heather's strengths include helping clients to articulate their business and life visions, develop aligned action plans to achieve six-figure and beyond goals. Her primary focus is in helping entrepreneurs identify sources for increasing the productivity and profit of their businesses. She is an insightful accountability partner who helps her clients stay focused and motivated while growing, changing, and enhancing their businesses, successes, and lives.

HEATHER DOMINICK

55 W 116th Street, Suite 120
New York, NY 10012
1 (888) 417-0283
info@EnergyRICHcoach.com
www.EnergyRICHcoach.com

CHAPTER NINE

Turning a Mental Breakdown into a Mental Breakthrough

An Interview with . . . **Tanya Brown**

DAVID WRIGHT (WRIGHT)

Today we're talking with Tanya Brown, youngest sister of Nicole Brown-Simpson. She is a life coach as well as an advocate life coach, speaker for mental health and relationship violence prevention. Her goal is to help others turn their mental breakdowns into mental breakthroughs. She uses her own experiences to help others; she has found key tools that have allowed her to manage life's undertow and subsequently create a more fulfilled life for herself. Tanya has a keen understanding of personal difficulties and concerns that may affect one's ability to enjoy life to its fullest. Her life coaching and speaking style are engaging and geared toward identifying, understanding, and proactively dealing with life's emotional pitfalls, disappointments, missed opportunities, and unrealistic expectations.

She addresses a variety of issues under the University of Life and believes that change is possible and approachable and that one can acquire proper management skills; life's challenges can develop into strengths. Her positive approach assists in creating an uplifting and inspiring presentation.

Tanya, welcome to *Stepping Stones to Success*.

TANYA BROWN (BROWN)

Thank you very much, happy to be here.

WRIGHT

So you have endured a significant amount of loss in your life as a young adult. What were a few of those life-altering events that made you the person you are today?

BROWN

Oh, where should I begin? I believe that it all started when I was a young teen. I'm the youngest of four sisters, and I wanted to be just like them. Denise is my oldest sister and was a supermodel with Ford Modeling Agency. Nicole, the rich, beautiful woman, married a famous football player. I thought she had everything. Dominique was the valedictorian, thin, and most popular. All of them were absolutely gorgeous and all were on the homecoming court—something I never was. I felt like, "Okay, where is my place in all of this?" I wanted to be like my sisters and I think that's really where it started. I didn't know where I belonged. Instead of just loving my own true, authentic skills and appreciating my own beauty, talent, and compassion, I was always trying to be somebody I wasn't. That carried on from childhood all the way up into high school. In high school was when a lot of tragedy happened in my life. I lost eight friends of mine during that time. It seemed like I was burying a friend every year, just from drunk-driving accidents, ski accidents, and ski bus accidents.

When you're that young—in your teenage—years you don't understand death; you don't understand loss. So it got to a point where I was burying a friend, going to school the next day, and moving on. I wasn't really coping with the loss, I was dealing with it.

Today I make sure people understand the difference between dealing and coping. I'm very careful with those two words. Dealing with an issue or a loss is sweeping it under the carpet. It's the same as saying, "Okay, this happened; now I'm just going to deal with it and move on," whereas coping is a skill that gets you through troubling, challenging, and life-altering times. Coping is a skill that needs to be learned and developed. For example, I needed to learn how to cope with the losses I experienced. Perhaps going into counseling or going into support groups could have really helped me, but I didn't know what coping skills were at that time.

The losses continued. Two years after high school, I lost my best friend, Harissa, who was a victim of a hit-and-run in Laguna Beach, California. I experienced my first bout of depression as a result of that tragedy. I was in a deep depression for two years and every single day my mother would post positive affirmations such as "I am beautiful, I am wonderful, I am smart, I am unique." Although they worked somewhat, my depression was so severe that I couldn't eat, I couldn't sleep, and couldn't get out of bed. I felt horribly guilty because I had lied to her the night before she was killed. I held that burden for so many years. That was in 1989.

What finally happened was I found comfort in food. Again, I didn't go into counseling, I didn't process the loss, I swept it under the rug, and I just went on. I tried to go on, especially after two years, but just could not. Eventually, I found comfort in food to get me through the pain. I became an overeater and battled with an overeating disorder. I hid my food like alcoholics hide their alcohol—under my bed, in coat pockets, in planters. I was able to keep my condition secret until my mom decided to clean under my bed. That's when she realized that there was a problem. She found empty boxes and dishes and I had ballooned up to almost two hundred pounds.

Then in '92 I was accepted to the University of California, San Diego. I fainted during my first day of college. I felt like this little fish in a huge ocean— it was just so overwhelming for me. I'm just from the small town of Laguna Beach. I had been sheltered pretty much my whole life, so this was really the first time I was on my own. I was living in my first apartment and going to college. I was just jumping in and doing it. Later, my friend, Holly, developed leukemia and died. Even though her passing was expected, it was still a loss and another pain that I had to endure. And I still had no coping skills.

Then, in '93, I found myself sitting in my apartment in Del Mar, California. My roommates were already gone for the holidays, the curtains were drawn, I had a glass of wine in my hand, and I was watching the old movie *Casablanca*. The fireplace was on, and it was only about one o'clock in the afternoon. I was alone—emotionally, spiritually, and physically. At this time I was really trying to figure out if I should I stay or leave UCSD. I had worked very hard to get into that school, yet I was failing. As I was sitting there, the phone rang and it was Nicole. She said, "Hey, Tanya! So Mama tells me that you're depressed."

"Nic," I said, "I'm *terribly* depressed. I have to make a huge decision whether to stay or leave UCSD." I was just so overwhelmed and just doing anything to escape it. "This is a very hard decision for me," I continued, "and I don't understand why I'm having such a hard time.

Okay," she said, "get a piece of paper and a pen."

When I told her I was ready, she said, "I want you to write this down: *delete the need to understand, we don't need to understand everything, some things just are.*" How true is that? We don't have to understand all circumstances.

I remember that—it was back in 1993. It was such a poignant piece of advice. She then gave me her "Nicole pep talk" and said, "So now I want you to go pack a bag. I want you to pick yourself up by the bootstraps and I want you to go up to Laguna and go Christmas shopping with Dita." Dita was what we called our mom.

"Alright," I replied. It was difficult, but I did it. It takes a lot of effort to pick up and move on when you are so down.

I think that little bit of motivation really helped me decide that UCSD is not for me, this lifestyle is not for me, and I'm going to make a change. I wanted to get through college alive and happy.

WRIGHT

So you experienced a huge life-altering event in your life—your sister, Nicole, was murdered.

BROWN

Yes. In 1994 Nicole was murdered. This drastically changed my life, my family's life, and it changed the way the world viewed and interpreted domestic violence and all forms of abuse. It woke the world up—if it can happen to her it can happen to anyone.

WRIGHT

In what ways did this emotionally impact you?

BROWN

There has been a lot of healing and a lot processing over the last fifteen years. I knew that I had a desire to go out and educate, revive and re-empower people in despair and who are overwhelmed and overextended. I'm the counselor in our family with the constant desire to help others help themselves. I have a desire and passion to counsel people, speak, educate, and empower everyone, but especially our youth and college-aged students. I enjoy this demographic because I was one who wanted to be liked by a boy, have friends, be liked, and get approval. I never wanted to disappoint anyone and I didn't want to be alone. I wanted somebody to take care of me; I was always like that.

Living your life co-dependently permits deceit to enter. I fell into unhealthy relationships, some controlling, some not. There are people out there who will prey on your weaknesses and one of those found me. During the most vulnerable times in my life, this person began to control me. He dictated the people I hung out with and when I had to be home. Later I found out that he had stolen all the money in my mutual fund. This deceit turned not only my life upside down, but that of my entire family as well.

Throughout the first five years after Nicole's murder, I continued to get into dead-end jobs just to pay the bills. These jobs did not satisfy me and they did not fuel my soul. They caused discouragement and depression because I knew I had a greater purpose. I wanted to go into our communities and educate and empower people, but out of respect for my family's decision to have my oldest sister be the spokesperson, I remained quiet and neglected my feelings. Again I stuffed my feelings, my emotions, my passion, and my purpose inside. I suppressed everything that I am inside.

I am a totally different person now. I gained courage and faith in myself. I'm driven now because I've experienced so much pain and loss in my life that I am truly filled with empathy for people who are in pain.

WRIGHT

During the time of the trials, you never believed in yourself to pursue speaking and coaching. Will you tell our readers why?

BROWN

One of the main reasons was respect for my mom and dad. Instead, I chose to remain quiet. I am not the type of person who goes against others' will. I respect others. I didn't have the courage to jump in and do a little something every day to reach my goal, which was to educate, empower, motivate, and inspire. This is what makes my heart beat and makes me breathe. There is so much despair, stress, depression, and anxiety in this world today. If I can share my story of trials, tribulations, and triumph with others and they are encouraged to change, then my job is done. I want to share with people that they can experience the light at the end of the tunnel—*if* they are willing to do the self-work.

WRIGHT

So why do you think you were lacking in faith in yourself and in courage?

BROWN

The lack of courage, faith, and belief in myself, along with being the "baby sister" everyone wanted to protect, all contributed to it, I think. I was the one who received things on a silver platter. I was the spoiled little "only child" pretty much, even though there were four girls. I really didn't know how to do things on a large scale such as starting my own speaking and coaching business. I didn't know where to start. I had all these great ideas. I had education, certificates, passion, and purpose, but I just did not know how to really conceptualize actually doing it.

I don't want to use the word "sheltered" per se, but things in general were always very easy for me. My mom even said to me not too long ago, "I wish I had raised you to be a little bit more self-sufficient." That says it right there.

I was clueless until I started to read books from those who were likeminded—people like Tony Robbins, Jack Canfield, and Oprah. I remember collecting Oprah magazines—anything to help me to get inspired inwardly first. I wanted to learn to have a love affair with myself first.

I truly believe God puts you in the perfect place at the perfect time. He knew that I wasn't ready. He knew that I had a lot of grieving, processing, and a lot of pain to acknowledge. Looking back on it, that's how I see it; going through it was discouraging.

WRIGHT

Let's jump forward to 2004. You were to be married and he cancelled four days before the wedding. What was all that about and how did you handle it?

BROWN

Yes I was to be married.

First I'll mention that I experienced another significant loss in 2001. It was my best friend Troy Choate. His death made a huge hole in my life. His death caused so much pain that was so insurmountable that it seemed surreal to me and many who knew him. I was closer to Troy than I was to my sister because Nicole and I lived two separate lives. She was in Los Angeles doing her mom/wife things and I was still at home; then I went to college in San Diego. Troy was my high school friend. He was the brother I never had. In 2001 he was at the Colorado River. He jumped off a cliff into the water and landed wrong. Except for his mom and dad, his entire family witnessed the tragedy.

For a day and half, Denise and my mom were trying to figure out how in the heck they were going to tell me. They knew this loss was going to be bad. I was in San Diego doing some outreach work. I came back to the place where I was staying, all excited about this fundraiser we were working on, when my sister said, "You need to sit down. Troy died."

That was a very significant loss in life; it was excruciating. I became horribly angry and I think this was a steppingstone that helped me begin my process of grieving all of my losses. I became horribly angry at God, even though I did have faith in God. I went to Troy's parents' house. I prayed and they prayed with me. Then, all of a sudden, the release of anger, pain, and despair was lifted from me and from that point on, I had a relationship with God instead of merely practicing a religion.

Then in 2004 I met a guy and we decided to get married. Four days before the ceremony was scheduled, he got cold feet and cancelled. He had thrown a prenuptial agreement in my face ten days before. I didn't care about signing one. I just wanted it to fair. I understand that people work hard and want to protect what they've earned. But, it just got too much for him. He continued to go back and forth with negotiations, but it just was not fair.

We had our family attorney look at it and she said, "You will be signing away what California is obligated to give you." Eventually, my ex said, "I can't do this." He just could not share and be fair in a relationship.

For one month I went into self-destruct mode—I drank and I popped pills. I had been on Klonopin to help me deal with Troy's death. Then, on October 9, 2004, we had a family friend over for dinner and he said something that triggered a significant emotion. I don't even remember what it was, but it was enough to make me snap—I snapped big time. I almost hit my dad and I called Denise names, which resulted in no communication for almost a year—and we lived under the same roof! (It took a year or so to regain trust and re-establish our relationship again.)

That night, under the influence, I was threatening to drive. At that time I went into my bedroom and I poured a bottle of pills in my hand. In that moment, my sister, Dominique, came in and I became scared so I scooped up the pills. I still took four and I said, "Get me the hell out of here!" (I have to admit, I used more profane language than that.) I continued on and repeated, "Get me out of here, because if you don't I'm going to hurt myself or someone around me!"

She took me to my girlfriend's mother's home where I stayed. The next morning she called me and said are you ready? And I knew exactly what she was talking about. On October 10, 2004, I was admitted into the Behavioral Health Center at South Coast Medical Center in Laguna Beach, California.

I was an inpatient for ten days and that is where I received my medical advocacy. I was put on medications and counseled. The scary thing during that time is that I was over-medicated on an anti-depressant and I began to go into a "manic" mode, figuratively speaking (with respect for those who suffer from manic episodes).

I cannot stress enough how critical it is for others to be their own advocate when it comes to their medication. Just because a doctor puts you on a medication, doesn't mean it is the right one for you. You have to pay attention to your body and how it reacts.

I believe that there are many people who need medication. But, I did research on medications and cognitive behavioral therapy. The combination of the two, are more effective than medication alone. I encourage people to do both. Medication will take the edge off, yes; but, coping skills need to be learned and implemented into daily living.

The inpatient program was very structured. We were encouraged to attend classes that were scheduled every hour, Monday through Friday. I chose to attend every single class. The program needed to be very structured because structure is very important for people recovering from anxiety, stress, depression, and other mental challenges. People who are making significant changes need structure; time management, goal-setting, problem-solving, communication, and other tools are needed to help them stay focused. I was basically a model student—I wasn't a patient, I was not going to fall victim to circumstance. I knew that I did not want to walk out the same person that came in, so I sat in every single class and took diligent notes. Instead of going into the kitchen and chit-chatting after class, I often went to my room and I would write in my journal. I processed, and did my self-work. I mean, I worked hard; I was a student of life, that's why I call it the "university of life."

I remember sitting in one of my classes and asking my occupational therapist, "What kind of therapy is this?"

"It's cognitive behavioral therapy (CBT)," my therapist answered.

"Whatever this is," I said, "it's working!" This form of therapy really does work.

WRIGHT

So when did you realize you needed to surrender to the Behavioral Health Department?

BROWN

It was the evening of October 9, 2004—the night I snapped. After ten days I was discharged as an inpatient and was admitted into an outpatient program the very next day. I didn't want to be the person I had become seemingly overnight. I needed more help.

On October 21, I went into the outpatient program. The morning of my first day, my dog died. It wasn't just any dog—he had been Nicole's Akita, Kato. Yet another chapter of Nicole's life I needed to bury. Attending the outpatient program was my job Monday through Friday—to work on myself, facing my pain and pushing down the brick wall that had held me back for so many years. It was there that I listened and I did my self-work and homework. I saved every note taken and every worksheet that was handed out. I created a binder that I still have today, because when I have down days, I can refer to it and remember where I was back then. If I'm having a bad day, all I have to do is remember where I was and it doesn't seem so bad. This does not mean that I do not have emotional moments, I do; but what is different now is that I am able to acknowledge my feelings and go through them, and now I catch myself. It may take me a few days or a week but eventually I tap into my coping skills.

In any event, my motivation and my inspiration still remained the same. I sat in my classes, eight o'clock until three every single day and did my self-work. As time went on, I realized that I was the one working on myself and nobody really understood it—nobody knew the process I was going through. I had to reframe the way I was thinking, the way I was feeling, and basically redo my life. I wanted to work on changing myself. I had a will and the courage to make changes and I had the time to do it.

WRIGHT

Is that the coping and self-care strategy you learned from that experience?

BROWN

Yes.

WRIGHT

So how has it ultimately influenced your life?

BROWN

Oh, that entire experience?

WRIGHT

Yes.

BROWN

It's made me a stronger and healthier person. I have always been a good person who always tries to do the right thing. I've always been a loving, kind, genuine, sincere person. Overall, this experience made me appreciate life so much more. It was so scary being in that dark place. But it helped me gain ownership of my own life. I encourage everybody to reach for that. In fact, I am frequently invited to speak at the outpatient program where I was a student. I want the patients to understand that if they believe in themselves, do the work, and take it seriously, they will be able to have a full-functioning and empowered life. There has to be a will to change, the will to do the self-work, and face the challenges that are holding them back.

Another aspect I learned was that my codependency and the need to be like everybody else, instead of embracing who I was, all went out the window only because I did the work.

When people are traveling through and experiencing tough journeys and have become a victim of circumstance, that's when I embrace them. I don't enable. I will never enable; rather, I empower. I encourage people—if they do the work, if they break through the brick wall that is standing in front of them, if they have the courage and a support network of those who love and care about them, true healing can begin. Until people are ready to break down that wall and face the pain, stress, anxiety, and/or depression, healing cannot begin.

I want to help people to acknowledge their despair, accept it, and surrender to the fact that they might need help. Please do it before it is too late. I don't want people to go through what I went through. It was a horrific experience. I felt the most excruciating pain; it was as though every nerve in my body was exposed and the wind was blowing on it every single day. I was filled with pain, with loss, with anguish, with anger. I never knew I had all these emotions bundled up in me. My message now is to inspire people and help them help themselves talk about what they are going through. If they don't, what gets stuffed down has to come out sometime and you never know when you will snap.

You must surround yourself with people who care about you, who love you, and who understand you. At that time, the people in my outpatient group therapy sessions became my support group because we were all going through some sort of tragedy. I sat on this story of struggle for five years. It is my personal story and it needs to be shared and heard by many.

Early in 2009, I received a phone call from a psychiatrist at the Behavioral Health Department at South Coast Medical Center. He shared with me how he went down to the outpatient program to acquire a success story patient to be their guest speaker.

I asked, "Who is your model patient?"

"You, Tanya Brown," was the response. After five years they remembered me. They remembered me because I worked so hard at changing myself. I spoke at a function they called "Dinner with the Docs." It gives local high school students an opportunity to meet doctors from the hospital. It was the first time my family ever heard me speak at an event on anything. That was when I received the support I had needed from my family. Not only did they listen to my story, but afterward they saw the teens come up to me sharing stories of their own such as: my girlfriend just tried to kill herself last week, my mom can't get out of bed because my dad's an alcoholic and she's falling into a deep depression. I was hearing these things from young teens and thought that there was no reason why they should be experiencing such turmoil.

So, I mustered up the courage and my friend, Lisa Mae Brunson, helped me write an article for an online magazine.

Now it's time to really focus on mental health and well-being issues. Primarily I need to reach out to the young kids, the parents, the corporate people who are overwhelmed, losing their jobs and killing themselves, and to the college kids who are overextended and not taking care of themselves because of added pressure to be perfect.

The number one cause of death on college campuses is suicide. Yet, for many years it was hazing. Kids, teens, and college aged students don't have time to have fun and be kids anymore. They are working on their resumes already when they are in high school. They need to be in the best class and be the best. When I was going to college students needed a 3.8 to get into a good school. Now they need a 4.5! What's that about? There is just too much pressure on people today.

Using the coping skills I learned, I finally understand how to manage my life. I learned how to control and contain stress, and I learned how to cope, with and identify the triggers that can set my emotions off. No one can get anywhere with that. However, I am human and I have my bad days, but with coping skills I eventually can gain back control.

WRIGHT

I can just hear the motivation. You received a bachelor's degree and aren't you working on a master's degree now?

BROWN

Yes. I finally completed my bachelor's degree, which was inspired by my hospital experience. I got my BA in Counseling Psychology, specializing in cognitive behavioral therapy. I then pursued my master's degree for one year. However, I temporarily withdrew for personal reasons.

Right now, however, I'm really focusing on launching my speaking and life coaching businesses. I am here to help others attain and maintain mental health and help them turn their breakdowns into breakthroughs. Right now this is my focus because I know it will save people's lives. People need to learn how to slow down and enjoy life. We're too quick to pop a pill in hopes problems will go away. We are a world where few of us have the tools to cope with life's ups and downs. People do not know how to breathe properly or manage their days because they are living too emotionally. They are not putting themselves first. It's okay to put yourself first. Without being healthy and happy yourself, how can others around you be? It's like the airplane safety announcement, "Please place the mask on yourself first, then assist others." This makes sense, right?

WRIGHT

So my final question to you is what made you ready to pursue your vision, goals, and turn your dream into a reality?

BROWN

I was ready and God knew I was ready, too. He wanted to use me and my own personal story of tragedy more than to live in Nicole's shadow. Nicole's murder and being a victim of domestic violence was an indirect experience. Even though it profoundly affected my family and the world—it influenced everybody for a lifetime—but I think my own experience is personal and powerful. I lived it, I felt it, and I worked through it, and I think that's when I began to believe. That is when I reached into my courage bucket and said, "Okay, this is what I need to do."

Another message is that I don't want other people to sit on their passion and their purpose. Everybody has a story inside them and they need to share that with others. You never know who may benefit or be saved from your story. People need help today and they need inspiration. My personal experience affected me greatly and it changed me forever. I came out on the other end a much better and stronger person.

If people who are reading this and are experiencing depression, anxiety, stress—whatever it is—talk to somebody; don't hold it in. I think that's one reason why we're seeing so much depression and suicide today. People are lost because they don't feel comfortable in talking to somebody about it; until they do, they're going to continue to suppress their emotions and that's their despair. Remember, what gets stuffed has to come out and mine came out in a really bad way. Had I known that counseling, group counseling, and talking to somebody would have helped, I would have done it, but I didn't know about those resources at the time. I always thought therapy was for the severely mentally ill. What I learned is that it is not—it is for everyone and anyone who needs to create harmony and peace in their life. Talk to somebody about it before it's too late.

WRIGHT

I really appreciate the time you've spent with me today. What a great dream and a great goal. I wish you so much success as you do this; God knows it's needed. You really honored us here today by answering these questions. I'm sure that our readers are really going to sit up and take notice. Hopefully someone who needs this advice will take what you've shared to heart; you might change someone's life for the better.

BROWN

I hope so; that's my goal.

WRIGHT

Today we've been talking with Tanya Brown, the youngest sister of Nicole Brown-Simpson. Tanya is an advocate, life coach, and speaker for mental health and relationship violence prevention. Her speaking style is engaging, as we have found here today. It is geared toward identifying, understanding, and proactively dealing with life's emotional pitfalls, disappointments, missed opportunities, and unrealistic expectations.

Tanya, thank you so much for being with us today on *Stepping Stones to Success*.

BROWN

Thank you, David.

ABOUT THE AUTHOR

TANYA BROWN, youngest sister of Nicole Brown-Simpson, is an advocate, life coach, and speaker for mental health and relationship violence prevention. She uses her own experiences to help others; she has found key tools that have allowed her to manage life's undertow and subsequently create a more fulfilled life for herself. Tanya has a keen understanding of personal difficulties and concerns that may affect one's ability to enjoy life to its fullest. Her speaking style is engaging and geared toward identifying, understanding, and proactively dealing with life's emotional pitfalls, disappointments, missed opportunities, and unrealistic expectations.

She addresses a variety of issues under the University of Life, specifically focusing on teens and college age students. Tanya Brown believes that change is approachable and that one can acquire proper management skills; life's challenges can develop into strengths. Her positive approach assists in creating an uplifting and inspiring presentation.

TANYA BROWN
949-278-5550
Tanya@tanyabrown.net
www.tanyabrown.net

CHAPTER TEN

Turning a Mental Breakdown into a Mental Breakthrough

An Interview with . . . **Dr. Deepak Chopra**

DAVID WRIGHT (WRIGHT)

Today we are talking to Dr. Deepak Chopra, founder of the Chopra Center for Well Being in Carlsbad, California. More than a decade ago, Dr. Chopra became the foremost pioneer in integrated medicine. His insights have redefined our definition of health to embrace body, mind and spirit. His books, which include, *Quantum Healing, Perfect Health, Ageless Body Timeless Mind*, and *The Seven Spiritual Laws of Success*, have become international bestsellers and are established classics.

Dr. Chopra, welcome to *Stepping Stones to Success*.

DR. DEEPAK CHOPRA (CHOPRA)

Thank you. How are you?

WRIGHT

I am doing just fine. It's great weather here in Tennessee.

CHOPRA

Great.

WRIGHT

Dr. Chopra, you stated in your book, *Grow Younger, Live Longer: 10 Steps to Reverse Aging,* that it is possible to reset your biostats up to fifteen years younger than your chronological age. Is that really possible?

CHOPRA

Yes. There are several examples of this. The literature on aging really began to become interesting in the 1980s when people showed that it was possible to reverse the biological marks of aging. This included things like blood pressure, bone density, body temperature, regulation of the metabolic rate, and other things like cardiovascular conditioning, cholesterol levels, muscle mass and strength of muscles, and even things like hearing, vision, sex hormone levels, and immune function.

One of the things that came out of those studies was that psychological age had a great influence on biological age. So you have three kinds of aging: chronological age is when you were born, biological age is what your biomarker shows, and psychological age is what your biostat says.

WRIGHT

You call our prior conditioning a prison. What do you mean?

CHOPRA

We have certain expectations about the aging process. Women expect to become menopausal in their early forties. People think they should retire at the age of sixty-five and then go Florida and spend the rest of their life in so-called retirement. These expectations actually influence the very biology of aging. What we call normal aging is actually the hypnosis of our social conditioning. If you can bypass that social conditioning, then you're free to reset your own biological clock.

WRIGHT

Everyone told me that I was supposed to retire at sixty-five. I'm somewhat older than that and as a matter of fact, today is my birthday.

CHOPRA

Well happy birthday. You know, the fact is that you should be having fun all the time and always feel youthful. You should always feel that you are contributing to society. It's not the retirement, but it's the passion with which you're involved in the well being of your society, your community, or the world at large.

WRIGHT

Great things keep happening to me. I have two daughters; one was born when I was fifty. That has changed my life quite a bit. I feel a lot younger than I am.

CHOPRA

The more you associate with young people, the more you will respond to that biological expression.

WRIGHT

Dr. Chopra, you suggest viewing our bodies from the perspective of quantum physics. That seems somewhat technical. Will you tell us a little bit more about that?

CHOPRA

You see, on one level, your body is made up of flesh and bone. That's the material level but we know today that everything we consider matter is born of energy and information. By starting to think of our bodies as networks of energy information and even intelligence, we begin to shift our perspective. We don't think of our bodies so much as dense matter, but as vibrations of consciousness. Even though it sounds technical, everyone has had an experience with this so-called quantum body. After, for example, you do an intense workout, you feel a sense of energy in your body—a tingling sensation. You're actually experiencing what ancient wisdom traditions call the "vital force." The more you pay attention to this vital force inside your body, the more you will experience it as energy, information, and intelligence, and the more control you will have over its expressions.

WRIGHT

Does DNA have anything to do with that?

CHOPRA

DNA is the source of everything in our body. DNA is like the language that creates the molecules of our bodies. DNA is like a protein-making factory, but DNA doesn't give us the blueprint. When I build a house, I have to go to the factory to find the bricks, but having the bricks is not enough. I need to get an architect, who in his or her consciousness can create that blueprint. And that blueprint exists only in your spirit and consciousness—in your soul.

WRIGHT

I was interested in a statement from your book. You said that perceptions create reality. What perceptions must we change in order to reverse our biological image?

CHOPRA

You have to change three perceptions. First you have to get rid of the perceptions of aging itself. Most people believe that aging means disease and infirmities. You have to change that. You have to regard aging as an opportunity for personal growth and spiritual growth. You also have to regard it as an opportunity to express the wisdom of your experience and an opportunity to help others and lift them from ordinary and mundane experience to the kind of experiences you are capable of because you have much more experience than they do.

The second thing you have to change your perception of is your physical body. You have to start to experience it as information and energy—as a network of information and intelligence.

The third thing you have to change your perception on is the experience of dying. If you are the kind of person who is constantly running out of time, you will continue to run out of time. On the other hand, if you have a lot of time, and if you do everything with gusto and love and passion, then you will lose track of time. When you lose track of time, your body does not metabolize that experience.

WRIGHT

That is interesting. People who teach time management don't really teach the passion.

CHOPRA

No, no. Time management is such a restriction of time. Your biological clock starts to age much more rapidly. I think what you have to really do is live your life with passion so that time doesn't mean anything to you.

WRIGHT

That's a concept I've never heard.

CHOPRA

Well, there you are.

WRIGHT

You spend an entire chapter of your book on deep rest as an important part of the reversal of the aging process. What is "deep rest"?

CHOPRA

One of the most important mechanisms for renewal and survival is sleep. If you deprive an animal of sleep, then it ages very fast and dies prematurely. We live in a culture where most of our population has to resort to sleeping pills and tranquilizers in order to sleep. That doesn't bring natural rejuvenation and renewal. You know that you have had a good night's sleep when you wake up in the morning, feeling renewed, invigorated, and refreshed—like a baby does. So that's one kind of deep rest. That comes from deep sleep and from natural sleep. In the book I talk about how you go about making sure you get that.

The second deep rest comes from the experience of meditation, which is the ability to quiet your mind so you still your internal dialogue. When your internal dialogue is still, then you enter into a stage of deep rest. When your mind is agitated, your body is unable to rest.

WRIGHT

I have always heard of people who had bad eyesight and really didn't realize it until they went to the doctor and were fitted for lenses. I had that same experience some years ago. For several years I had not really enjoyed the deep sleep you're talking about. The doctor diagnosed me with sleep apnea. Now I sleep like a baby, and it makes a tremendous difference.

CHOPRA

Of course it does. You now have energy and the ability to concentrate and do things.

WRIGHT

Dr. Chopra, how much do eating habits have to do with aging? Can we change and reverse our biological age by what we eat?

CHOPRA

Yes, you can. One of the most important things to remember is that certain types of foods actually contain anti-aging compounds. There are many chemicals that are contained in certain foods that have an anti-aging effect. Most of these chemicals are derived from light. There's no way to bottle them—there are no pills you can take that will give you these chemicals. But they're contained in plants that are rich in color and derived from photosynthesis. Anything that is yellow, green, and red or has a lot of color, such as fruits and vegetables, contain a lot of these very powerful anti-aging chemicals.

In addition, you have to be careful not to put food in your body that is dead or has no life energy. So anything that comes in a can or has a label, qualifies for that. You have to expose your body to six tastes: sweet, sour, salt, bitter, pungent, and astringent because those are the codes of intelligence that allow us to access the deep intelligence of nature. Nature and what she gives to us in bounty is actually experienced through the sense of taste. In fact, the light chemicals—the anti-aging substances in food—create the six tastes.

WRIGHT

Some time ago, I was talking to one of the ladies in your office and she sent me an invitation to a symposium that you had in California. I was really interested. The title was *Exploring the Reality of Soul*.

CHOPRA

Well, I conducted the symposium, but we had some of the world's scientists, physicists, and biologists who were doing research in what is called, non-local intelligence—the intelligence of soul or spirit. You could say it is the intelligence that orchestrates the activity of the universe—God, for example. Science and spirituality are now meeting together because by understanding how nature works and how the laws of nature work, we're beginning to get a glimpse of a deeper intelligence that people in spiritual traditions call divine, or God. I think this is a wonderful time to explore spirituality through science.

WRIGHT

She also sent me biographical information of the seven scientists that were with you. I have never read a list of seven more noted people in their industry.

CHOPRA

They are. The director of the Max Planck Institute, in Berlin, Germany, where quantum physics was discovered was there. Dr. Grossam was a professor of physics at the University of Oregon, and he talked about the quantum creativity of death and the survival of conscious after death. It was an extraordinary group of people.

WRIGHT

Dr. Chopra, with our *Stepping Stones to Success* book we're trying to encourage people to be better, live better, and be more fulfilled by listening to the examples of our guest authors. Is there anything or anyone in your life who has made a difference for you and has helped you to become a better person?

CHOPRA

The most important person in my life was my father. Every day he asked himself, "What can I do in thought, word, and deed to nurture every relationship I encounter just for today?" That has lived with me for my entire life.

WRIGHT

What do you think makes up a great mentor? Are there characteristics mentors seem to have in common?

CHOPRA

I think the most important attribute of a great mentor is that he or she teaches by example and not necessarily through words.

WRIGHT

When you consider the choices you've made down through the years, has faith played an important role?

CHOPRA

I think more than faith, curiosity, wonder, a sense of reference, and humility has. Now, if you want to call that faith, then, yes it has.

WRIGHT

In a divine being?

CHOPRA

In a greater intelligence—intelligence that is supreme, infinite, unbounded, and too mysterious for the finite mind to comprehend.

WRIGHT

If you could have a platform and tell our audience something you feel would help them and encourage them, what would you say?

CHOPRA

I would say that there are many techniques that come to us from ancient wisdom and tradition that allow us to tap into our inner resources and allow us to become beings who have intuition, creativity, vision, and a connection to that which is sacred. Finding that within ourselves, we have the means to enhance our well-being. Whether it's physical, emotional, or environmental, we have the means to resolve conflicts and get rid of war. We have the means to be really healthy. We have the means for being economically uplifted. That knowledge is the most important knowledge that exists.

WRIGHT

I have seen you on several primetime television shows down through the years where you have had the time to explain your theories and beliefs. How does someone like me experience this? Do we get it out of books?

CHOPRA

Books are tools that offer you a road map. Sit down every day, close your eyes, put your attention in your heart, and ask yourself two questions: who am

I and what do I want? Then maintain a short period of stillness in body and mind as in prayer or meditation, and the door will open.

WRIGHT

So, you think that the intelligence comes from within. Do all of us have that capacity?

CHOPRA

Every child born has that capacity.

WRIGHT

That's fascinating. So, it doesn't take trickery or anything like that?

CHOPRA

No, it says in the Bible in the book of Psalms, "Be still and know that I am God"—Psalm 46:10.

WRIGHT

That's great advice.

I really do appreciate your being with us today. You are fascinating. I wish I could talk with you for the rest of the afternoon. I'm certain I am one of millions who would like to do that!

CHOPRA

Thank you, sir. It was a pleasure to talk with you!

WRIGHT

Today we have been talking with Dr. Deepak Chopra, founder of The Chopra Center. He has become the foremost pioneer in integrated medicine. We have found today that he really knows what he's talking about. After reading his book, *Grow Younger, Live Longer: 10 Steps to Reverse Aging,* I can tell you that I highly recommend it. I certainly hope you'll go out to your favorite book store and buy a copy.

Dr. Chopra, thank you so much for being with us today on *Stepping Stones to Success.*

CHOPRA

Thank you for having me, David.

ABOUT THE AUTHOR

DEEPAK CHOPRA has written more than fifty books, which have been translated into many languages. He is also featured on many audio and videotape series, including five critically acclaimed programs on public television. He has also written novels and edited collections of spiritual poetry from India and Persia. In 1999, *Time* magazine selected Dr. Chopra as one of the Top 100 Icons and Heroes of the Century, describing him and "the poet-prophet of alternative medicine."

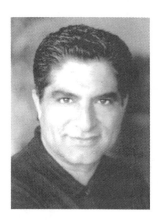

DR. DEEPAK CHOPRA

The Chopra Center
2013 Costa del Mar Rd.
Carlsbad, CA 92009
info@chopra.com
www.chopra.com

CHAPTER ELEVEN

Gratitude Positioning for Success: Your Personal GPS

An Interview with . . . **Laurie Moritz**

DAVID WRIGHT (WRIGHT)

Today we're talking with Laurie Moritz, a Reconnective Healing/The Reconnection Practitioner as well as a certified Practitioner of The One Command. She is also a member of Toastmasters International and holds the CTM designation. She is a past student and graduate assistant of Dale Carnegie Training and holds the Train the Trainer certification from Peak Potentials Training (T. Harv Eker, author of *Secrets of the Millionaire Mind*). She is also a spiritual life coach. Laurie has always believed that gratitude is a key ingredient of success.

Laurie, welcome to *Stepping Stones to Success*.

LAURIE MORITZ (MORITZ)

Thank you.

WRIGHT

Laurie, what is your definition of success?

MORITZ

My definition is that people who are reading this book are already successful because they understand that they want to be more. With this knowledge, everything is possible. The desire to be more is inherent in all of us, but not everyone takes action. Not everyone explores how to become who he or she wants to be and what he or she wants to create. Readers of this book are taking the first step.

The next step is to make a decision to apply the knowledge that you are receiving here. An important component of success is a belief in yourself that you can make changes and that you deserve to have what you want. Stumbling blocks for many are the limiting beliefs that "I can't do it" or "I can't have it." These beliefs stop you from taking action and moving forward. Being able to get past these beliefs is key to realizing your full potential.

WRIGHT

Why is gratitude so important in creating the life we want?

MORITZ

We co-create our lives and everything in it by the focus of our thoughts. If we give our attention to everything that is wrong or going wrong, that is what we will continue to create. By keeping our focus on everything we love and appreciate in our lives right now, we will attract more things that make us feel grateful—it's the *feeling* that matters the most.

Gratitude works and is supported by all of the universal laws—laws I learned about in Bob Proctor's *The Secret Science of Getting Rich*. You can't really speak about one law without speaking about the others because they all work in harmony and support each other. I have included an overview of some of the main laws that interact with each other.

The first is called the Law of Perpetual Transmutation. This law explains that the non-physical level of life is always moving into physical form. It explains how our very thoughts create ideas, ideas influence our emotions, and our emotions cause us to take action that creates the physical results. This whole process is driven by our energy in various states of awareness. When we are in our limited ordinary mind, our ability to manifest is contracted. When we're in greater states of awareness, our ability to manifest is expanded.

The next law is the Law of Relativity. Nothing is good or bad, big or small, until it is compared to something else. Be aware that there is always someone who is less successful than you are, and there is always someone who is considered more successful. It all depends on who you are comparing yourself with. For instance, if you start something new and you're still learning how to use this new knowledge or skill and you compare yourself to an expert, you're going to come up short—you're going to see yourself as lacking—this is using the law against yourself. Give yourself room to succeed, acknowledge how far you've come compared to where you began, and always remember to let this law work *for* you.

The last law that I want to mention is called the Law of Cause and Effect. For every action we take, there is a cause. Everything that we put out into the universe comes back to us. If we exude gratitude, which is an emotional, positive action, more good things come back to us, which is the effect. And when we keep the cycle in motion, our lives become more positive and the universe acts as a mirror of our behavior. With this law in mind, remember to always treat others with kindness, respect, and integrity. Concentrate on what you can do with positive energy and the effect will take care of itself.

WRIGHT

Why do you some people find it difficult to express and experience gratitude?

MORITZ

How many times have we heard "just think positive"? Well, here's the thing: we are so used to searching out and identifying what's wrong in our lives that it's difficult to experience gratitude and to actually recognize the good. I became aware that in the past I used complaining as a way to connect with people. Think about it—everyone seems to do this. We commiserate about the weather, the government, the economy, the stock market, and the list goes on and on. Complaining and focusing on the negative is epidemic. We forget that we have the opportunity to make choices. We actually can choose our thoughts and how we perceive the world, and we must remember that we have so much that we probably take for granted such as our families, modern conveniences, and the Internet, for example. We even take for granted our ability to walk on our own two legs and breathe in and out. We're often stuck in a groove, addicted to our habitual thinking—our way of thinking that says I'd rather be right than happy.

I know someone who loves to predict what's going to happen in her life. Now that would be great if she recognized that she had creative power, but she doesn't. She doesn't realize that she has this power and continually predicts what is going to go wrong. You can probably guess what happens—her prediction comes true and then she can say, "I just knew that was going to happen."

I've found that I prefer being right about the good things I'm attracting in my life. The opposite of complaining is gratitude and rather than railing against what we don't want, be thankful for what we do have and are experiencing. With gratitude you can change everything.

WRIGHT

How can I be grateful if I realize I'm not creating the life that I want?

MORITZ

I've come to realize that everything that has happened in my life has brought me to this point; my experiences have molded me into who I believe I am in this moment. We've all heard that everything happens for a reason, and it does. I am grateful for all of the hardships, the disappointments, and the wrong turns, because I'm here right now. Right now I realize that I not only created my past, but I'm also creating my present and my future. So everything that has happened has prepared me to be the person I'm becoming right now in this moment. It is also preparing me to become the person I want to be in the future.

WRIGHT

Well, how did you overcome your own perceived limitations?

MORITZ

To be honest, it's a process and I'm continually working on it. It's similar to peeling an onion, I get past one obstacle and then there is the next one.

There have been three major influences that have transformed my life and helped me to find my voice. The first was participating in Dale Carnegie

Training. Up until that time I didn't know how to express my ideas, either one-on-one and definitely not in front of groups of people. I didn't realize my own uniqueness and inherent talent and love of speaking until I'd taken that course. For the first time, I consciously experienced getting out of my own way. It showed me that I had tremendous courage and ability. I also realized how much my own unconscious programs play a part in keeping my perceived limitations alive.

I also learned that no matter how real fear can seem, it's really just an illusion. I heard a great acronym for fear recently—False Evidence Appearing Real (FEAR). Fear is always based in the future; it is not in the present or current moment. Over the years I've continued to peel the onion.

The next great influence for me was Rhonda Byrne's book *The Secret,* and it changed everything. Up until then I had no idea I had the power of co-creation. This knowledge put me on this fantastic journey that I'm now on. Her breakthrough, easy-to-understand information about energy and universal intelligence opened me up to new ways of thinking and living. I continue to evolve, to attract knowledge, resources, and tools that are transforming my life, right before my eyes, like this book for instance.

I also recently discovered The One Command teaching and it is recreating my relationship with my inner self, my family, and my finances. It is *the* most powerful technique I have experienced to date for rewriting the hard drive of my mind. I have had the privilege of meeting and working with the creator/author of *The One Command,* Asara Lovejoy. She has become my touchstone on what is possible for my life, in many new directions.

WRIGHT

Would you explain what "the greatness that resides within you" means in The One Command process?

MORITZ

Discovering how to engage in another portion of my own intelligence beyond my perceived limitations—an intelligence that is mine and contains all that is great within me including my own success DNA programming—was a very challenging notion, at first. Asara says, "You are largely operating in a very small sphere of influence, one that is defined by your Beta brainwave, which is your ordinary thinking mind in which you spend about 98 percent of your waking time, rather than your extraordinary intelligence, your Theta, universal mind. In Theta, you realize the greatness that you already have right within you, including your very own success DNA." Now, why wouldn't you want to live there? According to Asara, "We don't engage in our greater intelligence because: 1) we don't realize that we can and 2) the process of going into Theta consciously has to be learned."

Neuroscientists identify our Theta brainwave as our deep sleep state, especially our REM (Rapid Eye Movement) sleep. This is where we discharge our emotions and solve our problems. Our Theta brainwave is where our subconscious beliefs and programs reside. Processing our subconscious feelings, fears, and desires is so necessary that if you are deprived of your REM sleep, psychosis or worse can occur.

Consciously going into your Theta mind while awake is the power behind The One Command. Being in Theta has amazing properties of well-being, problem-solving, and creating what you want in almost seemingly miraculous ways.

Asara also shared that "Thousands of people have learned that they can indeed reach this Theta state while awake. They have learned to go from Beta to Theta in six easy steps; and while in Theta, issue the powerful statement known as The One Command. Imagine having a problem or a negative thought or belief that is constantly nagging at you that you can't ever seem to get around, or erase, or solve. Now, imagine that you can change the negative feelings and solve the problem instantly. I discovered how to do exactly that through The One Command." Now that is powerful and exceptional, and I also enjoy hearing about experiences others are reporting.

Here are a couple of experiences Asara shared that I especially like. The first is from a lady named Christine, who says, "I purchased *The One Command* several days ago and I have to say that this is one of the best books I have ever read. It is exactly what I have been looking for. I commanded to get out of my lease early and I got an e-mail from the landlord yesterday advising me that they are ready to start showing the unit to people to let me out of the lease early. This is great! I am also happy to report that I have started to feel the changes that are supposed to take place. It has a sort of magnetic sensation to it, and it is great."

The last one is from a gentleman name Suresh and here is what he had to say: "You may hear this hundreds of times a day, but I have to say it to you once more. Thank you so much for sharing this unique knowledge so generously.

Just when *The One Command* arrived some days ago, I felt a rush of certainty and presence in my being. In every line and word I feel your profound knowledge and wisdom. Reading it is like drinking more and more of this beautiful nectar. Yes, it's true, this I am. Yes, it's possible. Even what I thought unchangeable can change now. I've read many books about changing, the power of self, how to create attraction and money, and so on, and there were only three that really hammered me within the last ten years. The first was the book, called *Everything Can Change,* the second, *Ho'oponopono,* and the third is your book, but *The One Command* tops them all. The power emanating from this book is just beyond words." These testimonials are for the book called *The One Command,* by Asara Lovejoy.

WRIGHT

Why has The One Command process been such a powerful experience for you?

MORITZ

I read Asara's words that I have the power in my Theta mind to dissolve negative thoughts in an instant and simultaneously create a new thought that replaces the negative one. This new thought, emotion, and feeling then defines my reality in a new and expanded capacity and brings me new and masterful experiences. In addition, by doing so, I can create a way of thinking and being that realizes the greatness already within me. While reading Asara's book, I just had to know how to experience Theta and how to apply it in my life right now. I discovered the six easy steps to consciously access the Theta brainwave and, while there, command a new experience that then came back into the cells of my body, including my DNA, as a new belief about my life.

I'll explain the six steps in a moment, but first I'd like to answer the question about how this works. Many authors, including those you're reading in this book, have defined our ability to change the cells of our body even down to the DNA by our thinking. Our thoughts are described as almost amorphous fields of energy that create our possibilities and our limitations and are the filters of what we can accept or reject. We only allow ourselves to attract what we perceive as possible and repel anything else from our lives. We're already masters of our lives because what we think creates what we experience. Knowing that this is true makes it easy to understand that by changing the filters—the beliefs of what we think is possible—means we must have new experiences. It is 100 percent guaranteed.

What is unique to this process is doing this change work in your Theta brainwave. By making changes directly in your subconscious mind, you are, in effect, redesigning the thought filters of your beliefs; and as a consequence, you immediately attract new experiences. This is a biological and a physiological change in the neuronet firing sequence of your brain, the cells of your body, and your DNA. It is powerful and simple beyond belief.

WRIGHT

Would you share a personal experience of how you have used The One Command process?

MORITZ

I certainly can. My intuition had literally been a closed door to me for most of my life. Although I've continued to grow and expand throughout my life, I've always held myself back. I didn't trust myself; I'd learned that I couldn't trust anyone else either. I just couldn't understand why I still had such a difficult time opening myself up to people, trusting people, and mostly trusting myself. Through The One Command process, I learned that I had slammed the door on my own trust and intuition because of a violent childhood incident that I experienced.

When I was twelve years old, my mother and stepfather separated and my family was divided. He took his kids, and my older brother, older sister, and I remained with my mother. One day I was getting ready to go to school and my stepfather stopped by unexpectedly. He seemed very agitated and I sensed something wasn't right—something wasn't good about the whole situation. Reluctantly, I let him into the apartment and continued to get ready for school. A few minutes later, I heard shouting and then three gunshots. I ran from the apartment in hysterics, certain I was going to get a bullet in my back; I had no idea if my mother was alive or dead. Now, before we go any further, I do want to let you know that my mother did survive, but it's only now that my family is starting to come back together.

By opening that door to such trauma and violence, I'd also slammed the door on my own inner knowing. Somehow I felt that I was to blame for opening that door, and I felt responsible for the horrible outcome. Deep down I had decided that I didn't want to know anything in advance or recognize my intuition ever again. As traumatic as this experience was, I believed this incident is what set me on my path of self-discovery and healing. Through The One Command process, I reopened the door to my intuition and released the negative memories and judgments against myself in moments. What a relief that was, and now I know I can release any of the frozen emotions and fears that I've trapped in my body and my psyche.

I also used The One Command to write this chapter. I commanded that I would easily tap into my inspiration and attract the people and resources that I would need to create a meaningful chapter for this book.

WRIGHT

Is The One Command difficult to learn and apply?

MORITZ

Here is the really good part about this process; the six steps are laid out clearly in the book *The One Command*. The book also includes practice sheets to help walk you through this exercise first so that your body can actually physically learn how to go from ordinary, waking Beta thinking to extraordinary Theta thinking; and while in Theta, issue The One Command statement.

There are three parts to The One Command statement, and it starts with "I don't know how." This simple statement stops your negative thoughts in an instant. I want you to close your eyes right now and see how this works. Just think a negative thought, like "I hate doing exercises in books," for example. Then, mentally say, *"I don't know how."* Did you notice how your negative thought either disappeared or was reduced in energy? The reason this happens is because the brain cannot hold two ideas at the same time. The most common comment about this simple exercise is, "I felt so relieved that I didn't have to have the answer," which by the way we mostly don't in our Beta, worrisome, thinking mind and we always do in our extraordinary Theta mind.

The second part of The One Command statement is where you state what you want instead in present time, because there is only the now in the subconscious mind. I said, *"I trust my intuition to guide me in all areas of my life, I only know that I do now.*

The final part of The One Command is the blessing, which is *"and I am fulfilled."* So here is what it all looks like together:

1. I don't know how
2. I trust my intuition to guide me in all areas of my life - I only know that I do now
3. And I am fulfilled

Following is the six-step process that you use to access your Theta brainwave and state The One Command.

STEP ONE: GROUND

Grounding is where you come into your body, whether you're sitting or you're standing; close your eyes and just sense your physical body. Many of us spend nearly all of our waking moments in our heads. Instead of being in your mind and thinking, come into your body and feel your own energy (i.e., pulsations in your fingertips or toes and everything in between). Once you can feel your body, then visualize your energy going down your legs into your feet and then deep into the Earth and connect with the magnetic energy of the Earth. Once you feel grounded, you're ready to go to Step 2. (Remember, there is no right or wrong way to do this. Just trust that your body knows what to do.)

STEP TWO: ALIGN

Visualize the Earth's magnetic energy. Take a deep breath and visualize that energy being pulled up from the Earth into your feet. Take another deep breath and visualize that energy moving up your legs, up your torso, and into your heart center. Breathe in love and exhale gratitude. You're now ready to go on to Step 3.

STEP THREE: GO TO THETA

You do this by looking up under your closed eyelids, as though you were looking up into the universe. Your eyes will want to vibrate back and forth and go into an almost REM pattern, because they aren't used to rolling up so high for such a long period of time. This is actually a very normal thing for your eyes to do, so don't be alarmed. This physical act of raising your eyes up under your eyelids actually turns your brainwave from Beta down to Theta.

STEP FOUR: COMMAND

While in Theta, you make your One Command Statement. For instance, I could command:

1. I don't know how
2. I open my heart and mind to living in gratitude - I only know that I do now,
3. And I am fulfilled

STEP FIVE: EXPAND

While you still have your eyes rolled up in Theta, you expand on your idea. This is where you visualize or feel something even greater than what you've imagined for yourself. Then you direct that knowledge from the universe and what this new belief is for you.

STEP SIX: RECEIVE

This is where you receive this new knowledge. Keeping your eyes closed, let your eyes come down from under your eyelids and rest them in a natural place, then bring all of that new experience back down into your body. As you do so, imagine that you unwind, unwind, unwind (you are literally telling your DNA strands to do this and they're doing it) all of your old fears and beliefs, all of your negative emotions, everything that is keeping you stuck and then you rewind, rewind, rewind your new beliefs now and state, *"I am fulfilled."*

You can apply this technique to any life situation you want to improve, remove, or change, like increasing your flow of money, better relationships, elimination of post traumatic stress, health, and well-being. Asara often says that this can be the next best adventure of your life, and I encourage you to investigate the possibilities.

WRIGHT

How can I change my mind set to one of gratitude and achieve my personal definition of success?

MORITZ

The One Command is a powerful technique to use to get past negative beliefs that no longer serve you and literally release them from your mind and your very DNA.

I also have some additional tools to enhance The One Command, as I've learned that there is no one right way for every person to achieve success or to change his or her mindset. I believe that success is a journey; there is really no end point. When you're on a journey, it pays to have a compass or some form of navigation, hence your own personal GPS. I call it your Gratitude Positioning for Success.

Following are a few GPS tips and tools you can use to achieve your "attitude of gratitude." However, they will work only if you really work with them. I cannot stress enough how powerful writing down your intentions can be. Why is capturing our intentions in writing so powerful? Because it makes them real.

The first one is what I call the Gratitude Programming System. We can literally reprogram our brains for gratitude. For thirty days, write out all of the things you're grateful for, no matter how big or small and don't miss a single day or you'll need to start over. It's been proven that our brains reprogram themselves by repeating a thought or act over and over for thirty days straight.

You can also use The One Command to ask for more things to be grateful for. For instance, I don't know how I find more reasons to be grateful, I only know I do now and I am fulfilled. Or you can command that you understand what the feeling of gratitude is: I don't know how I feel and trust gratitude as useful and helpful in my life, I only know that I do now and I am fulfilled. You take yourself through the six steps and command away. Using The One Command automatically reprograms your brain, your body, and your DNA to attract and reveal more great things to appreciate.

The next tool is called Goals Plus Soul. This is where you create goals that resonate with you and define them specifically. Many people define success in terms of wealth or money. Everyone wants to be rich, but what you will come to realize is that it's the end result that you truly want. It would be great to have piles of money from floor to ceiling in your living room, for instance. But money just sits there, doesn't it? In truth, you actually want the freedom and the experiences that having money can provide such as taking care of your family, traveling, and so on. The only thing you cannot buy with money is time—it is precious and priceless. With that, it only makes sense that you want to spend your time on this planet providing a product or service that resonates with you and feeds your soul. You may not know what that looks like, but you do know what a product or service that does *not* resonate with you looks like. That's okay—contrast provides information about what we do want to be, do, and have in our lives. When you do find the product or service that fits you, your goals, and provides value to your clients or customers, you are in the flow. When you're in the flow, opportunities and synchronicities start to happen, and the road will rise up to meet you.

The last is called Go Post Success. This technique is important because we don't recognize all the things we're doing successfully already. For example, I'm a marathon runner and I used to think of running as something that I had to do; I never stopped to think that physical activity is a success catalyst. Not only do I feel great in having increased energy, but it's my best thinking time. I have wonderful epiphanies when I run.

Is there something that you do every day for yourself that you're not giving yourself credit for because it's just part of your routine? What I'd like you to do is write down five successes every day for thirty days straight. Remember: what you focus or put your attention on is what you will create. Keep your focus on your successes to create more of what you want in your life. Remember to mark the moment when you realize that you have created a success. This strengthens your belief in yourself that you are already successful each and every day.

Part of my nightly ritual is to write down five successes—five things to be grateful for, and three to five things to accomplish the next day. I create accomplish lists, rather than to-do lists because it makes me feel good instead of feeling stress or resistance. When I do this routine, I am sending out the intention of what I want to focus on the next day and my subconscious mind works for me while I sleep. It arranges my thoughts and ideas and puts the intention out into the universe to help me achieve my goals.

I am so excited for you! Whether this is the first time you've heard about The One Command and the Universal Laws or you're well versed, these techniques and truths will transform your life.

But there is one thing that you must understand: knowledge is not power until you've applied it. So, remember to take inspired action. Trust that you are becoming aware of your own power, and as you grow in this knowledge, opportunities will start popping up everywhere—opportunities that you would not have perceived if you were not on the right frequency to see them and say "yes" and embrace them. Say "yes" and be grateful for everything that comes to you and your life will transform.

ABOUT THE AUTHOR

LAURIE MORITZ enjoys empowering people through the use of The One Command. She is a certified practitioner of The One Command and holds the CTM designation from Toastmasters International. In addition to being a graduate and graduate assistant of the Dale Carnegie Training Course, she also holds the Train the Trainer certification from Peak Potentials Training (T. Harv Eker, author of *Secrets of the Millionaire Mind*). Laurie is also a Reconnective Healing/The Reconnection Practitioner and a spiritual life coach.

LAURIE MORITZ

319.731.0236
Laurie@ReconnectToBalance.com
Laurie@RunningSpiritCoaching.com
www.ReconnectToBalance.com
www.RunningSpiritCoaching.com

CHAPTER TWELVE

NOTE TO SELF:
Remembering What You Already Know

An Interview with . . . **Linda Edgecombe**

DAVID WRIGHT (WRIGHT)

Today we're talking with Linda Edgecombe, CSP. Linda is an internationally renowned award-winning humorous speaker, trainer, best-selling author, and professional speaking coach. She energizes every audience as she leads people to loosen up, lighten the load, and laugh. Inside all the laughter, Linda encourages people to find the meaning in what they do and let go of what's not working. Her audiences are inspired to shift their perspectives on life, work, and themselves. She has been featured in the *Wall Street Journal* as an expert in shifting perspectives; her message is as welcome as a deep belly laugh and as profound as an honest look in the mirror.

Linda, welcome to *Stepping Stones to Success*.

LINDA EDGECOMBE (EDGECOMBE)

David, it is my pleasure. I love and appreciate being a part of this project.

WRIGHT

So you state that motivation is a physics equation. What do you mean?

EDGECOMBE

I believe that motivation does not come from me or anybody else standing in front of a room blabbing at people. Motivation comes from all of us, individually, by literally putting one foot in front of the other and moving into something. When that happens, physics takes over because inertia takes effect. When you move on something, it takes on a life of its own—the snowball effect. So being a physics equation means that you have to put some energy into something and move on it, and it starts to unfold and move forward. Just blabbing about it doesn't do it.

WRIGHT

You start your presentations by asking the question: are you doing the best you can right now? Why do you start your presentations with that question?

EDGECOMBE

When I speak, one of the first parts of my agenda includes this question because I want people to realize that we all have a lot on our plate and that it's a choice. I ask them to actually write down, in first person to themselves, "How am I doing?" I then make sure they write down the word "considering." I say, "Considering what?" What I mean is, considering literally everything you're choosing to put on your plate right now.

We all pile a lot of stuff on our plates, and most everything we pile on is a choice. How we respond to everything on our plate is definitely a choice.

WRIGHT

Why do you think people pile so much on their plates these days?

EDGECOMBE

I think there are two reasons why we pile so much stuff on. Number one, when you have a lot of stuff going on—you're volunteering here, you're working half-time, full-time, or double-time, working in your schools, and in your churches, in your communities, and you're coaching this sport and that activity, and driving your kids—it's all very admirable. You look good when you're really, really busy. People around us are impressed that we are managing all of this, so they give us lots of really good feedback for being so busy.

The second reason I believe that we pile so much stuff on our plates is because at some level, whether it's conscious or subconscious, you know you can't do it all, so being really busy is a great out. It's much easier for us to get out of committing to something because we're so busy than it is to say "no" in the first place. In the meantime, however, because you're so busy, you get great feedback, you get great accolades—wow, you're very impressive!

If I ask my audiences that question, I'll also ask, "What's the most common answer to the 'how are you doing' question?" In chorus, they'll all say "Fine," then they'll respond with the word "busy." "Oh I'm fine. I'm fine, but I'm busy." See, "fine" to me is a word that we've all become accustomed to. It is very nondescript—it doesn't have to go anywhere because most of the time we don't really want to go there. Because of manners or being cordial, we ask people how they are doing and they respond, "Fine and busy."

WRIGHT

Tell our readers about your thoughts on "Life's Ultimate Goal."

EDGECOMBE

I actually believe there are two ultimate goals, but the first one that every one of us goes after, day after day, year after year, whether we are working or doing other things, is *happiness*. Often I'll ask my audience, "Who's been doing this work for [whatever organization it is] for the last five years, ten years, twenty years or more?" I try to find out who in this group has hung in there the longest. Sometimes it's thirty-eight years, sometimes it's forty-two years. Are they seeking happiness? I feel this is the goal we are all going after every day. Now, not all of us use the words "happy" or "happiness" because for some of us, those words may just be a little bit too trite or too thin or whatever the word might be. Some people might want to use the term "inner peace" or self-satisfaction or a sense of contribution. I use the word "happiness" to encompass those concepts because most people understand the word happiness.

The other piece around happiness, which is rather funny, is that although we are going after it every day, most of us don't have a clear picture of how we define that word individually for ourselves. I try to encourage people to think about their own recipe for this crazy thing called happiness—where do you hang your soul when you're stressed, what makes you say, "Ahhh," what kinds of smells, scenes, situations, and experiences make you feel happy? I want people to really think and start to document their recipe. I get them to think about the big and small things that make them feel good. Most of us have some pretty general ones that are common. We want to do well at work. We want to have a healthy family and we want to be healthy ourselves. We want a nice place to live and lay our head down at night. But there is a lot more to the happiness recipe. I usually try to get them to dig a little bit deeper when asking about life's ultimate goal.

One question I often ask is, "When was the last time you had one of those days where 'the stars were aligned' for you?" All of us have our ideas and images for this kind of a day or moment. For some people it might be on the water in their boat, it might be fishing, maybe hiking up in the hills somewhere, or skiing on a beautiful winter day. Maybe you find it during a dinner party with some friends and you find the conversation at that moment fantastic and you say, "You know what guys, it doesn't get any better than this!"

Now, I've read different things over the years about this thing called happiness, and there are different theories of thought around how many of those "it doesn't get any better than this" moments we need in a year. Probably a half a dozen to a dozen max is great. You don't want them every day because if you had them every day, you wouldn't appreciate them as much. But the crazy thing about this is, that when you're clear on the recipe, "the stars tend to line up" and you will recognize the "it doesn't get any better than this" moments quicker.

WRIGHT

So tell us about life's second ultimate goal.

EDGECOMBE

If the first one is happiness, the second one, I believe, is that when you leave this world (and for the most part, one never knows when that is going to be), you want to leave with as few regrets as possible. I'm not a big believer in the no regrets thing because that's extreme to me, but I think as few regrets as possible is more powerful for people.

I love the movie, *The Bucket List*. As you are reading this chapter, I am literally headed to Nepal to do one of my "bucket list" items—hiking up to base camp on Mount Everest. I don't want to regret that I never took this opportunity to achieve one of my goals.

We all have un-dones. This includes phenomenal writers, musicians, managers, small business owners, comedians, and parents. All of us have some stuff we want to try just for the sake of trying it. What gets in the way of our going out there and trying stuff, for the most part, is a crazy ailment called "perfectionism."

If you suffer from the ailment of perfectionism or if you were brought up with the idea that if you can't do something well, don't do it at all, you have a great reason to not try at all because both are great excuses. I use the word "excuse" very passionately and people don't like it, but they're great excuses not to move on anything. It's never going to be perfect, but who gives a rip whether you're the best at something or not? Now, I justify that thought with my personality style, which is a very eclectic. I'm very ambitious, but I'm all over the board. I'm a scatterbrain and I'm not very detailed, but I'm ambitious, so the only way I get things done or accomplish anything is I have become a compulsive goal-setter.

What I know about this is that *it's* not about the goal. It's never about the goal, but you don't know what it *is* going to be about until you actually start out and move on the goal. In the middle of going after the goal it turns into something else. So when I say who cares whether you're the best photographer, the best musician, the best whatever, that's irrelevant—the point is to just move on it and see what unfolds with as few regrets as possible.

WRIGHT

Your new book has a section title called, "Are You on the Deferred Life Plan?" So what do you mean by that?

EDGECOMBE

Most of us culturally are raised on the deferred life plan, meaning that we are raised to put things off until something better comes along. Whether it's more time, more money, a better body, better relationships, a better job, you procrastinate. You have kids and the kids are grown and yet you still keep putting off the stuff you want to do until something else happens. Most of us have this problem. We keep deferring and we're okay with that. We finish high school and we say, "As soon as I finish college [or university], then life will actually start to kick in." Then we complete university and we think, "Okay, maybe if I actually got that job then I'd feel better about myself." So we get that job, and we begin thinking, "Well, actually, if I was making a bit more money—" Then we start going after promotions. Now we start thinking. "If I had a person in my life, then I'd feel more fulfilled." We meet the person, then, as I always say, you both sit down over a bottle of wine one night and say, "Well, if we actually had kids, then we'd really feel fulfilled as a family." Then you have the kids and say, "Okay, well, when the kids graduate and move out of the house, then we're going to - ."

We just keep pushing it off. We basically keep pushing the carrot out there, and wonder why at thirty-five (usually it's a little later, maybe forty-five, fifty-five, or sixty-five) we begin to resent this crazy thing we call work or the life we've created. We're thinking, "Why am I not doing the things I want to do?" Most of us (in most countries I've ever worked in or spoke in) are culturally living our lives on this thing I call the Deferred Life Plan.

WRIGHT

Can people really have the life they say they want, or is that just a bunch of personal development jargon?

EDGECOMBE

I think it comes down to how you look at the life you have. I don't know why I was raised with the ideal or the philosophy that I have, but I don't believe that life has to be hard—everything in life does not have to be hard for it to be real. I have family members who feel if life comes too easy to you, you're cheating or something.

I look at life with the mentality that it rolls out and plays out, actually very, very well for me. It always has and I expect that it always will. Now, don't get me wrong, I do massive charity work in the country of Nepal and believe me, the plight of people there is very, very different from my circumstances, living in a very prosperous country. However, when I talk to the girls and women in Nepal, they don't see themselves as having a terrible life. They see themselves as very happy, very cheerful, day to day. I think we create exactly what we want and that's a mindset.

I was speaking in Orlando last week and met a couple who hiked to base camp on Mt. Everest last year, so of course I asked them lots of questions. The woman was from St. Petersburg, Soviet Union, and in her Russian accent, she said, "Just remember, Linda, you must have a positive attitude when you're hiking. There are going to be some tough days for you but you must keep a positive attitude." I said, "Thank you," realizing that I talk about this stuff all the time, but it was a reminder to me that I'm going to need that little voice in my head on a few of those days. So is it hooey to have the life you say you want? You know what? I (and I'm sure you're no different than I am), surround myself with pretty great people and my energy feeds off their energy.

WRIGHT

Is having fun and laughing a long-forgotten memory of something we've done in another life?

EDGECOMBE

Well, it depends on the person. I pride myself on being a humorous speaker, that's how I've marketed myself for years, it's a big part of the program, so I have become very good at nurturing funny. I see things funny and I see things funny fairly quickly—I actually call it "finding your own funny faster." It's a skill you have to acquire if you tend to see the dark side more quickly than the light side. Let's say, the reason that you do see the dark side is because it's become your habit. I tend to see the funny side and laugh very easily because it's become my habit.

If I take a fitness class or a yoga class (usually its yoga because the stretches hurt for me), when I'm in those situations I laugh; it's like a default for me.

Having fun and laughter is something that some of us need to grow and nurture. I always say that when you're having a tough day or a tough week, don't go rent *Silence of the Lambs* again, or watch another *CSI,* not that they're bad shows but they just aren't pick-me-ups. If you need a little more humor, you have to create opportunities to surround yourself with humor—watch a funny show, listen to a great comedian. When you're on a long road trip, start to nurture your "funny bone"—your sense of humor and look for road signs that are ironic or different or funny. Looking for "funny" is a skill—it's a habit that takes a bit of practice.

WRIGHT

So why do you think we go from being teenagers whose most common answer to every question is nothing, to being adults whose most common answer is "I'm too busy"?

EDGECOMBE

I have teenagers—a fifteen- and a twelve-year-old. I'll ask, "So what are you guys doing?"

"Nothing," they'll answer.

"Well," I'll ask, "who are you hanging out with?"

"No one."

"Where are you going?"

"Nowhere."

They don't want to answer you. Then we become adults and it goes like this:

"So what are you up to Linda?"

"I'm busy. Oh gosh, I'm busy!"

As I said previously, it's a state I think that probably in the last twenty years we have come to admire. We've come to think highly of the Baby Boomers who are usually really busy.

If you're a Baby Boomer and you work with twenty-somethings, you'll probably agree that people in this generation look at their life very differently than Boomers do. (I'm a forty-nine-year-old). Our work ethic is different because we bought in differently. The younger generations have bought into a lifestyle that is, with all due respect, probably healthier than the one those of us who are older bought into. We, however, judge their work ethic as lazy. We give people a tough time if they decide they've got to leave work early because they want to do something for themselves. We judge them but it's just a cultural way of how they live their lifestyle compared to the way we do. People who are in the Y generation see having a life outside of work as important as having a career.

WRIGHT

What steps do you think we can take to getting more energy than we've ever thought possible?

EDGECOMBE

To me energy is very simplistic. I came out of the university with a degree in Physical Education and Recreation and the big soap box that I've stood on for years is movement. It's not complicated, even though we've somewhat complicated it. The truth is that we all need to move. If you want more energy, the number one thing you can possibly do for yourself is to move your body more.

I say that you've got to think of it in terms of getting more oxygen in your blood system, versus thinking, "Oh man, I've to go running." If you're a walker or a jogger or a biker or a swimmer or a gardener, a golfer, or whatever your thing is, think of it as getting more oxygen in your bloodstream.

One of the best things, those of us who are forty-five and older can possibly put in our bodies to live well into your eighties and nineties energetically, with some vibrancy, is oxygen. You have to think in terms of increasing circulation in your body. The number one thing for energy is movement, so when you're exhausted and if you're the kind of person who sits a lot during the day, it's critical, especially from lunchtime on, to get up and move whenever you get a chance.

I speak at conferences and conventions all the time and the most exhausting thing these people do besides stay up later than they normally do, is sit all day. They go home and their family and spouse thinks they've been on a holiday, but in fact they're exhausted. The number one step for energy is definitely movement.

Number two for energy is laugher. To increase laughter, you have to find more funny things, nurture your sense of humor, whatever style of humor you have. When you laugh, you have this great drug that surges through your body called endorphins. The amazing thing about laughter is that it energizes you and it calms you down at the exact same moment. When you need a bit more energy and you're feeling a little bit in a slump, that's when I say definitely go and rent a movie that makes you howl; hang out with friends with whom you can find some levity and look for the funny.

The number one ingredient for energy is movement, and the number two for energy is laughter.

The third way to increase energy is a little different than the first two. It's about literally turning off the chatter—turning off the noise—and taking some time to be in the moment. It would be great if this was done every day, but at the very least once a week, just get to a place where you can hear yourself think. For some of us this might be prayer, for others it might be meditation, soaking in the bathtub, taking a walk, going fishing, going someplace quiet, or having self-reflective moments. Within all of us are the answers we need, all the questions you ever need to ask, all the creative thoughts, and the inspiration. It's all there if we'd just get to the point of quietness. If we can just let it resonate, it will completely reenergize us.

WRIGHT

Most people shy away from the "accountability" word. What makes your program so simplistic and enables participants to accomplish the things they've been shoving in the back corners of their lives?

EDGECOMBE

The word "accountability" itself has been a hot word for the last probably ten or fifteen years. There was accountability in education for a while, and then accountability in health care. Then people had to be accountable in their jobs—they were required to be more accountable, taking credit or admitting fault.

What I do in my program evolved by happenstance. One day, many years ago, I was speaking to a room of five hundred people—90 percent men, most of them blue-collar. I threw out a challenge thinking that stereotypically ("men" and "blue collar"), they were not going to do this. I said, "I want you to e-mail me with your to-do list for next week. On that to-do list I want you to give me a couple things that have a bit more meaning for you than what you regularly would write. I don't mean the, "I have to go to work and get my kids to their sports activities, or whatever. And by the way, if you e-mail me, I'll e-mail you back." I was very wrong with my stereotypical beliefs.

Okay, so I thought, "Oh yeah, who's going to do this?" Well, I got about three hundred and eighty e-mails the next week. I was floored. I thought to myself, "This is very interesting. Why would they have responded to that?" So next, of course, I started reading the e-mails. Remember, I had promised to respond to them all.

It was amazing what they shared. Ever since then, every group I've spoken to, I've sent out that challenge. I've put a little bit of format to the process, but I do it every time I speak and that's been more than seven years, so we're talking about thousands and thousands and thousands of e-mails. I usually put the challenge out with a deadline to e-mail me by the next Monday. I've read from those thousands of e-mails that this little challenge helped people be more accountable.

All of us have stuff in our heads; I force them to write a few things down while they're there in the audience. I'm a nobody to them, so I'm not threatening. I then have them send this e-mail and they write, "Wow, I can't believe it!" All I want them to do is to see how simplistic being accountable is when there is nothing else attached to it.

It doesn't matter whether they do it or they don't do it, but what they prove to themselves is how easy it is to go after something that they want and what that does for them. That's actually the fourth step in the whole energy process. When we start doing things we love to do, aside from our day-to-day jobs, it energizes us. It makes us look at our work differently, and it starts to break down some of the low level resentment we have toward this crazy life we've created. I hope that makes sense. I encourage everyone reading this to e-mail me with their to-do's (info@lindaedgecome.com.).

WRIGHT

You say there is some science behind getting your goals down on paper. How is this so?

EDGECOMBE

As I said in the last question, all of us have ideas in our heads—we all do. Often, at our job we're required to write down what our goals are for the month or the year. Very few of us ever write down goals for ourselves personally, outside of work. The fact is that when we have ideas and we put them down on paper it makes a difference. And I mean *handwrite* them—there is a connection between thinking about what we want to do and handwriting it on paper, not just typing it on a computer. By just handwriting our ideas, even if we don't look at it again, I've read that we've got a 50/50 chance that we'll do something about it, just because we've taken it out of our head and put it on paper and it's sitting there somewhere.

Writing goals is very simplistic. You've brought it to the forefront of your brain; that's all you've done—you've brought it into your consciousness and into your awareness of the day. Most of us never write our ideas down because we feel if we write them down then what if we don't do it? Who cares? Just write them down.

Now, if you go and tell somebody, "I'm thinking about going for a few more walks this week," then you've got an 80 to 85 percent chance that you'll go and do it. Most of us don't like the fact that we've told somebody we're going to do something, because we feel that we then *have* to do it. This is accountability— "What is somebody else going to think about me if I don't do what I say I'm going to do?" The truth is nobody is thinking about you because most of us think primarily about ourselves, right?

So that's really why, in my latest book, I ask readers on the very first page to go directly to page 129 and answer the question there. When they are finished answering the question, I ask them to come back and read the rest of the book. I literally want people to act on something right then so they can prove to themselves how simple it is to get the ball rolling. So the science is to get your goals out of your head, on paper, and tell somebody what you want to do, and then things will start to happen. What really is amazing is things start to happen even faster than you expect them to happen.

So if you are a goal-setter, you've had something in your head, you've written it down, you've told somebody, and you've accomplish your goal quicker than you expected, you might think, "Whoa, that happened way faster than I thought! Now what?" It's the "now what" that scares the heck out of most of us. The "now what" requires us to probably stretch a little further because we realize that we can do more. We realize that we're more capable than we originally thought we were. It is the *energy* that is required in the "now what" that really frightens people.

WRIGHT

The title of your most recent book is *Shift or Get Off the Pot: 26 Simple Truths About Getting a Life*. Would you tell me about this sassy title?

EDGECOMBE

When I was growing up, my mom used to have this favorite saying. I can't use the real word but you can figure it out. Anyway, Mom just couldn't stand it if we were sitting at home humming and hawing about what to do. She would just say, "Make a decision and get on it already." I'm a very shoot-from-the-hip, candid person and there is no question that I like being a little bit edgy in my humor, so I knew I couldn't just write a book about the *Twelve Steps to Getting a Life* or something like that. I had to come up with something that was a little bit more "in your face." I do believe in "the just move on something already" approach. I really do believe in that philosophy, and it gets me some attention.

WRIGHT

When I introduced you as Linda Edgecombe CSP, the CSP stands for Certified Speaking Professional. I understand that there aren't many of those in the world—four hundred or five hundred. Is that right?

EDGECOMBE

In Canada, there are about twenty-five of us and there aren't many women. As you know, it's an accreditation in our industry. I've been speaking now for twenty years and it's quite a tough accreditation process. You need to be outstanding in the business. I'm serious about the business and I love the business. I could talk about the business forever because I'm very passionate about it. I know how fortunate I am that I get to do what I do. So when you earn accreditation, as anybody does in whatever profession you are in, you feel proud because you worked hard. I certainly felt pride when I achieved my Certified Speaking Professional Designation.

WRIGHT

What a great conversation we've had here today. I've really enjoyed it and I really appreciate the time you've spent with me. I'm sure that our readers are going to get a lot from this chapter.

EDGECOMBE

I hope so too.

WRIGHT

Today we've been talking with Linda Edgecombe, Certified Speaking Professional. She helps people loosen up, lighten the load, and laugh. She encourages people to find the meaning in what they do and let go of what's not working.

Linda, thank you so much for being with us today on *Stepping Stones to Success*.

EDGECOMBE

My pleasure.

ABOUT THE AUTHOR

LINDA EDGECOMBE a Certified Speaking Professional, is an internationally renowned award-winning humorous speaker, speaker's coach, and best-selling author. As a professional, with a degree in Physical Education, Linda brings twenty years of recreation, employee Wellness, Lifestyle, and corporate consulting experience to her programs. Quoted by the *Wall Street Journal* as an expert in "Shifting Perspectives," Linda has the ability to help audiences reset their lives professionally and personally. Change has never been this painless.

LINDA EDGECOMBE

2770 Reyn Road
Kelowna, BC
888-868-9601
info@lindaedgecombe.com
www.lindaedgecombe.com
www.shifttopaidspeaking.com

CHAPTER THIRTEEN

The 4 P's:
How Mature Portfolio, Project, Process, and
People Management can Enhance Performance

An Interview with . . . **Bradley A. Malone**

DAVID WRIGHT (WRIGHT)

Today we're talking with Bradley A. Malone, President of Twin Star Consulting Company, a project management and organizational effectiveness consulting company. Brad has managed numerous large hardware, software development, and integration projects and has directed many project management process implementation and improvement efforts for major corporations globally. He develops and instructs courses in basic and advanced project management principles and application for the Project Management Institute (PMI), and InfoComm International. He has provided instruction worldwide to over twenty thousand course participants from numerous corporate and governmental organizations. He leads project management audit teams for commercial and government clients and consults with a wide variety of clients on project and quality management implementation issues.

Mr. Malone holds the Project Management Professional (PMP) designation from the Project Management Institute and is a standing member of PMI's Educational Member Advisory Group and PMP Process Audit Committee. He holds a Bachelor's of Science degree from the United States Air Force Academy and a Master's of Art in International Affairs and Business from the University of Dayton.

Brad, welcome to *Stepping Stones to Success*.

BRAD MALONE (MALONE)

Thank you. It's a pleasure to talk with you today.

WRIGHT

So what have you discovered about organizations that are not as productive, effective, and efficient as they could be?

MALONE

David, I've found in my more than twenty years of management and consulting experience that leadership will attempt to improve their companies in one area, but often do not take into account the ramifications of those actions in other areas. For example, they may try to improve their processes through a program like Lean or Six Sigma, or attempt to improve their project management practices. What they often don't do is look at their organization holistically. They'll actually set up conflicting practices and metrics between their improvement programs.

They'll say, "We're going to put into practice better portfolio management," and yet they won't change any of their vice presidents' or directors' incentive packages to align with that improved portfolio management system.

They'll say, "We're going to run our projects better," and yet they won't talk to their resource managers and get them to align and allocate human resources to make sure that they're assigned to the correct projects effectively.

In order to become more mature in its operations and projects, leaders must look from a holistic approach to managing what I'll call the four P's— their Portfolio, their Projects, their Processes, and their People. Leaders who manage these four P's well—and those who refer to it as mature management—truly become effective. There is not a lot of drama; they just make things happen in a smooth and organized fashion. They don't eliminate the chaos that sometimes occurs, but they manage themselves through it well.

I use the word "mature" throughout this discussion to portray leaders in companies or organizations who truly think holistically, then act in alignment with those thoughts. They measure their companies' processes objectively and improve them continuously. Maturity has nothing to do with the age or size of an organization—it primarily has to do with the maturity of its executive management team (again, age is not a determinant factor).

WRIGHT

So why are the four P's so important?

MALONE

When used together, Portfolio, Project, Process, and People Management, look from a holistic viewpoint into an organization. They are interrelated and need to be aligned, cascading from the executive management level down to the individual person working within the organization.

The following questions should make sense and have an inherent integrity to them: Why is the organization here? What value is it providing? How does it determine, select, and prioritize its projects? What processes are developed and used in a repeatable way to start to create efficiencies? How does it reward its people for the right behavior? How does it incentivize and improve on the processes to maximize their efficiency?

In mature organizations I have seen this cascading approach—this interlocking alignment. When you look at it from a holistic and systemic viewpoint, most people understand and know why they're there. They see that their behaviors and motivational metrics align with the purpose, the projects, and the processes of the organization. I really think that all four aspects combined have to be in place for an organization to truly be run effectively and productively.

WRIGHT

So the first P is portfolio management, how do you define the portfolio?

MALONE

A portfolio is comprised of everything that the organization is doing. This can include a combination of recurring operational tasks and non-recurring projects. This can be compared with your organization—you'd have people answering the phone on a daily basis, but you also have this particular book project—a non-recurring activity. So a portfolio is all of the work that is currently occurring in the organization, whether it's operational—something that is repetitive or ongoing—or whether it's projectized, meaning that the work effort has a definite beginning and specific product, service, or result at its conclusion.

Leaders can manage their company's portfolio most effectively when it establishes clear criteria for why either an operation or a project should be inside of the portfolio or why they want to select that endeavor to begin with. How does it align to the purpose and strategy of the organization and how does it create value to the organization? Does that mean market share, profit, or a reduction in costs? Then truly selecting projects based on those criteria, making that selection process transparent, making it visible, and showing people—

from executive management to those working within the projects and operations—that these are the ten criteria, they match and align to the goals and objectives of the organization, this project was vetted against those criteria, and therefore it was approved and selected.

The next piece in how you make a portfolio effective is through prioritization. What often occurs within organizations is that leaders will select ten projects or endeavors and say these are the things we're going to work on this quarter. The challenge is that the managers of the resources and the people working on those projects will wonder about the priority of the many projects assigned to them. So, many organizations select a portfolio but then they don't prioritize it. What happens is that the people at the lowest echelon in the organization will prioritize these very strategic and important projects based on their own workload and their own prioritization criteria. These criteria can be what they like to do best or the people they like the most or what they don't like to do. This is where resource management really has to tie into the management of a prioritized portfolio.

WRIGHT

So what are the most common problems regarding portfolio management?

MALONE

I think that lack of communication would be the first problem; people don't overtly communicate. Senior management intuitively understands what they have in their minds when they think certain projects are the important things to do, but they don't make and keep that portfolio visible to their resource managers or employees. So there aren't large charts on walls that say these are our five goals, this is our portfolio of projects, and this is how we're doing on them. They don't cascade the project responsibilities from the top strategy all the way down to the bottom task—displaying "This is why we're doing these things."

Showing the value of those selected endeavors as they approach maturity or approach completion gets people excited, saying, "What I worked on today increased our profit" or "What I worked on today reduced our costs" or "What I worked on obtained ten more customers." There is not a direct linkage in most companies between the strategies down to the portfolio and down to the daily work of the people. People lose their focus on things they don't see visibly and then they tend to do work that isn't adding or producing value.

A second problem encountered in portfolio management is the non-alignment of metrics. People respond to what is being measured—performance, compensation, etc. All too often companies begin initiatives and never consider performance objectives or compensation plans because that's an annual process and isn't timed well with the start of new projects. The portfolio communication says to do one thing, but the incentive structure tells people to do another, causing confusion and inefficiencies.

A third problem that often occurs is that the portfolio is held off in the distance and managers will assign their people to work on what I call "drive-by's." The boss comes by and says, "Hey, do you have a minute?"

The person answers, "Sure." That minute now turns into an hour that just took the employee away from the value added work, which was in the portfolio, to do something that was convenient for somebody else (the manager in this example).

So the key is communication of the portfolio and visibly showing what the company doing about it.

A fourth problem is that most managers don't see the vital role they have in managing the portfolio, and therefore also don't see the consequences of not managing it. People look busy, but are they actually doing work that will accomplish the organization's strategy and purpose?

WRIGHT

The second P is Project Management. What makes managing projects so different?

MALONE

David, I've been teaching project management for about twenty years worldwide and I think that it's a true paradigm shift for most people to really understand what is different about a project versus an operation.

The definition of a project is "a temporary endeavor undertaken to create a unique product, service, or result that is progressively elaborated." There are three distinct differentiators contained within that sentence. The first is that a project is often time-based, which means it has a definitive beginning and a deliverable at its end, whether that deliverable is a product, a service, or a result. The end of a project is often usually a constrained one, which means someone has attached a target date to the completion or there is a deadline to it (e.g., an Olympic opening ceremony). Operations tend to be repetitive and ongoing, whereas in a project we're going to go build something only once—we're not going to go build it repetitively forty or fifty times as in a manufacturing line. So that's the first differentiator—it's time-based. Given that it has a constrained endpoint, everybody has to define when "completed" is "actually finished" from the beginning of that project. What I find in a lot of projects is that people understand that there was a deadline to the project but do not have a clear understanding of the completion criteria of the deliverable.

The second differentiator is that projects always have a level of uniqueness in them.

An example of uniqueness is a book project with a new author and a new publisher. Those two pieces would be unique. Other unique factors could be that the company will also ship it to a new destination and use a new shipping agent. The more uniqueness that enters a project, the more risks and uncertainty will occur, and the more unknown factors will creep in. All those unknowns will then interfere with the parameters of the project because the future can't be foreseen with certainty.

Another way of describing the uniqueness of projects is that they are almost always fictional occurrences because they're future-based. On the other hand, operations tend to be past and present-based. Processes have been done the same way many times and what is going to occur next is predictable. Depending on the level of uniqueness, projects always have newness to them. We may have done some of this before, but we need to understand what the differences are and the magnitude of the associated risks.

Many people try to manage projects as though they're an operation (predictable). They base their estimates as though they're the same and that the future, even though unique, will be the same as before. "Well, we did something like this two years ago, and we didn't track how much effort it really took or how much it really cost or who did it. But it ought to only take a month; that sounds about right." Then that month's time frame becomes an expectation and constraint that everybody measures the success of the project against. The project team says, "Well, I guess we've only got a month. We'll do the best we can." But the intent of the project wasn't really about the month time frame at all—it was about a quality deliverable that got lost in the communication.

The third differentiator regarding a project is that it is "progressively elaborated." This is a phrase that basically means all projects will change in some way during their lifecycle. This is because they are future occurrences that have uniqueness and unknowns within them. Projects are a type of adventure. They are explorations into what is possible, with people coming to a clearer understanding as the project evolves of what the deliverables will ultimately be, the true effort and costs that will be required, and the associated timeline or duration. So as we begin a project, people find "That wasn't quite what I was thinking. It's good, but I would like to change this aspect."

Change always occurs in projects, but one of the myths about projects is that they should never change. An operation should never change, unless it can be improved, but a project always has changes occur within it. What happens in a lot of projects is that people make small changes but they don't tell their managers that the changes were made because the project wasn't supposed to change. What happens then is that the project shifts and is reshaped along the way, but everybody is under the expectation that it was supposed to stay the same. The project was expected to match the original estimates that were based on often undocumented hypotheses.

What happens next is a "do-over cycle." People say, "We didn't get what we wanted because we never really knew that what we thought we wanted wasn't going to be achieved anyway. Now that we do know, we'll have to do it again; but don't tell anybody." They also didn't take the time to have mature conversations throughout the project and say, "We now know more than we initially did. How do we now make this change to the project to make the deliverables better, and how do we make this change to use these resources better?"

These three differentiators—temporary and often constrained time frame, varying levels of uniqueness, and the inevitability of change— distinguish a project from an operation.

What I have found in most companies is that senior management often has an idea of a result, but has little understanding of the magnitude of planning and effort required to make that result real. Another myth of projects is that if an executive dreams it, it's somebody else's job to make that dream come true. What I have also found is that most companies aren't like Disney movies—the dreamed projects rarely occur as envisioned.

WRIGHT

So what makes up a project?

MALONE

We talked about the differentiators of a project versus an operation earlier. Now we'll talk about the major elements. There are five key elements which comprise a project. I use metaphors to make this explanation more powerful and more tangible. Envision a project as a pyramid. That pyramid has three primary sides, but it also has a volume to it and it also has a base. These five elements—the three sides, the volume, and the base—are what actually comprises a project. Each of these elements can be linked to a set of corresponding questions.

Before the project even starts, it needs to have a purpose that should be defined at the inception of the project and measured after the completion of the project. The purpose of the project is its reason for existence—"Why are we doing this?" This purpose can be measured in a number of ways: value, profit, return on investment, increased efficiency, cost reductions, and so on. The purpose is defined by the project's customer, and ultimately must be measured by that customer after the project is completed. The project itself will only deliver the potential to achieve the purpose—the customers themselves usually have to operate differently in order to fully achieve the purpose.

An example would be a project involving the purchase of a book on diet and exercise. I have a book in mind with an associated budget and a time frame to purchase it in. But the purchase of the book itself will not make me lose weight and be healthier—the result of the purchase will only produce value once it is put into use.

A major challenge in a lot of projects I've seen is that the people working on the project's deliverables have no clarity on the purpose or value of the project—its reason for existence. Instead, they think that the purpose will be achieved by the deliverable itself. They are then preoccupied with the timeline and/or the cost and the organization does not ultimately achieve the value of the project's deliverables.

The first major side of a project is the scope and it defines the deliverables—"*What* is it we're going to build, *what* is it we're going to deliver? *What* are we going to create and then leave behind?" It can also ask the question, "*What* are we *not* going to build?"

The second major side of the pyramid is the time side, which involves two questions. The first question is a process-oriented one: "*How* will we do that?" The answer to this question gives us the activities and the tasks we're going to have to accomplish in order to create the deliverable. The second question of the time side is concerned with the duration: "*How long* will it now take to do this and is it constrained or not?" If a project has an external constraint, like the publishing of a book so that it can be released prior to the start of a school year, then we have a project that is a *"By When"* project and the question becomes "We have to publish this book *by when?*" When the time element is constrained, we've made that side of the pyramid hard—inflexible.

The challenge with many projects is that they initially were "how long" projects—the timeframe was somewhat flexible. But because someone put a target date out there, everyone begins to believe the project's time frame is now constrained, and those in charge of the project's resources begin to view the project as a "by when" project. They will often hurry to "meet the date" and will often affect the quality of the deliverable and reduce the likelihood of achieving the purpose or value of the project.

The third side of the pyramid is the cost side, and cost isn't just viewed in a monetary sense but it's also the amount of effort to be expended by the resources involved in the project's activities to create the deliverables. This side is also concerned with two questions. The first is a resource-based question: *"Who* or *What* do we need to accomplish this activity or create this deliverable?" In a large construction project those resources are concrete, metal, conduit, drywall, plumbing, bulldozers, cranes, tools, as well as the people required to order, inventory, build, and clean up the construction site.

If I have more of an information technology project or a business process improvement project, then the resources are the people who are going to work on that project as well as some of the people who are being affected by the project's deliverables. These people are involved in requirements, testing, training, and implementation. Their amount of effort needs to be estimated and should be tracked, giving rise to the question *"How Much?"* either in quantity of materials, hours, or monetary measures.

What I find in a lot of companies is that they place people on the approved projects but they don't take into account the actual amount of effort it will take to accomplish the required activities. Most organizations underestimate the amount of effort required to perform activities, and usually the estimates are based on best-case assumptions or conditions.

The volume of the pyramid makes up the fourth element of the project and is the level of quality inherent in that project. Quality is really driven by all three of the pyramid's sides and it also interrelates to all three sides. It answers the question *"How good?"* This question must be asked of all three sides: Scope, Time, and Cost.

The deliverable to be created must have a measurable level of quality, not only the quality of the deliverable itself but also the quality of its usage. This ties the deliverable to the purpose or value of the project.

One of the key aspects of projects that are often missing is aligning the quality of the deliverable to the purpose of the project within the organization. This is where projects often tie to portfolio. The deliverable that the project created must align to a goal and objective and should be measured in terms of value achieved versus just being measured against time and cost. The activities or tasks required to define, create, build, test, train, and implement the deliverables also have a quality perspective.

Did the project team actually think through how to go build, design, test, train, and roll out the deliverable, or did they just say, "Go, you build it the best way you can." This aspect of quality defines how good/effective the processes inherent in the project were in delivering a quality product or service.

The third aspect in terms of quality is the competence of the human resources and the quality measurements of the raw material resources. The incoming materials must have a level of inherent quality that match the level of quality desired in the deliverable output. The people resources must have a level of quality that is measured by their competence and motivation. Does their competence align with the project's activities? Does their competence also align with the value that the project is supposed to be generating?

What I find in many projects is that we put good people on them but we don't really tell them how to properly go do the work to meet the specified deliverable, neither do we tell them why they need to be doing the work properly to achieve the intended result.

The middle of the pyramid, the quality element, often becomes very amorphous because we're not defining it in very clear discrete terms. How will we measure the quality of product? How will we measure the quality of the process? How will we measure the quality of the people?

An example, for those of us who have children, is when we told our children to clean their room. Did our children really clean their room or did they make their room just look clean? Usually, what I find is that children learn how to make their room look clean based on what they think the standards of their parents are. If they have high standards, the room will be clean. If they have lower standards, the room will not be as clean. But did we ever instruct them on how to measure "clean" before they started? Rarely.

The other situation that occurs is when we're not provided standards of goodness, we just start to build using our own. I was a kid who liked thins clean, so I had a pretty clean room. My brother was not; he would just shut the door and say, "It's just not a good idea to go in there." Which way was better?

So the challenge is often that the individual quality standards of the person working on your project will dictate the quality of the activities and the deliverable. If you're building a house or if you're building an IT system with multiple resources, all these resources have different personal quality standards. This can cause a problem because outsourced resources' quality standards are not linked to the customer's standards neither are they attached to the purpose of the project.

The fifth project element is *Risk*. Risk makes up the foundation of the project—its stability and predictability. Its question is *"How sure?"* and takes into account how much we know regarding the conditions and assumptions of a particular project. The more similar a project, the more predictable we should be regarding its level of effort, activities, duration, and outcome. Therefore, the project should have a sense of stability, just as a pyramid needs to sit on a firm foundation. The more unique a given project (e.g., different materials, different customer, different project team resources), the less predictable the outcome and the less firm the foundation. In order to make the project more stable (less risky), the project will typically have to revise one of the other key elements—increase cost, increase time, decrease quality, or decrease scope.

A well managed project must be kept in balance and maintain its integrity. If an organization is to be able to keep a project in balance, it must establish and communicate a level of flexibility in at least one of the primary elements: Scope, Time, or Cost. This flexibility is determined by prioritizing the three major elements (scope, time, and cost) through a series of questions:

- Which primary element is most important?
- Which can vary? (This is based on priority.)
- By how much? (This is based on uncertainty—the more unique, the more flexibility required.)
- Which is constrained? By whom?
- What are the variance thresholds?
- Has this priority been communicated? To whom? Is there agreement?

This fundamental understanding of what comprises a project, as well as its purpose or reason for existence, is rarely fully discussed by the participants within a project, which is a key reason why a majority of projects start to go awry.

WRIGHT

So why do most projects miss delivering the intended results?

MALONE

I think the primary reason is that the project's customers and participants don't really know neither can they fully communicate what the intended results are supposed to be in clear and measurable terms. People spend a lot of time in projects worrying about the time and cost elements because they're easy to measure. They may worry about the deliverable having all of its components and they will talk about those concerns, but they don't talk a lot about the result to be achieved from that deliverable's usage.

As an example, let's say a manager decides to install a new piece of software because this new software will make everybody's job easier and better. But there is little conversation about how to measure "easier and better" and little measurement being done on how people currently do their job. The manager just believes that this software will make it all "easier and better." The project itself then becomes about installing the software within a specified time period for a certain cost. The software is delivered and turned on. It's on time and within the budgeted cost. But were the operations people who will use the software fully trained in how to use it, and were they given an understanding of why they would want to use it? Were their performance metrics changed? Did the manager understand how much it cost to run the old software before and how many minutes it took to actually run what the people had to do before? Was it tracked and measured after the installation? What I find is that what was measured was that the software was delivered on time and on budget, and then about six months later a conversation like the one below takes place:

"You know, that software isn't working right."

"What do you mean it's not working right?"

"Well, nobody is using it."

"Did you even ask them whether they wanted it?"

"Well no, but it was new, so it had to be better."

Yet if you look at the performance criteria—the criteria originally used to incentivize the people who will ultimately have to use the software—it wasn't changed, and no one managed how that project aligned with the purpose of the organization or the value to be achieved for the organization.

I think that many executive managers fixate on the project itself versus measuring the value and must learn to assign responsibility for using the new system, not just implementing it. It's incredibly important to have a purpose for a project's existence from the very beginning and to set up metrics and responsibilities early on. They should determine how to measure value, if that value was achieved, who will be conducting the measurement, and who will be responsible for achieving the aligned outcome.

Another reason the intended results are missed is the lack of a sanctioned project management methodology. It creates a standard, a vocabulary, a language, and a process to which everyone involved can identify with and predict. Without a proper methodology, the project will be undertaken without predefined rules and it will be difficult for everyone involved to know how the steps fit together. There are many methodologies in the marketplace; an organization needs to ensure that the methodology chosen and used is in alignment with the level of discipline in its culture, the level of communication structure, and is in alignment with the authority, roles, and responsibilities of executive managers, resource managers, project managers, and team members.

Too often, organizations let the project management office or department or the information systems department select and build an onerous methodology with tons of forms that will never be supported by executive management or used by the resource managers.

WRIGHT

The third P is for Processes. Will you explain process management?

MALONE

There are a lot of programs out there that speak to the term "process" in more words than I'll use today—programs such as Lean, SigSigma, Business Process Engineering, and so on. How I view process is that it is just how we do things—it's as simple as that. If you watch people and how they do something, you can measure their effectiveness and efficiency. You can look for areas to improve, steps that don't add value, and delays or waiting time that could be removed. But it all starts simple, and we perform hundreds of processes every day, often without conscious thought.

When I teach, I use simple everyday occurrences to explain concepts instead of diving right into the work environment. There's quicker understanding and less judgment. At work, people often feel that process identification can be viewed as threatening or judgmental. People might think, "They want to know exactly how I do what I do—"

So with that in mind, this morning I made a pot of coffee. I have a drip coffee maker, therefore I put the paper filter in the basket, then measured the coffee into the filter, then added the water into the reservoir, and then I put the pot underneath. There are some people I know who put in the water first, then the filter, then the coffee. Both involve a slightly different process, but in the end, they achieve the same result.

How do you do it at home?

WRIGHT

It depends on whether or not I have a Bunn Coffee Maker. I do.

MALONE

That does make a difference. If it's a Bunn, you've got to put in the water last and use a different container because a Bunn operates differently from a typical drip coffee maker. Most coffee makers heat water that is being poured into them at the time, and there is a delay between when the water is poured in and when the heated water enters the filter area. The Bunn has a reservoir of water always heated, so the water being poured in displaces the heated water, which almost instantaneously enters the filter and the pot underneath. Now, if you had never had a Bunn Coffee Maker and had been given one as a gift, did you know to put the water in last with a separate container so that you didn't make a mess all over the kitchen counter? Did you find out that you had to put in the water last in a good way or the hard way?

WRIGHT

In a good way, in my case.

MALONE

There are some people who figured it out the hard way—they were people who put the water in first and the water went all over the place.

WRIGHT

Some of my friends have experienced that when using my machine.

MALONE

Now we have an opportunity for understanding a simple process and making improvements to it. What I find in a lot of companies is that almost every person learns it the hard way. You have to look at how costly that is. In the example of the Bunn Coffee Maker, how wet did everyone make their kitchen counter?

We also need to look at processes from an organizational perspective, not just an individual perspective. If ten people are all going to be making coffee, then they need to look at and understand the machine, its supplies, and determine the best way to make good coffee. People need to be proactive—let's think about it, let's talk about it, let's measure it, and then let's document and standardize it. I'm not talking about making non-thinking robots out of people, but I am talking about how we need to consciously look at how we do things.

A lot of organizations spend an incredible amount of time and money documenting perfect world processes and yet they don't really look at how their people do it now on a daily basis and how they can just make small and incremental improvements on the things they do currently.

WRIGHT

So how does a company improve its processes?

MALONE

First, we want to understand why a process is in place and its purpose. This should tie into portfolio management—achieving value in alignment with the organization's goals and strategies. If we're doing something on a daily basis or we're doing it in a project, we should stop to ask: why are we doing this, what's the intent behind it, and what's the value being achieved? Second, let's really measure what we're actually doing, not what we think or wish we were doing.

I've trained and consulted around the world. What I find in many organizations (and this is typically a North American phenomena) is that people don't like to be measured. If you ask someone how he or she does something, the person will ask, "How do you want me to do it?" We just want to watch how people actually perform what they're doing. I've found that most people think you're judging them when you measure them. They need to understand we're not measuring *them*, we're measuring the process. They are just one component in the process.

A lot of other cultures in different regions of the world don't have the judgment factor when it comes to measuring processes. They just say, "You want me to write down what I do, and then we'll get together collectively or we'll get some good people in the room, and we'll improve on it." Again, "improvement" is based on the value they are trying to achieve, not based on ego, "doing it my way" or "being right." So mature leaders document and incrementally improve their company's processes in a nonjudgmental fashion, attempting to take out waste, or steps that do not add value.

I'll give you an example of a typical process where the participants had little understanding of the process but were caught inside a continuous loop of re-learning. It's the Easter holiday, and two children are watching their mother prepare a ham for dinner. Their mother gets the ham out of the refrigerator, puts it on the cutting board on the counter, and cuts off both ends of the ham. She then puts it in the pan and into the oven.

One of her children asks, "Why do you cut off both ends of the ham?"

Her mother answers, "That's just the way we cook ham at Easter."

Her other child asks, "Why?"

"Well, you know who would know that? Let's talk to Grandma. She'll be here soon."

When their grandmother arrives, the children ask, "Grandma, how do you cook ham for Easter?"

"Well," she answers, "you cut off both ends and you put it in the pan and you put it in the oven."

"How come?"

"That's just the way we cook ham at Easter."

The children, now smiling, ask, "Where did you learn how to do it that way?"

"My mother—your great-grandma—is going to come later today and we can all ask her."

So their great-grandmother arrives and is seated at the table with the rest of the family. As she is eating a piece of the ham, the children ask, "Great-grandma, why do you cut both ends off the ham before you cook it?"

Great-grandma smiles and answers, "Well, honey, the pan was too small."

That's the way it is in many organizations. Something is put in place by one employee, or generation. It is followed by other employees and the employees after that until the reasoning behind the process is lost, and the potential value is often lost as well. It's inherent within a mature organization to periodically and objectively, which doesn't mean judgmentally or robotically, look at how people are doing what they are doing and then align that to why they're doing what they're doing.

WRIGHT

The fourth P is people. This is a big topic, so what do you focus on?

MALONE

Yes, it's a huge topic. What I tend to focus on within the structure of the four P's is how we manage the people inside of the organization—those working within the processes supporting the operations and projects that are part of a well-defined and measured portfolio.

The questions to focus on are: How do we set objectives that people can meet? How do we set up clear and definable metrics? How do we manage the utilization of those resources effectively? How do we motivate and incentivize people to meet those objectives?

The first aspect in how we effectively manage resources is to establish and communicate alignment for our people that lets them understand the big picture of the organization. It lets them understand the priority of what they're working on and gives them direct correlation in how it aligns with the value that the company is generating.

The second aspect is creating processes inside the organization where people have meaningful work to do. "Meaningful" means that they can see that what they're doing contributes to the purpose and value of the organization.

The third aspect is giving resources the opportunity to improve how they do the work they do, as well as giving them an opportunity to improve themselves in other areas also.

What I find is that most human beings are incredibly creative, yet a lot of us spend our creativity trying to work around the processes that are put in place for us instead of systematically measuring and improving the processes.

Leaders in a mature organization need to channel that creativity toward creating value, allowing their resources to see the link between their actions and that value, and then reward people for creating enhanced productivity and performance. I find in many organizations that we've made people into machines. They are cogs in a major wheel. What they are working on has lost its purpose, it doesn't have value, it turns into just a job, and therefore their brain just checks out. That's a sad commentary, but it stems from the lack of a holistic view of the strategic portfolio to begin with: "Why am I here and what value am I adding?"

WRIGHT

So how does a mature organization effectively manage its resources?

MALONE

It's the alignment of a visible portfolio of operations and project, linked with measured value-added processes, combined with people who know why, how, and where they make a difference.

Leaders in a mature organization establish a priority to its work that shows value toward its strategy. The resource managers are responsible for the allocation, assignment, and utilization of the actual resources that are working on the projects or within the operation. They have to align their resource allocation and their resource utilization based on the company's portfolio. They also have to be held accountable for managing the work processes, creating improved ways that people do work that add value to those projects and operations, which ultimately add value to the portfolio.

WRIGHT

Do you include people as a resource?

MALONE

Absolutely—especially when it comes to projects. In projects, people are often the key resources. I think if you look at an operational line, like a manufacturing plant, the machines will literally run themselves once the process is established. It has to be maintained by people, but the manufacturing process itself is pretty self-sustainable.

Projects create something new or they create something that is different than before. It takes a lot of mental horsepower and often physical labor to do a project well. So I view the human resource as the most valuable resource on a project and it therefore ought to be treated as such. This is very different from saying that they are just a robot inside of a piece of machinery.

WRIGHT

So where do leaders in organizations typically go awry when managing resources?

MALONE

They don't align the actual assignment of their people with the purpose or why they're there. They also tend to overuse their key people. "If you're really good at doing X, then we're going to make you do Y also, since you ought to be good at that, too. So you get to keep doing X but you also have to do Y, and, oh, by the way, we just hired Joey and you have to take care of him, too, and teach him how to do part of your X job in your spare time." And now the employee has no spare time. So we take our best people and give them more roles. This is very much a North American phenomenon; other cultures grow their people very differently. They don't assume that because one person is very good technically or functionally that he or she will be a good manager or will be somebody who can take on new things. So we create too many roles for our people, with little or no prioritization, which creates a feeling of attention deficit disorder or a feeling of being overwhelmed by the task. People can't focus on what they're doing now because they keep thinking about all the other tasks they should be doing, which causes a lot of wasted time and frustration. Since they're also very good at what they do, somebody else is coming to them every five minutes and asking for them to do something else. They start many tasks but not many are finished, which, again, causes frustration. This goes back to the portfolio management conversation where there is no standard prioritization system, yet everything is important and must be done now. It also goes back to the process management conversation where there is no standard way of doing or training.

I find that people are often measured on how busy they are, versus how productive they are. I was recently working with a company and the president said, "I want people who put in lots of effort." I asked him to define that. He said, "I want them working from seven in the morning until ten at night." I asked him whether or not he would know if they got anything valuable done. He replied, "Well, I'll know it's effort." Given that he was rewarding effort, I more fully understood why he had lots of busy looking people spending lots of hours, who weren't creating a lot of productive value, and who actually had built in a lot of chaos and waste into their system.

When I asked his people what they spent most of their time on, they replied, "Re-do's and tasks that make us look busy." It was a very demoralized company because people felt that they weren't valued, they didn't have a say in how to do things better, and the metrics and rewards system wasn't in alignment with the results they needed.

WRIGHT

People confuse motion with progress, don't they?

MALONE

Absolutely. I think that this is a worldwide phenomena but I find that in the United States we've taken some of these things and created a nightmare. We reward people based on what's easiest to measure, but not always on what is most important to measure.

WRIGHT

Would you distinguish for our readers the difference between competence and behavior?

MALONE

Yes. Competence and behavior are often collapsed. Many managers put the two together, so when someone is not doing something correctly, managers don't look at it and ask, "Is it because they're incompetent or is it because they're just choosing to behave that way?" I define competence as the ability to function to the standards established in the process.

My wife and I have two sons: a five-year-old and an nine-year-old. I'm not going to ask my five-year-old to wash the dishes by himself; it just wouldn't make sense. But if he did want to learn how, and he started doing the dishes and he spilled or dropped some things, he's not behaving poorly, he's just not competent enough yet to do the dishes—he's just five years old. What's interesting is people will say, "Well you shouldn't expect him to be able to do the dishes, he just turned five." I absolutely agree, however, we sometimes expect thirty-year-old or forty-year-old or fifty-year-old people do work that they've never done before; and because of their age, we expect them to do the work correctly the first time. When they don't, you'll hear, "They're not doing it right, they need to be motivated" or "They're just not that good." Those are incorrect assumptions. They need to be trained and mentored and be allowed to learn the same way we allow our children to learn, not expecting perfection right away or chalking up their poor performance to poor behavior.

What I also find is that if we tend to take our most competent people and overwork them by giving them additional roles and responsibilities, we will give the training responsibilities of our new people to the least competent people. No one wants to have incompetent people on their project, so they will train the newest people in all of the incompetent people's poor practices. We've then created a model of tolerating and rewarding mediocrity or incompetence. Many people are not competent to do the work they're asked to do, and I'm not confusing competence with stupidity as many people do also. They're not purposely doing something poorly, it was how they've been trained (or not trained) to do the work.

I would look at basic behavior as either the willful alignment to the established standards or the willful disobedience to those established standards. Behavior manifests itself from the motivation behind how you do what you do once you're inside the process—it's your attitude. Ignorance is definitely about competence, not behavior. Entitlement, laziness, ambivalence, and ethics manifest themselves as behaviors. So what I look at in terms of competence ought to be based in the process. If you have a Bunn Coffee Maker,

I need to teach you that you put in the filter, then the coffee, make sure the pot is underneath, and then the water.

WRIGHT

Right, especially the pot underneath!

MALONE

Yes, *especially* the pot underneath. Now, if I put water into the Bunn machine the same way I do at my home and didn't know it was different and water starting coming out all over the counter, would I be behaving poorly or did I just not know? The challenge is to determine which occurred. Unless they investigated more thoroughly to understand what occurred, many people would say something about my behavior, "Oh, Brad is always making messes" or "Brad doesn't care about other people's stuff." It had nothing to do with behavior—I just didn't know the Bunn operated differently.

Now, if I purposely smack the coffee pot hard into the machine and cracked it, that would be behavior. I knew better than that, and that is a willful act of disobedience to the established norms and process. This is where motivation structure comes in, in terms of providing incentives to behave in a way that is aligned with the values and the ethics of the company and then discouraging the behaviors that don't.

I have found two very good references in this vein of thought. I find that the simplest references are the ones that work the best. Ken Blanchard is a key person in terms of developing competence using the Situational Leadership model. This model explains in a very straightforward manner how to train and motivate people based on their developmental level, not based on how I feel comfortable interacting with them. There are four primary leadership styles based upon task behavior (directive) and relationship behavior (supportive):

1. TELLING: Giving specific instructions and closely supervising.
2. SELLING: Explaining your decisions and providing clarification.
3. PARTICIPATING: Sharing ideas and facilitating the decision-making.
4. DELEGATING: Turning over the decision-making and implementation.

I would love to delegate dishwashing to my five-year-old, but that would be irresponsible on my part. In order for him to build confidence, both from a competence and relationship perspective, I would have to move through all four quadrants of the Situational Leadership model based upon his growth, not just my schedule or desires.

The second piece that I look at is motivation and behavior. And Aubrey Daniels captures cause and effect in a straightforward manner in his book, *Bringing Out the Best in People*. Daniels specializes in creating effective performance measurement systems. Every behavior needs to have consequences. These consequences can be used to increase that specific behavior, through positive reinforcement (getting something they want) or negative reinforcement (taking away something that they don't want). We also need consequences that decrease behavior; punishment (getting something they don't want) or a penalty (losing something they have and want).

Those four aspects drive everybody's behavior. Now, the challenge is that those types of consequences don't drive other's behavior as they drive my behavior. What I find in many organizations is that leaders try to motivate their people based on the motivation structure that works for the leaders instead of the motivation structure that resonates with their work force. They must understand from their employees' perspective which of those four models work for them in each and every case. It may be the opposite of what works for the leaders. It doesn't mean the employees are bad people, doesn't mean they're wrong, it just means that they need different incentives.

In the last ten years, and especially in the United States, we've taken away most of the consequences that decrease bad behavior. I'm not saying that it's good to put penalty and punishment back into the mix but the carrot-and-stick approach was around for a long time because it worked when applied appropriately. When you take away the stick (not as though you ever want to or have to use it), then you allow a number of people to get away with behaviors that are not in alignment with the behaviors the organization wants.

Managers in many organizations condone poor behavior by not addressing it appropriately using the correct structure. They also don't grow their people's competence in a supportive and productive way that aligns with the desired processes. This has a lot to do with the organization's culture and how its managers either take or abdicate responsibility for their role in determining the strategy, the portfolio, the projects, and the processes. It also has to do with whether they give their people the opportunity to experiment when improving processes or make them afraid to make a mistake and shut down both creativity and forthrightness. Leaders in mature companies basically make sure that everything aligns with the vision and mission of the organization as well as the values and ethics of that organization.

WRIGHT

So what is the intended outcome of the holistic application of the four P's?

MALONE

I think you can add more P's to the model here to describe its intended outcome, and Productivity is one. When people actually feel engaged in their work and they know they are contributing through a value-added process, there is less waste in the system. Also, when there is less wasted effort in the portfolio (i.e., we don't have projects that don't make any strategic sense and we don't have "hobby projects"), then the productivity factor of the resources and the productivity factor of the organization are only going to go up. What you'll also see is Performance, so more value-added effort will equate to more value being created. You will get greater results, you'll get greater efficiency, you'll get greater effectiveness, and you'll reach the organization's goals quicker. Because people have that alignment, they have streamlined and effective processes, their projects are planned and executed well, and they're trained well, their competence is high, and their behaviors are being aligned. If you're a for-profit company, your Profit will also increase. This is due to your productivity being high and your performance being high. The amount of waste that will go out of the system means your business expenses will go down and your overhead costs will go down. Even if your price point stays the same, your profit margin will go up.

If you're a not-for-profit organization or if you are inside of an overhead portion of the organization, as Information Systems departments usually are, then it will allow for more throughput—Productivity (getting more done) and Performance (getting more value). You can accomplish more work—not more work like taking blood from a stone, but more value-added work. By having an aligned portfolio, projects that are planned well and that make sense are measured correctly. Value-added processes are standardized and continually improved upon, and people who are allocated in alignment with that portfolio on to their projects, who are confident and competent in performing the processes, and whose behavior is either continually reinforced or disincentivized.

I think these three results—Productivity, Performance, and Profit, are the minimum that will occur. I've been working the last five years very diligently on this model and I've seen enormous results in the companies that have truly taken them on and made this happen, so I know it's a system that works.

WRIGHT

What a great conversation, Brad. I really appreciate all the time you've taken with me to answer these questions. You've given me a lot to think about and I'm sure that you've done the same for our readers.

MALONE

Thanks David. I appreciate the opportunity.

WRIGHT

Today we've been talking with Bradley A. Malone. Brad is the President of Twin Star Consulting Company, a portfolio and project management and organizational effectiveness consulting company. He has directed many portfolio and project management process implementation and improvement efforts for major corporations, governmental organizations, and small businesses worldwide. He leads portfolio and project management audit teams for commercial and government clients and consults with a wide variety of clients on portfolio, project, process quality, and people management issues.

Brad, thank you so much for being with us today on *Stepping Stones to Success*.

MALONE
Thank you, David.

ABOUT THE AUTHOR

BRADLEY A. MALONE is President of Twin Star Consulting Company, a project management and organizational effectiveness consulting company. Brad has managed numerous large hardware, software development, and integration projects and has directed many project management process implementation and improvement efforts for major corporations globally. He develops and instructs courses in basic and advanced project management principles and application for the Project Management Institute (PMI), and InfoComm International. He has provided instruction worldwide to over twenty thousand course participants from numerous corporate and governmental organizations. He leads project management audit teams for commercial and government clients and consults with a wide variety of clients on project and quality management implementation issues.

Mr. Malone holds the Project Management Professional (PMP) designation from the Project Management Institute and is a standing member of PMI's Educational Member Advisory Group and PMP Process Audit Committee. He holds a Bachelor's of Science degree from the United States Air Force Academy and a Master's of Art in International Affairs and Business from the University of Dayton.

BRADLEY A. MALONE

344 N. Elm St., Third Floor
Hinsdale, Illinois 60521
(847) 890-3609
brad@twinstarconsulting.com
www.twinstarconsulting.com

CHAPTER FOURTEEN

Navigating Change
An Interview with . . . **Denise Kaku**

DAVID WRIGHT (WRIGHT)

Today we're talking with Denise Kaku. Denise offers somatic leadership coaching services and organization development consulting to individuals, teams, and organizations. She is a Certified Somatic Coach and associate of the Strozzi Institute with extensive experience in all phases of organization effectiveness. Ms. Kaku has a master's degree in Organization Development from the University of San Francisco and has advanced coaching training. She is a former certified public accountant and Internal Revenue agent. Ms. Kaku serves on the Board of the Professional Women's Network. She has been a presenter at the International Coach Federation Conference, the National Organizational Development Network, the Bay Area Organization Development Network, and various other local organizations. She has designed and delivered public workshops on communication, goal-setting, and managing change.

Denise, welcome to *Stepping Stones to Success*.

DENISE KAKU (KAKU)

Thank you, David. I'm very pleased to be with you.

WRIGHT

So what got you interested in transitions?

KAKU

Having gone through many transitions myself—a divorce, empty nest, a new marriage, a job buyout, and career switch—I started developing different ways of coping with these changes. I became very curious in my coaching work with leaders, executives, and teams on the many ways people resisted change. I noticed how different people cope with change and manage major transitions at work and at home.

My decade-long study and research on resiliency, adapting to change, and navigating major life transitions have given me general areas to look at when helping others cope with major changes. I generally approach these conversations with clients from a framework of asking questions around care of the body, mind, and spirit. In particular, I look at one's capacity for taking action and exploring new possibilities as necessary.

Given that the Baby Boomers are starting to retire and entering a whole new phase in life, it is particularly important to have a tool kit of ideas and choices for entering, what I call, "the third age." The first age covers our childhood years and growing into adulthood. The second age covers our adult focus on establishing a career and family. The third age is that horizon of time after midlife.

The current Boomer population may be getting older, but they are much too young to retire. As they exit a major career track and finish raising children, there can be a general feeling of not knowing what else is left in life. What's next? I think it's a precious time to rewire our life in a way that has greater joy and a deeper sense of satisfaction. For some it may be a time to step up to an unrealized dream or desire that one never had time for before. Or it could mean building a legacy to leave the next generation. It may be a time of service or giving back and could involve mentoring or teaching. In any case, this time of life can be the most fulfilling, provided we consciously look at and create it for ourselves.

WRIGHT

I'm curious, what's the difference between change and transition?

KAKU

Change is a specific event—something that causes us to pause and rethink our automatic behavior. We are creatures of habit as human beings and we tend to stabilize and create routines in order to function. Events that alter our normal way of operating wake us up to the invisibility of our unconscious routine.

For example, a change event might be our children leaving home. A child leaves home and suddenly all the activities that revolved around child-rearing have disappeared. That leaves an empty space for us to recalibrate and ask, "Now what do I do; how do I fill my time?"

"Transition" refers to the actual process of adapting to that change event. There are no right or wrong ways of adapting to change, so transition is really a personal process that each individual gets to uniquely develop. Our personality will influence this transition process as well as our temperament, values, and specific lifestyle preferences. Of course, exercising our free will and mapping out our options is crucial to making good personal choices. How we go about making friends with any major change, wanted or unwanted, can be challenging and stressful.

The key is to realize that we experience transition in phases and different moods attach to each phase. There is a likelihood that each of us will go through a period where our mood drops. It could take the form of a depression or feeling lost. It may have elements of grief. For some, I think that creates a little bit of a panic or concern. But when we realize this is part of a normal process of letting go of something that used to be and getting ready to experience something new, we can calmly navigate the waters of change.

Bill Bridges wrote a book on transitions where he outlined a three-stage model of transition consisting of endings, the neutral zone, and beginnings. What is useful is knowing that although we as humans don't necessarily go through those three phases sequentially, we do experience different emotions around letting go of the past and embracing the future. As time progresses, we miss the past less and less. It is not uncommon to experience emotional swings as we adapt to change. We still are creatures of our routines and when they're altered or disrupted it causes us to think and to take stock. One may even experience a crisis of values or wonder what should be done with the rest of one's life. It can feel like being cast adrift without a paddle, so to speak.

I know when my father died eleven years ago I went into a tailspin because I never had experienced the death of someone close to me. I think that's where I really started to get this notion that there are different ways for us to move through changes. This evolved into a study of resiliency, optimism, and positive thinking. I read about happiness and researched the many ways people moderate their lives so they create more happiness, even in times of unwanted change or economic stress like we're currently experiencing.

So change and transition is definitely a topic that lives in each of us at many points in our life, and just to know that distinction is helpful because changes don't necessarily happen in a planned way; they can be triggered and foisted upon us, like a job buyout or a job downsizing. At the same time we have many choices in how we react, respond, and adapt to those changes.

In the language of somatics, or looking at the body, change feels like a grab or a push that puts us off balance. We get to choose how to respond to the force of that change. Sometimes it's just an easy, quick corrective action. Other times there may be struggle or suffering. My coaching clients have used different movement practices that keep them centered, open, and connected to what they care about.

WRIGHT

Will you give me some examples of transitions?

KAKU

Oh, absolutely; there are many. I've mentioned a few—divorce, the death of a loved one, loss of a job. Other common transitions that require adapting to change include experiencing a major illness—our own or that of a family member. Another transition could be that we decide to change careers because where we are no longer serves us. A change in economic circumstances or an empty nest in our family life are also common points of transition. Military service or reentry into civilian life after serving in the military can be a major transition. So anything involving a change in our circumstances or in our identity is definitely an opportunity to develop good transition strategies.

WRIGHT

So, I know what leadership coaching is. What is somatic leadership coaching?

KAKU

Soma is Greek for the body, and somatic coaching is a way of looking at individuals in how they lead their life. It involves looking at their energetic presence or their leadership presence, so to speak.

Have you ever been in a social setting where you've seen somebody walk in the room and his or her presence is so large in the way the person moves that you think, "Wow, that person must be somebody important?" Well, that's "leadership presence." It's that kind of indefinable thing—the essence of a person as he or she enters a room. It's how people carry themselves, how warm and inviting they appear to others without uttering one word. That energetic presence communicates volumes to people. Do they convey confidence? Are they comfortable in their body? Do they act authentic and congruent with what they are saying?

Part of what I like to do when I work with leaders is to have them really get a sense of how they feel in their body and to really see themselves in how they move and connect with people. Some of that is done through some physical exercises that we do together in partnership so they get a better sense of how they carry themselves. We don't walk around with a mirror looking back at ourselves or take a video camera and make video tapes of ourselves, so how do we know when we project confidence and tranquility or agitation and distress?

We can get a deeper sense of how we are physically feeling by honing our mental observer. This skill of noticing what is happening in real time—what we're sensing, feeling, or thinking—has a physical influence on our body shape. Even though we don't actually see ourselves as we move through life, we can get a better sense of how alive we feel by training our observer to notice what we are thinking and feeling. What causes us to get engaged or detached? Somatic coaching really does give an advantage to those who wish to accelerate their ability to be authentic and excited about what they do, and be connected to what they care about.

WRIGHT

How does your specialty coaching apply to people's lives?

KAKU

Through developing our ability to be an astute observer of our moods and emotions as well as the thought patterns we think, many opportunities appear for generating new habits that serve us better.

A prime opportunity for establishing new habits is when a major change has occurred or when we are experiencing a major blockage.

For example, I worked with a manager who was very arrogant and distant. He wanted to advance up the corporate ladder but was stalled out. His body appeared very closed and aloof. As we talked, he said he didn't want people to know his personal business, so he was very private. The way he moved and stood sent a message to everybody to stay away and not approach him. When he walked down the office corridors, people would back off. It's very difficult to lead people when they are afraid to approach you. His energetic presence was threatening.

What we worked on was increasing his approachability. He had to get a better sense of connection to himself and who he was and then observe how he connected with others in casual conversations. He discovered what was okay to reveal to others about his leadership style and personal work ethic. He allowed himself to be human at work and this changed his ability to connect with coworkers. He was promoted and developed new relationships both inside the corporation and in his personal life.

What changed was that he started to develop a whole new way of interacting at work that shifted him into a much more likable stance because he was being more authentic. He was able to open to the natural person that was previously held in check and now could come through.

This can be difficult to conceptualize without experiencing it, but it's like coming home to oneself and feeling really comfortable in your skin. You don't have to spend any time or energy being guarded or protecting yourself or living up to a certain image of the way you ought to be versus just being naturally who you are.

My client clarified his beliefs and rules for living and modified them to fit his life today. A major shift occurred in his way of being in the world and he is much happier and more successful.

WRIGHT

I'm a bottom line guy. Will you give me some benefits of somatic coaching?

KAKU

Somatic coaching works with one's ability to get out of the head and into the rest of the body. When I ask clients to describe what sensations they are feeling in their body I often get opinions and thoughts about what's going on in their head. We often lack a vocabulary to describe sensations in our body. A huge benefit of somatic coaching is bringing a fuller sense of living in one's body as opposed to one's head.

There is great wisdom in our body if we only pay attention. Our bodies tell us when we are stressed. We get headaches or backaches or tightness in the shoulders. Stress may show up as a stiff neck or churning stomach. Many experience shallow breathing. In extreme cases, life-threatening illnesses appear, such as high blood pressure, heart attacks, diabetes, or ulcers.

Our bodies tell us when we are happy or calm. There is a sense of ease, lightness, and expansion. Our voice is not strained and the pitch is lower than when agitated. From a body that is balanced and centered, we are able to problem-solve more creatively. Our daily interactions are more pleasant and nourishing. Struggle and arguments are minimized and a flexible, open, and accepting way of being emerges. Less energy is spent defending or being right and an attitude of curiosity generates interest and insights.

The benefits of somatic coaching are that people learn how to be more discerning observers of themselves. They become more focused and aware of their ability to make intelligent choices about what really matters to them. They learn to recenter themselves when they get off balance by practicing belly breathing. This brings more oxygen into their system and helps them refocus and think clearly. Through journaling, meditation, and physical exercises, one can access and identify beliefs, self-talk, and habituated thinking patterns that need attention. To the extent we fiercely examine our desire to grow and change and commit to taking new actions, we are able to create a life of well-being and satisfaction.

Invariably, coaching conversations touch on time management. For example, we can either choose to be at the mercy of phone calls and requests and reacting to what is urgent but not important, or we can be discerning and choose to put our time and attention on what really serves us. Looking at how one responds to requests or demands or general pressures of life really does inform one of how we use our time.

One of the major benefits of somatic coaching is developing a deeper sense of one's self and how to self-correct and self-generate in ways you choose, as opposed to being on automatic overload, feeling stressed, overwhelmed, and out of control.

WRIGHT

Would this change be manifested in body language?

KAKU

Absolutely, as well as in your physical energetic presence. People notice your mood before you ever open your mouth to speak. We are actually very transparent to others. How we move and carry ourselves speaks volumes. So if we want to be perceived as confident and calm, it helps to check our thoughts and scan our body for tension. Is there ease of movement? Are we breathing naturally? Are we feeling settled?

Comments from my clients that indicate somatic coaching has had an effect cluster around feedback that usually says they are different. It may be in the mood that they convey or eye contact, but it's also about how they carry themselves, their posture, and breath. They stand taller. Their face is not pinched, their jaw is relaxed, and their gaze is softened. Their shoulders are dropped and relaxed. Their breathing is natural and full, not labored or shallow. There is an absence of constriction or nervous twitching. They appear more comfortable and natural. They seem to light up with excitement and enthusiasm when engaged in conversation.

During periods of transition, our body may experience being literally off balance. When I left my last job, I experienced dizziness and light-headedness. I was feeling disconnected from my body. I went through a period of questioning my identity and missing the structure and relationships from that job. I was in a whole new territory without a map. I had an empty slate with the scary task of choosing how I spent my days. Because I had read and prepared for my job transition, I knew there would be adjustments to make but until you actually go through one, it's hard to predict how your body will respond. My response when my Dad died was very different from when I left a sixteen-year career. Both were difficult and each took a different way of adapting to the change event. In the former, I tackled the loss head on and mapped out specific steps to take—grief therapy, grief support group, journaling. In the latter event, I ramped down my activities over time from being super busy to gradually having more open spaces of time that I could call my own. I reorganized my life by taking a year off to rest, start a consistent exercise regime, and purposefully slow down. I looked at areas of my life that had been neglected and made a list of desires.

Life experiences shape our body as well as our thinking and our emotional range of expression, but we can always modify it, and with a coach, it just accelerates the change process.

WRIGHT

Denise, who would be your dream client? To put it in another way, who uses your services?

KAKU

Well, for many years it was executives, managers, and leaders moving up the corporate ladder, but many of my current clients are experiencing major life changes. I am attracted to those clients who are sitting at a crossroads in life, grappling with major change. I am in my own transition into this wonderful third age and I love helping others move gracefully through these turbulent times. I continue to work with business leaders but I work with smaller businesses now and nonprofit organizations. It's an exciting time for me because it's opened up a much wider range of clients.

My primary dream client is one who is willing to play in this arena of the body, and really get a deeper sense of aliveness and joy in how he or she moves and feels. Painful things happen to us, but suffering is optional. We get to determine the level of suffering in our lives, if any, since it is merely our interpretation and response. We can always choose a different response that eliminates the suffering; it's our choice.

WRIGHT

What a great quote. It makes the concept easy to understand. What makes it so hard for people to change, given there are so many benefits to it?

KAKU

Well, we're changing all the time in spite of ourselves. Our physical bodies are always making new blood and new skin. But what is interesting is that we create habits of thought and habits of action, some of which were shaped unconsciously. Any time we want to change, it requires effort and thoughtfulness. First we must become aware there is a need to change. For the involuntary change events, it can be easier to change because we are forced. The loss of a job eliminates our routine of going to work each weekday. The structure of our life is fundamentally altered. The work routine is gone and the rhythm of life must change. There are people who like a lot of novelty and change and others who prefer routine. Either way, it requires us to stop, reexamine, reflect, and then choose a new course or path of action.

This stopping to recalibrate can be uncomfortable, depending on what kind of change we're talking about. It may take time to figure out what to do or determine what we want. A change may require time to decompress and release the old. Some changes we adopt too quickly and others require much time, depending on the scope and nature of the change event.

There is always an in-between stage that can be very unsettling in adapting to change. This in-between time is after letting go of the old and before embracing the new. I've experienced it as a range of emotions from "the dark night of the soul" or fear of the unknown, to boredom or lack of energy. This is also a time of great opportunity since everything is shaken loose and we get to shape a new way of being and doing. This is a time of emptying so we may refill with fresh ideas and exciting new ventures. It is a time to release old beliefs and ways of being so that we can feel more alive, animated, and committed.

A simple transition is like learning to drive a car. At first it was very difficult, but then it became automatic as we practiced over time. If we were injured and couldn't use one of our legs, driving would be difficult, and we'd have to relearn.

When routines get disrupted or no longer serve us, creating new habits requires discipline, determination, and diligence. Habits either unintentionally happen when we procrastinate, or are intentionally created to serve us well. New habits become embodied with repetition, attention, and energy. We can look at mundane habits like our morning routine or e-mail management. The purchase of an iPhone caused me to rethink how often I check e-mail now that my phone signals me each time a new e-mail arrives. How we manage that information coming into our lives is important and we're either reactive or we're in control.

WRIGHT

Considering the title of this book, *Stepping Stones to Success,* what prompted you to submit a chapter?

KAKU

Well, most of all, the timing was right. I was ready to step up to this because I have been writing a book on navigating transitions and it's still in progress. This chapter represents a brief summary of some ideas I've been exploring during my interviews and gathering data. Also, the title was compelling. *Stepping Stones to Success* is a perfect title for a somatic coach who helps people take more powerful actions in stepping forward.

It was a convergence of many things that pushed me in this direction. It's time to step up and turn my back on negative excuses that block my progress. We all have those negative voices or the critic in us. The challenge for myself, as well as my clients, is quieting that critic but not silencing completely because it serves us at times. It's useful to notice when our critic stops us from doing what we really want to do.

WRIGHT

Why do you think the topic of transitions is so popular now?

KAKU

I think life is moving at warp speed and we're continuously bombarded with opportunities to change. We're living longer and healthier so we have more options and choices in our lives that require a transition of some kind. All of that is pushing us in the direction of learning how to adapt and be resilient to the changes happening around us. Those who don't adapt miss out.

There is a whole new world out there on the Internet that was not available a decade ago. The way of doing business is changing with online marketing. The Internet is so rich in information and the technology is advancing so rapidly that it calls us to be more responsive. Consider the popularity of Twitter and Facebook, for example. Whole new social networks are being built. There isn't a day that goes by when my husband and I aren't on the computer researching information, making purchases, or learning via teleclasses, and it's all at our fingertips. Our world is becoming much smaller and more connected. How we accept and adapt to those changes with grace, dignity, and discernment, really does speak to the quality of the life we have and the trajectory we take in achieving our dreams. Anything is possible.

WRIGHT

Well, what an interesting topic. I could talk with you all day about this. I appreciate all the time you've taken to answer these questions. You've given me a lot to think about and I'm sure our readers will enjoy this chapter as well. I appreciate your participation in this project.

KAKU

Thank you. It's been my pleasure.

ABOUT THE AUTHOR

DENISE KAKU offers somatic leadership coaching services and organization development consulting to individuals, teams, and organizations. She is a Certified Somatic Coach and associate of the Strozzi Institute with extensive experience in all phases of organization effectiveness. Ms. Kaku has a master's degree in Organization Development from the University of San Francisco as well as advanced coaching training. She is a former certified public accountant and Internal Revenue Agent. Ms. Kaku serves on the Board of the Professional Women's Network. She has been a presenter at the International Coach Federation Conference, the National Organization Development Network, the Bay Area Organization Development Network, and various other local organizations. She has designed and delivered public workshops on communication, goal-setting, and managing change.

DENISE KAKU

P.O. Box 2025
Carmel, CA 93921
831-905-6359
Denise@KakuConsulting.com
www.KakuConsulting.com

CHAPTER FIFTEEN

Develop a Disciplined Life

An Interview with . . . **Dr. Denis Waitley**

DAVID WRIGHT (WRIGHT)

Today we are talking with Dr. Denis Waitley. Denis is one of America's most respected authors, keynote lecturers, and productivity consultants on high performance human achievement. He has inspired, informed, challenged, and entertained audiences for more than twenty-five years from the boardrooms of multi-national corporations to the control rooms of NASA's space program and from the locker rooms of world-class athletes to the meeting rooms of thousands of conventioneers throughout the world.

With more than ten million audio programs sold in fourteen languages, Denis Waitley is the most listened-to voice on personal and career success. He is the author of twelve non-fiction books, including several international bestsellers. His audio album, "The Psychology of Winning," is the all-time best-selling program on self-mastery. Dr. Waitley is a founding director of the National Council on Self-Esteem and the President's Council on Vocational Education. He recently received the "Youth Flame Award" from the National

Council on Youth Leadership for his outstanding contribution to high school youth leadership.

A graduate of the U.S. Naval Academy Annapolis, and former Navy pilot, he holds a doctorate degree in human behavior.

Denis, it is my sincere pleasure to welcome you to *Stepping Stones to Success!* Thank you for being with us today.

DR. DENIS WAITLEY (WAITLEY)

David, it's great to be with you again. It's been too long. I always get excited when I know you're going to call. Maybe we can make some good things happen for those who are really interested in getting ahead and moving forward with their own careers in their lives.

WRIGHT

I know our readers would enjoy hearing you talk about your formative years. Will you tell us a little about your life growing up in the context of what you've achieved and what shaped you into the person you are today? Do you remember one or two pivotal experiences that propelled you on the path you eventually chose?

WAITLEY

I believe many of us are redwood trees in a flowerpot. We've become root-bound by our earlier environment and it's up to each of us to realize that and break out of our flower pot if we're going to grow to our full potential.

I remember my father left our home when I was a little boy. He said goodnight and goodbye and suddenly I became the man of the family at age nine. My little brother was only two, so I had to carry him around as my little shadow for the ensuing years. To this day my kid brother has always looked at me as his dad, even though there is only seven years' difference between us. He'll phone me and ask what he should do and I'll tell him, "I'm your brother, not your father!"

Our dad was a great guy but he drank too much and had some habits that took a firm hold on him. He never abused me and always expected more from me than he did from himself. I had a push-pull—on the one hand, I felt inadequate and guilty when I would go to succeed but on the other hand, Dad kept feeding me the idea that he missed his ship and I'd catch mine. The only thing I could do to get out of that roller coaster impact was to ride my bicycle twenty miles every Saturday over to my grandmother's house. She was my escape. I would mow her lawn and she would give me such great feedback and reinforcement. She told me to plant the seeds of greatness as she and I planted our "victory garden" during World War II. She told me that weeds would come unannounced and uninvited—I didn't need to worry about weeds coming into my life, they didn't even need to be watered.

I said, "Wow! You don't have to water weeds?"

"No," she replied, "they'll show up in your life and what you need to do, my grandson, is model your life after people who've been consistent and real in their contribution as role models and mentors."

She also told me that a library card would eventually be much more valuable than a Master Card. Because of my grandmother reading biographies of people who'd overcome so much more than I was going through, I thought, "Wow! I don't have any problems compared to some of these great people in history who really came from behind to get ahead." I think that was my start in life.

I went to the Naval Academy because the Korean War was in force and you had to serve your country, so the best way was to run and hide in an academy. If you earned enough good grades you were put through without a scholarship or without money from your parents. Since my parents didn't have any money, it was a great way to get a college education.

I became a Navy pilot after that and learned that if you simulate and rehearse properly you'll probably learn to fly that machine. But much of it has to do with the amount of practice you put into ground school and into going through the paces. As I gained experience being a Navy pilot, I eventually decided to go on and get my advanced degree in psychology because I wanted to develop people rather than stay in the military. I pursued a program where I could take my military and more disciplined background and put it into human development. That's basically the story.

I earned my doctorate, I met Jonas Salk, and Dr. Salk introduced me to some pioneers in the behavioral field. Then along came Earl Nightingale who heard just a simple taped evening speech of mine and decided that maybe my voice was good enough, even though I was a "new kid on the block," to maybe do an album on personal development, which I did in 1978. It surprised me the most, and everyone else also, that it became one of the bestsellers of all time.

WRIGHT

Being a graduate of Annapolis and having been a Navy pilot, to what degree did your experience in the Navy shape your life and your ideas about productivity and performance?

WAITLEY

David, I think those experiences shaped my life and ideas a great deal. I was an original surfer boy from California and when I entered the Naval Academy I found that surfer boys had their heads shaved and were told to go stand in line—everyone's successful so you're nothing special. I found myself on a team that was very competitive but at the same time had good camaraderie.

I realized that I didn't have the kind of discipline structure in my life that I needed. I also discovered that all these other guys were as talented, or more talented, than I was. What that shaped for me was realizing that the effort required to become successful is habit-forming. I think I learned healthy habits at the Academy and as a Navy pilot just to stay alive. To perform these kinds of functions I really had to have a more disciplined life. That set me on my stage for working more on a daily basis at habit formation than just being a positive thinker only.

WRIGHT

In our book, *Stepping Stones to Success,* we're exploring a variety of issues related to human nature and the quest to succeed. In your best-selling program, *The Psychology of Winning,* you focus on building self-esteem, motivation, and self-discipline. Why are these so crucial to winning and success?

WAITLEY

They're so crucial they're misunderstood. I think especially the term "self-esteem" is misunderstood. We've spent a fortune and we had a California committee on it—we formed the National Council on Self-Esteem. What has happened, in my opinion, is that self-esteem has been misused and misjudged as being self-indulgence, self-gratification—a celebrity kind of mentality. We've put too much emphasis on the wrong idea about self-esteem.

Self-esteem is actually the deep down, inside the skin feeling of your own worth regardless of your age, ethnicity, gender, or level of current performance. It's really a belief that you're good enough to invest in education and effort and you believe some kind of dream when that's all you have to hang onto.

What's happened, unfortunately, is that we've paid so much attention to self-esteem it's become a celebrity and an arena mentality kind of concept. Most people are "struttin' their stuff" and they're celebrating after every good play on the athletic field, whereas, if you're a *real* professional, that's what you do anyway. A real professional is humble, gracious, and understands fans. I think that what we've done is put too much emphasis on asserting one's self and believing that you're the greatest and then talking about it too much or showing off too much in order to make that self-esteem public.

The real self-esteem has two aspects: 1) Believing that you deserve as much as anyone else and that you're worthy. Someone may look at you and tell you they see real potential in you. If you can feel that you have potential and you're worth the effort, that's the first step. 2) The second step is to start doing things to give you confidence so that when you do something and learn something it works out and you'll get the self-confidence that comes from reinforcing small successes. That combination of expectation and reinforcement is fundamental to anyone who wants to be a high achiever. That's what self-esteem is really all about—deserving on the one hand and reinforcing success in small ways to get your motor running and feel the confidence that you can do better than you have been.

Fears crop up and get in the way of our motivation. In my case I was afraid of success. Nobody had ever succeeded in our family and because they hadn't, I felt inadequate to be able to succeed. Whenever it would show up around the corner I would think, "Well, this is too good to be true for me—I don't deserve that." So I would feel a little bit doubtful of my abilities. When I would succeed, there would be an attendant, "Yelp!" I would feel because I would not believe I deserved what I had achieved.

I think fear is the thing that gets in the way of our motivation because we're all motivated by inhibitions and compulsions. You should be motivated more by the result you want rather than the penalty. That's why I've always said that winners are motivated by reward of success rather than inhibited or compelled by the penalty of failure. If you get this conviction that you're as good as the best but no better than the rest—I'm worth the effort, I'm not Mr. Wonderful, I'm not the center of the universe but I can do some things that I haven't done yet—and then apply this motivation to desire rather than fear, that is when self-discipline comes into play.

I'd have to say, David, I could spend the entire interview on self-discipline because I missed it as one of the most important ingredients in success. I've always been a belief guy, an optimism guy, a faith guy, and all the self-esteem things but I think, as time went on, I forgot the amount of discipline it takes for anyone who is a champion in any endeavor. I think I'm back on that track now.

WRIGHT

I can really appreciate the Flame Award you won from the National Council on Youth Leadership for helping high school leaders. I've got a daughter in college and I know how difficult and important it is. But in some circles, self-esteem has gotten a bad reputation. For example, in many schools, teachers won't reward high achievers for fear of hurting the self-esteem of others in the classroom. Many people feel this is not helpful to these children.

In your opinion, where is the balance between building healthy self-esteem and preparing kids and adults to cope and succeed in a competitive world?

WAITLEY

I think that there has to first of all be some kind of performance standard. A good example is the Olympic Games. The idea of the Olympic Games is to set a standard that you've tried to live up to in your own way as a world-class person, realizing that there can only be so many Olympians and so many gold medalists and so on. I think, on the one hand, it's really important to have standards because if you have a standard, then you have something tangible to shoot for or to measure against.

I think there's a problem, however, in that only so many people can be medalists and win medals at the Olympics. One of the reasons that the high jump bar, for example, is set so that everyone can jump over it the first time, is to experience the feeling of success that first jump produces. The feeling of success is working in the competitor before the bar is raised to world record height and to much higher standards than even the normal Olympian.

I'm one who believes in testing. It's difficult when you have a "No Child Left Behind" concept because many times today we're going pass/fail. We're moving people up through the grades regardless of their performance simply because we don't want them left behind and therefore feeling that they're not able to function simply because they can't compete with some students who've been given many more opportunities to succeed than others.

Having said that, I'd say that healthy self-esteem is gained by giving specific stair-step, incremental, bite-sized pieces; perhaps there needs to be several different standards set. Usually the grading system does that and the point system does that where you have someone who has a four point three grade average because of all the extra credits they're taking. Then you have those with a three point eight and then those who are just barely passing. Unfortunately then, what that does is enable only a few people to get into universities and the others have to go to community colleges.

What I will have to say, however, is that we in the United States have to be very careful that we don't dumb down or lower our standards for excellence in our schools. Traveling as much as I do, I have discovered information about this. For example, there are 300 universities in Beijing alone—just in one city in China. The way it goes internationally is that the public schools in Japan, for example, are much more competitive than the private schools. If you're in Japan going to a public school, you have to really perform up to the highest standards in order to ever think of qualifying for any kind of university. You'd have to go into a vocational school if you didn't compete in higher standards in public schools in Japan. The same thing is true in Singapore, China, and in the developing nations.

We have a situation brewing here where we've got global developing countries with really high standards in English, mathematics, engineering, and science. And we have educators in the United States who are more concerned about making sure that the self-esteem of an individual doesn't get damaged by this competitive standard. I think we have to maintain standards of excellence.

I wish we had kept dress codes in schools. I have found schools that have marching bands. A certain amount of uniformity not only encourages greater athletic performance but higher academic standards as well. The same is true globally. There's an argument that if you put kids in uniforms, you're going to limit their creative thinking. The truth is, if you can standardize the way people appear in their style, then you can focus more on substance—their experience, imagination, contribution, and their study. The core of an individual rather than the surface of an individual can be developed much better. It would be great if we could combine the more disciplined aspects of the developing countries with the more entrepreneurial, creative, free-thinking aspects of our society, which means we're critical thinkers (i.e., you throw us a problem and we'll try everything we can possibly think of to solve it). In the developing countries they'll use a textbook or an older person's experience rather than using critical thinking.

We're very entrepreneurial here in America, but I'm very much concerned that our standards are being lowered too much. If we're not careful, we're going to take our place in the future as a second-rate educational country and therefore forfeit the idea of being a technological and market leader.

WRIGHT

I also hear grumbling about motivation. I'm sure you've seen business people roll their eyes a bit at the mention of listening to "motivational" tapes or CDs. Some tire of getting all hyped up about change or sales goals, for example, only to lose their excitement and fail to reach their goals. Are they missing something critical about the nature or application of motivation?

WAITLEY

I really believe they are, David. I think they're missing the idea that what you *want* in life turns you on much more than what you *need* in life. Too often business managers even today focus on the hard skills because they say that the other skills are "soft skills." Well, there's no such thing as a hard or soft skill because you can't separate your personal from your professional life anymore. You get fired more for personal reasons—for being late, for your habits, for you hygiene, your behavior, your anger. This idea that technical training as opposed to motivation is the way to go is misguided.

I have found that employees are excited and are full of desire and energy because management listens to them, reinforces them, is interested in their personal goals, and is interested in keeping them inspired. That inspiration is what we remember. So, when we go to a meeting we remember how we felt about the meeting, not the specifics of the meeting.

I think this emotional component—keeping people's energy and desires foremost and doing a desire analysis of employees rather than just a needs analysis—is very, very important. I often think this is lost in the idea that we're giving a pep talk, or a quick fix, or a Band-Aid when, as Zig Ziglar has mentioned so many times, "Motivation is like taking a bath. You take a bath every day and you might say why take a bath—you're going to get dirty anyway." But the very nature of doing it, and doing it on a habitual basis, makes this positive energy continue to flow and motivation becomes habit-forming. I think you need a lot of it to keep these habits of excellence or else you'll just be running scared—you'll be afraid not to do well because you'll lose your job.

Believe it or not, we have a lot of employees in America who are working harder than they ever have before so they won't be fired. That's not really the way to go after a goal—constantly looking through the rear view mirror trying to cover your behind.

WRIGHT

If you don't mind, I'd like to change the focus a little to the topic of self-discipline. People seem to know what they should do and how they should change, but they just can't discipline themselves to take the necessary steps to do so. What is the secret to becoming a disciplined person?

WAITLEY

I think the secret is to get a team, a support group, a mastermind group because not only is there safety in numbers but there's accountability in numbers. When we are accountable to one another to maintain a certain standard of discipline, it's much easier to work out if someone else is getting up at six-thirty in the morning with you. It's much easier to have a support group if you're interested in maintaining a healthier diet, for example, because the temptations are irresistible to procrastinate and to fall off the wagon. That's why I believe you need a team effort.

It also has to be understood in an immediate gratification society that there is no "success pill" that you can swallow. There is no quick way to get rich and get to the top. There is this steady ratcheting to the top and that's why I think leaders need to say it's going to take us about a year to get any permanent change going. So, I think we should all understand there may be a little dip in productivity as we start this new program of ours—a little dip at first and a little uncertainty—but over time, over about a year, we're going to become like an astronaut or an Olympian. We need to engrain these ideas so they become reflexive. It takes about a year for an idea or a habit to become a reflex. This idea of being able to do it in twenty-one days is misguided. I don't think it takes twenty-one days to learn a skill. It may take twenty-one days to learn to type, it may take twenty-one days to begin to learn a skill, but it takes a year for it to get into the subconscious and take hold.

I think we have to learn that discipline is practicing on a daily basis for about a year so that it will become a habit—a pattern—that will override the old inner software program.

WRIGHT

I'm a big believer in the greater potential of the individual. I remember a fellow—Paul Myer—who helped me a lot when I was a young guy. He was in Waco, Texas, with a company called Success Motivation Institute. You may know him.

WAITLEY

I know him very well. Actually, he's one of the icons and pioneers in this entire field. He and Earl Nightingale were the first ones to ever have a recorded speaking message other than music. Earl and Paul were pioneers in audio recording and I have still a great respect for Paul. I spoke for his organization some time ago.

WRIGHT

He personally helped me a lot when I was younger and I just really appreciated him. In your book and program, *Seeds of Greatness*, you outline a system for nurturing greatness. Will you give us a brief overview of this program?

WAITLEY

It's taken me thirty years to get this thing to where I want it. I wrote the book twenty years ago titled, *Seeds of Greatness*, and sure, it became a bestseller but so did *One Minute Manager, In Search of Excellence, Iacocca,* and every other book at that time. I have trouble keeping that thing pumped up.

Over the years I've found that *Seeds of Greatness,* for me, has been a system. What I've had to do is go back through all the mistakes I've made as a family leader. I knew I was a father and not a mother *and* father so I had to find a mother who was also a good clinical psychologist and who had worked with every form of behavioral problem. We put our efforts together so that we had a man and a woman as family leaders with clinical and other experience who could give parents or leaders of the day a certain track to run on where they could coach their small children and adolescents on a daily basis.

I provided a perpetual calendar that gives coaching tips of the day—what I call "sign on the day" and "sign off the day"—for parents to use to communicate with their kids. Then I had to put nineteen CDs together—audio tracks—that covered these "roots and wings," which I would call the "core values" and the more motivational or, if you will, ways to set your kids free.

The idea of parenthood should be to lay the groundwork, make it safe to fail an experiment, and then send them off on their own as independent, not codependent, young adults so they can reach their own destiny. I divided it into "roots of core values" and "wings of self-motivation and self-direction" and tried to balance the two so that whether you're from a blended family, or a single parent family, and whether you're structurally religious or whether you're spiritually religious, it would work, regardless of your personal core belief system.

I'm very happy that we've finally put together a self-study program that can be taught by the authors or by people who are licensed facilitators. It's something that a family leadership group could take and work on their own at their own speed by watching, listening, interacting with their kids, and using a combination of a written book, the audios, the DVDs, and this coaching calendar to maybe put it all together so that over a period of six months to a year they might be able to effect some changes in the way they interact with their kids.

WRIGHT

Sounds great! Before our time runs out, would you share a story or two about your real life coaching and consulting experiences? I know you've coached astronauts and Super Bowl champions as well, haven't you?

WAITLEY

Well, I have. I've been lucky to work within the Apollo program in the simulation area. I found that simulation prevents failure of the first attempt. In other words, if you're going to go to the moon and they're going to shoot you up a quarter of a million miles up and back in a government vehicle, you had better have your rehearsal down and really pat. The astronauts teach you that the dress rehearsal is life or death. The Olympians teach you that at the moment you go to perform, you need to clear your mind so you can remember everything you learned without trying—you develop muscle memory and reflex.

Twenty-one years ago when Mary Lou Retton was doing the vault, she needed a nine point nine five to tie the Romanian for the gold medal in women's all around gymnastics. I asked her what she was thinking about when she went to vault and she said, "Oh gosh, I guess what everyone thinks about—speed, power, explode, extend, rotate, plant your feet at the end. When the pressure is on I get better just like drill. 'Come on, Mary Lou, this is your moment in history!'"

I thought, "Wow! That's not what everyone thinks. What everyone thinks is, 'Thank God it's Friday,' 'Why me?' 'Don't work too hard,' 'Countin' down to Friday,' 'Looking to five P.M.,' 'Romanians are better trained, probably on steroids,' " So I get these stories of Olympians who have internalized this wonderful running the race in advance and simulating as well.

I guess the one story that I'll share is about a ten-year-old boy. In about 1980 this boy came to a goal-setting seminar. He told me that none of the people who had paid their money were really working on their goals. They were really thinking about what they were going to eat and golf. I gave him a work book and told him to go back and do what they were supposed to do and write down his abilities and liabilities, what he was going to do this year and next year and five years from now and twenty years from now. He got all excited because he thought it was this wonderful game that you can play called, Write the Future, or Describe the Future.

So he ran back and worked on the project and forty-five minutes later he astounded the adults in the audience by saying he was earning money mowing lawns and shoveling snow so he could go to Hawaii on the fourteenth of July to snorkel on the big island of Hawaii's Kona Coast. Then he said next year he'd be eleven going into the fifth grade and he was going to build models of what was going to be a space shuttle and he was going to begin to learn more about numbers and math. In five years he'd be fifteen and as a tenth-grader. He said he would study math and science because he wanted to go to the Air Force academy—he was all excited about that. I asked him what he was going to be doing in twenty years and he said he'd be an astronaut delivering UPS packages in space.

I forgot all about him and twenty years later, sure enough, I saw him on the *Today Show* as they showed a picture of an astronaut on a tether line pulling the satellite into the bay of the space shuttle. I thought, "My gosh! This kid did what I only talk about in the seminars." He was a living, breathing example of someone who was focused on this. I said to my family, "Look at what he did!" And they said, "What have *you* been doing for the last twenty years?" I said I was a goal tender. They told me I should be a goal achiever too.

WRIGHT

What a great conversation. I always enjoy talking with you. It's not just uplifting—I always learn a lot when I talk with you.

WAITLEY

Well, David, I do with you as well. You've got a great program and you do a lot of good for people who read and watch and listen. I think you give them insights that otherwise they would never get. I'm just grateful to be one of the contributors and one of the members of your global team.

WRIGHT

It has been my sincere pleasure today to visit with a truly great American, Dr. Denis Waitley.

Denis, thank you for taking so much of your time to share your insights and inspirations for us here on *Stepping Stones to Success*.

WAITLEY

Thank you very much, David.

ABOUT THE AUTHOR

DENIS WAITLEY is one of America's most respected authors, keynote lecturers and productivity consultants on high performance human achievement. He has inspired, informed, challenged, and entertained audiences for over twenty-five years from the board rooms of multi-national corporations to the control rooms of NASA's space program and from the locker rooms of world-class athletes to the meeting rooms of thousands of conventioneers throughout the world. He was voted business speaker of the year by the Sales and Marketing Executives Association and by Toastmasters International and inducted into the International Speakers Hall of Fame. With over ten million audio programs sold in fourteen languages, Denis Waitley is the most listened-to voice on personal and career success. He is the author of twelve non-fiction books, including several international bestsellers, *Seeds of Greatness, Being the Best, The Winner's Edge, The Joy of Working,* and *Empires of the Mind.* His audio album, "The Psychology of Winning," is the all-time best-selling program on self-mastery.

DR. DENIS WAITLEY
The Waitley Institute
P.O. Box 197
Rancho Santa Fe, CA 92067
www.deniswaitley.com

CHAPTER SIXTEEN

Using Soul Influence as
Your First Stepping Stone to Success

An Interview with . . . **Karen Keller Ph.D.**

DAVID WRIGHT (WRIGHT)

If you met Karen Keller Ph.D. in passing, you'd immediately want to connect again to continue the conversation. She's passionate. She's inspirational. She changes lives with her penetrating wisdom. In short, you'd definitely want to add her to your professional network of women who are go-getters—make that a Rolodex of influential women. You see, this psychologist cum peak performance executive coach turned entrepreneur is determined that women learn how to claim their power using their greatest natural gift: Soul Influence.

Karen came to be known as "The Influence Expert" after her uncanny insights into human behavior helped to affect state policy decision-making in the courtroom and seal multi-million dollar deals in the boardroom. Armed with a PhD in clinical psychology, she went on to earn the coaching industry's highest status of Master Certified Coach through the International Coach Federation in 2003. She is also a syndicated newspaper columnist. Her weekly advice column, "Ask Dr. Keller," offers custom workplace solutions for healing relationship rifts and catapulting careers. She's recently created a new business,

Karen Keller International, Inc., focusing solely on programs and products that teach women how to use influence to get what they want. The result is that her phone is ringing off the hook with calls from women who want advice on how to be more successful from the courtroom to the boardroom to the bedroom, and all points in-between. Is that correct?

KAREN KELLER (KELLER)

Absolutely, David. And thank you for that wonderful introduction.

WRIGHT

I've noticed that it's women especially who cringe when they hear the word "influence." Webster's tells us that "influence" is the capacity or power of a person to be a compelling force to produce effects on the actions, behavior, or opinions of others.

KELLER

I think women in our generation may have been taught that influence means manipulation. And the reason I say that is because for twenty years, overwhelmingly it's been the women clientele in my private practice—whether they're recent MBA grads, moms, or business owners and CEOs—who, whenever I say "influence," get this shocked look on their face.

The first words out of their mouth are, "Oh, *no*. I could never have power over—"

Understandably, too many people equate influence with dominance, because if you re-read that definition, that's exactly what it says. Nothing could be further from the Truth—and that's Truth with a capital T (remember, Webster was a guy). So for our discussion, let's get our words and meanings correct; because when you shun influence, you shun power.

WRIGHT

That sounds intriguing.

KELLER

It is. Power is both intriguing and *very* useful. You're born with all the power on the planet. This is why we read so much nowadays about being made of the same stuff as the sun, the moon, and the stars. I mean, who really knows what the heck that means? I'll tell you: It means we're all made from one pulsating, powerful energy. It's the Universal Wisdom bestowed in each of us by the Grand Overall Designer. It's the energy that enables you to breathe, beats your heart, and pumps your blood. It's the same energy that, as Deepak Chopra says, creates a trillion cells that are each completing bodily functions simultaneously that we're not even aware of. We don't have to be aware of it because it works perfectly. It's Infinite Intelligence that's all-knowing, all the time. And you have complete access to it. That's called Soul.

And if you don't influence it—allow it, acknowledge it, lasso it, direct it and use it—if you block it with too much food, wine, television, overspending, anxiety, and depression, it's as if your Power doesn't exist. The message you're sending to your natural Power is, "You don't matter and I don't need you."

Influence means congruency. I like to call it "inner fluency." The success of your inner fluency is measured by the exact degree of the beliefs you hold in your heart, the thoughts you think, the words you say, and how the actions you take line up. Think of the dancers in *A Chorus Line*. Not a toe was out of step; if it were, they wouldn't make the cut. Your life is no different. Are you cutting it? Is what you do day after day in alignment with what you tell yourself you want?

Join the two, and Soul Influence is about how to tap into your true power and make it work for you. Other synonyms for Soul Influence could be inner influence, inner power, Self influence.

I would add that influence has to do with getting what you want, getting what you need, and helping others get what they want and need.

WRIGHT

That sounds like the title of this chapter.

KELLER

Yes. Originally I wanted the title to be "Influence It, Get It and Keep It: What Every Woman Should Know About How To Direct Her Thinking, Get What She Wants . . . And Keep Creating More Good." But that wouldn't fit on the cover page. "Using Soul Influence as Your First Steppingstone to Success" really nails it because Soul Influence is the absolute core of everyone's personal success story, which is this thing called Life, of course.

How much do you want to accomplish, prevail, triumph, be a hit, be next, prosper, love, connect, inspire, evolve, and live a life of bliss?

"Truth stands outside the doors of our souls, and knocks"—St. Gregory of Nyssa.

WRIGHT

Soul Influence works for everyone, then, not just for women?

KELLER

Yes. There's no gender in the mind of the Grand Overall Designer. Philosophy, beliefs, thoughts, words—these are also genderless. It's humans who assign them meanings that don't really exist.

What I've found in twenty-five years of mentoring both sexes in clinical psychology and life coaching is that men spend much less time than women do thinking about their attractions, connections, and intentions—their "inner world." The truth is they're people just like you and I who've learned the art of Soul Influence. Anyone can do it!

WRIGHT

What is the essence of soul influence?

KELLER

I asked one of the stars of *The Secret*, Dr. John Demartini, that question and he stated the concept so beautifully this way:

The Soul is the: "Spirit of Unconditional Love and the Study of Universal Laws and the Source of Universal Light. The soul is the radiant wisdom emanating from the source of our truest being that wisely guides us to act through love. The soul (Spirit of Unconditional Love) is the synthesis and synchronicity of all complementary opposites expressed in human behavior. The Soul influences our wavering mind by whispering, guiding, and inspiring it to the balanced truth of wisdom and love"—Dr. John Demartini, Philosopher, Author, Healer and Personal Transformation Specialist: (www.DrDemartini.com).

WRIGHT

Why does soul influence matter?

KELLER

It matters because it's the technique that gets you to the real-world actualization: "With God, all things are possible." This is why it's the first steppingstone to success. How you tap that power is to know who you are and constantly affirm your passion and purpose. The practice of Soul Influence is to have an awakened soul.

WRIGHT

Was there a time in your life when you really felt your soul awaken?

KELLER

I remember when it began. It began in a 1977 Chevrolet Nova hatchback with my firstborn, Beth, who was just six months old. My husband and I were travelling from Grand Forks, North Dakota, fifty miles north to a small town called Grafton during one of the worst snowstorms of the century. The temperature was approximately ten degrees below zero. We were driving in the kind of snow that makes noise when it hits the ground. Big, icy flakes were coming down in torrents when, all of a sudden, the entire car got dark. The engine was still running, but the dashboard lights and headlights were dead. We were on a country road with no street lamps. Surrounded by pitch black darkness, it was impossible for my husband to drive the car.

My first thought was, "Oh my God, we're stuck in a blizzard in the middle of nowhere and we're going to freeze to death!" Fear gripped my heart. I turned to look at my daughter in the back seat. She looked like an angel, in deep sleep.

All I can say, David, is that I was a complete nervous wreck. I didn't know what the hell was going to happen. Physically, I couldn't drop to my knees, but mentally I dropped and asked (actually I think I begged) for God's help. In fact, I took out my rosary and began praying.

My world opened up and for a moment I felt a connection to a peaceful source beyond my imagination. Right then and there I met my Soul. In that instant all was quiet and I could feel it—the peace was palpable. Wow. How could I go from one extreme state of mind to the other? It was indescribable.

What happened next was unbelievable—unbelievable but true. When I opened my eyes, a halo of light had appeared just beyond the front of the car. We had light that showed us the road where there was no snow or wind. It was as if we were driving through a tunnel where it was snowing everywhere around us. My husband and I were silent. We knew—we knew it was God's messengers of light.

That halo stayed with us and guided us as we drove all the way into town, a good fifteen miles. The moment we turned onto a road with a streetlight, the halo disappeared. We arrived safely at our destination, with no headlights. The next day we found out there was a short in the car's electrical system and had it fixed.

But we knew. We knew in that dark moment that all we had to do was simply trust and follow the light. I rode in a state of gratitude and bliss. My daughter slept the whole way.

The smoothness, the calmness, the serenity is the language of the soul. I'm pulsating right now—after twenty-two years, I can still feel the experience. There is an energy field within each of us. It's the most powerful energy in the Universe. Even though I tapped into it unknowingly, I was blessed that night with a memory that will forever be etched in my soul, as well as my heart.

WRIGHT

The light literally illumined your way.

KELLER

And literally saved our lives. When we can get to a moment of grace and surrender, it changes everything. The surrender itself is the igniting of the soul energy. And then it shines. In that moment, I ignited my soul. And because of that, God answered with a miracle that awakened me to all of its potential.

WRIGHT

I'm reminded of the story Jack Canfield tells in *The Secret*. He described how, with one thought, a way can be made out of no way. What he says in the movie is to think of a car driving through the night. Even though the headlights only go a hundred or two hundred feet ahead, you can make it all the way from California to New York driving through the dark because all you need to see is the next two hundred feet in front of you.

So you would agree we can live our entire life this way?

KELLER

Yes. That's precisely what it takes to experience soul influence. And women especially can be so good at it. I think we need to be, now more than ever. The world—the planet—is calling to us to stop hiding our light! That's why my life purpose is to inspire and empower women to live their highest vision in a context of love and joy.

As you can imagine, that experience changed my life forever. I was the context, not the content. That's what Jack means. You see, if I were the content, then I'd know everything and I'd have all the answers.

Using soul influence, we are the answer. We don't "get" it, we "be" it. I was allowing and trusting myself to be influenced by God!

WRIGHT

What affect did *The Secret* have on you?

KELLER

Besides nearly falling off my chair watching Jack's uncanny storytelling? Profound. I think the *The Secret* may very well be the best modern-day teacher in the science of influence that there is.

There's soul influence (inner) and human influence (outer). With its recipe of

1. Believe
2. Ask
3. Receive

The Secret touches a little bit on both. But it's missing the vital nutrient women need to digest for success.

WRIGHT

What's that?

KELLER

Self-consent. Women are brought up in an "other permission-based" society. No matter what that culture may be, no matter where we're living. It's a collective consciousness. There is a very narrow band of acceptable behavior for women. I call it a "behavioral corset" that's fashioned from psychological, sociological, anthropological, and illogical factors. Whether it's a home environment, school system, or religious institution, many of us were brought up not to think in a certain way, say certain things, or take actions that would benefit us because they were outside "the norm" and "different from the status quo." We were taught to not think, talk, learn, or excel too much.

For example, some families teach that education is for men only. "Your brothers are going to college, and if there's money left over, we'll talk about college for you." And even that's a big maybe. (Thankfully, that wasn't my experience.)

Education is just one issue—the tip of the iceberg. Almost every instance in a woman's life can be stifled due to this nasty habit of permission-based thinking because our lives are lived thought by thought. I call it a "nasty" habit because it destroys our dignity, esteem, and evolution.

There is a lot of research showing that for women to be effective they need to be perceived as likable. It's not the same for men. Society says women need to please socially. The message to women is: when we are giving something to someone else, we are feminine; when we are asking for something from someone, we are not. We're taught that "nice girls don't ask." Well, if you don't ask, how can you get?

To be fully self-realized or "self-actualized" (as Maslov calls it), then we must generate feelings—not emotions, but rather, obtained and directed thoughts to stir the energy of the soul. If we don't give ourselves permission to feel good, then we can never manifest what it is we truly want. All creation is based on feelings. When joy is repressed, our lives are limited.

I want to be a kind person—to be attuned to others' needs. But I also need to ask for what I want. Being true to myself—and to all women—depends on it.

You may have heard that our entire life is programmed into us between the ages of two and eight. This is where the "control" and "power-over" others thinking is born. Although all children have limits (mostly physical) in an adult world, women don't escape this mindset without some new information and what I call "brain training"! So, believing that we have to have permission from outside of ourselves is the antitheses of success. Can you imagine? What if you never get it?

"Some people live a life of ninety years and some people live one year ninety times"—Karen Keller.

WRIGHT

What is control, exactly? It seems a little confusing because we hear it used as both a positive and a negative. Controlling others is bad while self-control is good.

KELLER

Great question. In everyday language, control is having authority over somebody else because you're afraid, you're insecure, and you don't want others making the decisions because you're afraid those decisions will threaten your survival.

Whenever you're acting from fear, you're acting from the EGO—Edging God Out.

"The ego has two objectives. One, it wants to own everyone or everything it comes into contact with. And two, it always wants to be right"—Dr. Wayne Dyer.

Now, when you have influence, self-dominion, the ability to think and act in a certain way because you know you bring to the table a level of wisdom that's called for in a certain situation—that's another thing entirely. Influence is a level of thought and communication mastery that benefits yourself and others. I mentioned that earlier, remember? So these degrees of differences need to be understood.

Let's take an example from my coaching practice—handling money in a relationship. It's an issue I see all the time and an especially trendy topic in today's recession. If your partner is careless with money and you're not, you need to have a conversation because clearly the behavior is not working. It's very likely that loose spending will sink the financial ship.

Influence is wise. You want to address the situation, without controlling the other. So you might say, "We have a problem here." No accusation, no attack. Notice I didn't say "You have a problem."

Now the reality is that a lot of people can't even have a conversation about money. They immediately get into fear—fear, like love, is a vibration—and the brain goes into what I call "The Terrible Twos" and the next thing you hear is, "Nobody's going to touch my money!" Am I right? Isn't this what usually happens?

Here's where the power of influence steps in. Influence helps you negotiate. Where there's control, there's no negotiation. Agreeably, what I'm talking about here can be treacherous waters.

What I want you to understand is that there is a difference between bringing qualified (purposeful) influence to the table and being the authority. I would coach my client this way: Be wise. If you know this is going to push hot buttons (hot buttons are always labeled "Insecurity"), speak in the plural. "We've got to work together . . . We've got to do a better job with our finances because—" Make it an "our" problem, not a "your" problem. The empowerment in influence is all-encompassing. It's in everybody's favor. Influence enhances. And the results, quite frankly, can be enchanting. When we get into the process of Soul Influence, you'll see that it's a totally new format for life.

WRIGHT

And manipulation?

KELLER

Similar. Control and manipulation are for personal gain.

Manipulation causes harm because it comes from the place of fear. Ultimatums, far too popular in our culture, are bad news. Anytime someone starts "parting the Red Sea" between you and your good, you're in trouble.

Communication that starts with "if" is a threat. Relationship by threat . . . control by threat. Threats are viruses. They're intended to kill by trickery, bluff, deceit—any form of maneuvering that another person uses to get his or her way. For example: "If you don't do this." "If I don't get that." "If, if, if" from someone else means "ouch, ouch, ouch" for you.

I guarantee that if a spouse or relative is controlling you, there are other people in your life controlling you as well.

Entire generations of women, however, got their needs met by communicating through manipulation. It's just a fact that mothers and grandmothers walked around angry their entire adult lives in an effort to get what they wanted. If you have a mother in her seventies who communicates in this way, it's unlikely she's going to grow up psychologically and join you in a conversation about Soul Influence, for instance.

I recently heard an interview with Ruth Reichl, former editor of *Gourmet* magazine, about her memoir, "Not Becoming My Mother: and Other Things She Taught Me Along the Way," published in April 2009.

Ruth said she thinks that there are many women whose mothers had very sad lives. She reveals her own pain at discovering that her mother, who was born in 1908, was thwarted in every possible way. She was smart, educated, and bored to death. What her mother wanted most was for Ruth not to become like her. She wanted Ruth to become more.

Let's look at what happened to middle-class women in the last century. They got the vote. They were supposedly emancipated, but they didn't know what that meant or how to do it and there weren't any teachers to show them the way. We got our first generation of female doctors and lawyers, or at least they had the promise of becoming white collar professionals. So there was immense frustration of power or the promise of power, and the inability to act on it.

On top of that, during World War II, women proved competent in the workplace. When the war ended, they were told to, "Get out, give the jobs back to the men and go home and tie on your apron strings."

I think a lot of women were confined and, of course, this is going to generate grief.

The part that moved me the most was when Ruth revealed how her mother (at age seventy), finally got on the path to self-assurance and independence. In her diary, Ruth's mother writes, "My mother has been dead for twenty-five years. Why am I still letting her tell me what to do?" And she just exorcised her mother and let herself be herself.

This is a rite of passage all women must go through. You can see that "collective consciousness" I talked about—we take on the thinking of everyone around us. Ruth's mother had been told by her mother that she was too homely to be successful. She wrote in her diary that her parents didn't offer her hope and forbade her from becoming a doctor.

Determined not to repeat the cycle, Ruth's mother told her, "When you find yourself, you will be beautiful."

Of course, relationships between mothers and daughters are very complicated. I think this is especially true for my generation because we have a great disparity of opportunity between the two generations.

WRIGHT

What was your relationship with your mother like?

KELLER

My mother was an incredibly wise woman. She only had a high school education, yet she knew so much about how life works. Mom raised me with hope and had a tremendous influence on my successes in life.

But even though I could talk to her about anything, even I wasn't immune from "permission-based" thinking. I don't know why I thought I had to earn my mother's love, she was tremendously skilled at loving me unconditionally. Although we shared the same core values, I carried around this gnawing feeling that I would be disappointing her if I didn't take her advice. I finally couldn't take it anymore and told her. Without batting an eye she laughed and said, "Honey, I expect you to be different than I am. All I can offer is what's in my mind. Certainly you're going to do things in your own way. I did things differently than my mom and my mother-in-law! My generation was different from yours and it'll be the same with your daughters and on and on."

To her it was a leaf falling from a tree. To me, it was thirty years of self-talk seeking her approval and permission. *I didn't have to be like my mother and could still have her love and respect! It was a life-changing ah-ha! moment.*

I see this mother-to daughter-relationship dynamic all the time in my practice. Mothers are taught to be controlling—we don't want our daughters to leave us, so we make ourselves secure. Of course, that leaves them being insecure!

What's missing—and how I coach mothers and grandmothers—is to practice being forthcoming. All daughters need to be told that they can be who they are and that they're still worthwhile, valuable, and loved. They don't need Mom's approval!

With my own two daughters, I'll throw in my own two cents. And I've learned to ask, "Well, what is it you want to do? What outcome do you want?" I like to think I've given them the freedom to think and ask questions.

And of course they both use Soul Influence.

WRIGHT

What do we need to know to prepare ourselves for the Soul Influence Experience?

KELLER

Your success can be in your deliberate and conscious creation. This happens effortlessly when you have focus and intention on meeting yourself with the daily practice of Soul Influence. What we're doing is bringing our inner vibration in harmony with our life's desires. In our Western society, this can sound a little strange at first. Soul is consciousness. It's my belief that the soul is the true essence of who you are. When you look into the mirror, you see an image of yourself. It's a body, a shell. It's not who you *really* are. Your soul is the person inside of you. Oftentimes your soul is radiated through your personality; your personality is your outer spin. Both can affect how you relate to others and to yourself. Fortunately, no two souls are alike.

You may be questioning the benefits of acknowledging the existence of your soul. Well, if you're a spiritual being expressing itself through the instrument of a limited physical (human) body, wouldn't you want to know how to live a complete life?

In order to do that, you must honor all of you. As we've already seen, women are living what I call "half-baked lives" in the outer realm. Men get most of the validation, women tend to split from their power and fragmented living is the result. You can never be successful at a mind-blowing level of creation operating from soul distraction.

When a woman invites her soul level into her daily life, she radiates source energy, pure light, confidence, courage, strength, and unconditional love for herself and others. Your inner soul is the vehicle from the source of true wisdom and guidance that can never be destroyed, altered, or taken away.

That's because the soul is powered by God. This phenomenal place of unlimited resources (some call it "the well") is accessible twenty-four seven, three hundred sixty-five. Once you start using soul influence you'll start to feel, see, and experience a world that you never thought possible. You'll be creating your life on a whole new level.

I want to suggest that anyone reading this learn to use the phrase "up until now." When you find yourself talking to yourself in a way that seems true, yet doesn't offer up your highest good, just turn it around. Turn "I've never made the money I've deserved" into "I've never made the money I've deserved *up until now.*" "I always choose the wrong men to date" becomes "I always choose the wrong men to date *up until now.*" You can change your perception with just those three little words.

Life was never meant to be a struggle. Your purpose is to use your talents and abilities to be happy, joyous, to achieve your spiritual potential, and become all that you can be during your physical time here on the planet—a beautiful extension of the source of all creation.

So Soul Influence is actually a co-creation process between you and God. You're not in it by yourself.

WRIGHT

"Up until now" shows that we can turn every life situation into a positive one. For twenty years here at Insight Publishing, I've had the great pleasure of interviewing many thought leaders—some of the best and most respected in the world. A common theme has been that purpose isn't about becoming the president of a company, winning awards, or saving the world. It's more about affecting people and the planet in a positive way.

KELLER

Yes. Soul Influence will have a positive effect on you and others because it's about giving your life meaning. We hear stories every day about the millionaire or celebrity whose life is rife with problems or who may even have committed suicide. The root cause is not a lack of money or prestige; what has no meaning, perishes. It's a Universal Law. When your life has meaning, you're "in fluency." You will be happy, no matter what the stock market averages, unemployment, or divorce rates.

I love using the term "act out." When I was a clinical psychologist, my clients had all kinds of "behavior problems" that were mucking up their lives. Using the Diagnostic and Statistical Manual of Mental Disorders (a 943-page textbook that identifies scores of pathological states but no healthy ones) as my guide, it was clear they were "acting out" as a societal norm. Essentially, they were just "acting out" from fear and what they knew how to do *up until the point where they learned something* new. (You can't know what you don't know.) Now that I've shifted my practice from one of psychologist to coach, I teach my clients to go within, then "act out" from their Soul Influence!

If you ever want to see a soul expressing itself, just look at the work of an artist or watch a dancer move to music. They're tapped in. Unencumbered. Nothing is hindering their essence.

I used to own a business called "Keller's Kids" where I taught seventy students piano and other lessons. The truth is, they taught me. The level of non-conversation closeness we shared stirred a shift in my perception and ability for intimacy. They helped make me the teacher and speaker I am today with their level and type of energy. These adorable children exuded pure love, and soon my own vibration matched it. When I was away from my students, I felt myself wanting to feel that energy more and more. For a woman who was pre-med, in college, and lived from her data-driven head, this was a big realization. People think we absorb others' energy. We don't. We match it. Soul Influence lets you be *more* of the energy you want to experience in the world. (By the way, that's especially helpful when we're at family gatherings and we find ourselves stepping into a zone of negativity. You can choose to use the process of Soul Influence in the moment and stay above the fray through the energy of light and love.)

Those kids made me see that my abilities were meant to help people achieve their own soul's purpose of being all they can be. By tuning into *all* my natural sensory and activating soul influence, my life evolved. I became a Master Certified Coach. I was able to leave two very successful businesses, my private therapy, and execute coaching practices to transform my gifts to match my soul's purpose as an Influence Life Coach for women.

In your daily practice, you'll be tapping in to Source energy and aligning our feelings with our greatest good. As you use Soul Influence every day, you'll notice that your life consists of eleven senses acting on your behalf, whether you're aware of them or not.

PHYSICAL ENDOWMENT:
- Sight
- Sound
- Taste
- Smell
- Touch

MENTAL EMPOWERMENT:
- Imagination
- Intuition
- Perception
- Memory
- Will
- Reason

WRIGHT

That's interesting. I think we're all familiar with the first group of senses. We don't hear much about the second.

KELLER

One day our schools will evolve to teach us about our entire selves, not just the physical senses. For now, we must empower ourselves. What science shows is that the brain and the body *do not* differentiate between sensory images from the mind as opposed to those in reality. That's the secret of Soul Influence!

"The leaders in the past who had the secret wanted to keep the power and not share the power. They kept people ignorant of the secret. People went to work, they did their job, they came home. . . . They were on a treadmill with no power, because the secret was kept in the few."—Dr. Denis Waitley, psychologist and trainer in the field of mind potential.

"If you want to tap into the power of the soul and live a life of passion and potential, then you first have to remember that you *are* a soul here and now"— John Holland, *Power of the Soul: Inside Wisdom for an Outside World,* pub. Hay House, January 2007.

There are many ways to connect to your soul. Sitting in the silence, prayer, meditation, singing, working on a creative project, journaling, or doing anything that gives you joy and keeps you so engaged that you lose all sense of time (physical).

The rewards of Soul Influence are Infinite. You can:

- Improve your relationships;
- Make the most of your creativity;
- Enhance your career;
- Receive divine guidance on important decisions;
- Feel more connected to nature;
- Break free from the "what will other's think of me?" "It's too late," and "I'm a failure" syndrome;
- And do, be and have anything you really want!

Soul Influence daily has five immediate benefits to help you create what you want:

1. Allowing your highest good
2. Hearing God or your inner voice for guidance and direction
3. Mindfulness to overcome distraction
4. Belief in the impossible
5. Permission to actualize your dreams

Congratulations on making the decision to experience who you *really* are!

The following daily practice allows you to tap into your inner self, acknowledge that spiritual character inside of you, and give her (or him) a voice in your outer expression.

What you'll need to begin:

- Find a quiet writing place free from distraction.
- Have a copy of the following *Soul Influence Daily Guide*, one for each day.
- Clear your mind of daily worries, concerns, and plans.

SOUL INFLUENCE: INNER WISDOM GUIDANCE FOR SUCCESS IN AN OUTER WORLD

DAILY GUIDE

Date _____

Relax, get comfortable, and sit upright in a private space. Gently bring your attention to your breath. For five to fifteen minutes, simply allow your mind to have no thought activity.

Write the following affirmations:
I trust my intuition and myself.
I now notice when my inner voice is speaking to me.
I attract all that I need in my life that is for my highest good.

What Truth does my Soul want me to know? (*Listen for a small, still voice that's whispering the Truth about You.*)

I am so happy and grateful now that—(*allow yourself to accept your heart's desire*).

Today I am sending out vibrations of—(*describe the energy field you want to create this day*)

Thank you, Grand Overall Designer, for giving me the gift of creating my perfect day.

WRIGHT

Are there instances when Soul Influence doesn't work?

KELLER

No. It's guaranteed, and not because I say so! It's guaranteed because the Grand Overall Designer ordained it. It's effective to the degree you use

it. Get interested in you! If you find you can't move beyond your past conditioning to allow your well-being, it's perfectly okay to seek the counsel of an experienced professional, whether that person is a therapist, coach, or someone like myself who's both.

It's part of my purpose to assist others in any way I can. I move them to another level, and in this way, I help their souls evolve.

**99 rockets of desire fill the sky,
Each one expands the universe and doesn't ask why.**

**Visualize your desire with focus and intention,
Then follow your bliss, Soul Influencer, and pay close attention.**

**The universe is guiding you to your every desire,
Believe in yourself and you will fly higher.**

STAND BACK!
I am sending
off rockets
of desire!
© Andy Dooley

WRIGHT

Do you practice Soul Influence with your clients?

KELLER

Absolutely!

WRIGHT

Karen, what's your mission?

KELLER

Missions are chockfull of so much goodness! Remember that behavioral corset I mentioned earlier? For many women, it hits them where it really hurts—their pay check. I'm determined that women make as much money as men for the same work. Influence is about negotiation. This is the number one material world hang-up for women—asking for what you want and getting it. The latest frontier in the effort to achieve pay equity in the workplace is the gender divide in how men and women approach negotiations and their attitudes about the worth of their work is. More money brings more freedom.

Of course, all of my talks, workshops, CDs, and online seminars teach women the art and science of Influence they can apply in any circumstance.

Now more than ever before, when you empower women you transform the world because we're a demographic completely connected to each other by technology. Now we must connect through thought influence.

There's no better way to have a miracle this day than lighting the whole world. It just takes one interaction to transform a person's life or belief system. Affecting someone's life in a positive way is what Soul Influence is all about—embracing life and living from your soul—learning, growing, loving, sharing, and constantly evolving!

You have the power to vibrate, shine, and illuminate. Start where you are and become all that you are.

WRIGHT

We're coming to the close of our time together. Karen, I could talk with you all day. You've certainly opened my eyes about Influence and its potential life-changing effect. I appreciate all you've shared with us here today and I promise to put Soul Influence into action.

KELLER

Thank you, David; it's been a pleasure and a privilege. And remember, everyone: *Influence It!*™

All my love to you.

ABOUT THE AUTHOR

KAREN KELLER PHD is passionate, inspirational, and she changes lives with her penetrating wisdom. In short, you'd definitely want to add her to your professional network of women who are go-getters—make that a Rolodex of influential women. This psychologist cum peak performance executive coach turned entrepreneur is determined that women learn how to claim their power using their greatest natural gift: Soul Influence.

Karen came to be known as "The Influence Expert" after her uncanny insights into human behavior helped to affect state policy decision-making in the courtroom and seal multi-million dollar deals in the boardroom. Armed with a PhD in clinical psychology, she went on to earn the coaching industry's highest status of Master Certified Coach through the International Coach Federation in 2003. She is also a syndicated newspaper columnist. Her weekly advice column, "Ask Dr. Keller," offers custom workplace solutions for healing relationship rifts and catapulting careers. She's recently created a new business, Karen Keller International, Inc., focusing solely on programs and products that teach women how to use influence to get what they want. The result is that her phone is ringing off the hook with calls from women who want advice on how to be more successful from the courtroom to the boardroom to the bedroom, and all points in-between.

KAREN KELLER, PH.D.
Karen Keller International, Inc.
333 Moser Drive
Bronson, MI 49028
800-408-6888
info@Karen-Keller.com
www.Karen-Keller.com

CHAPTER SEVENTEEN

Secure Your Success -Do What You Love
An Interview with . . . **Linda Brown**

DAVID WRIGHT (WRIGHT)

Today we are talking with Linda J. Brown. She sees herself as the spark setting fire to the tinder that begins as a dream; she says "ignite a fire in your life!" Linda is a business coach and consultant; she's passionate about helping women entrepreneurs develop successful businesses. Her role is to offer support, help build a structure, and develop the strategies that will make the business thrive. She says, "In these tumultuous times it can be very comforting to know that there is someone on your side. A professional coach is just that, you're the 'ace in the hole,' champion, cheerleader, and soothing presence to breathe a sigh of relief with."

Linda Brown, welcome to *Stepping Stones to Success*.

LINDA BROWN (BROWN)

Thank you, David.

WRIGHT

So if you were starting a new business right now, what would you do first?

BROWN

Looking back at how I started my last two businesses, the first thing I would do is put my team of advisors together sooner. I'd get them on board before I even began the business. I've found that having advisors there to bounce ideas off and to go to when suddenly something wasn't working saved a lot of time. That's the big thing I would do differently. The one thing I did right was I hired a business coach from the outset, and with her help I was able to streamline my business in a much shorter time frame so that within six months she was no longer just my coach, she became my mentor. The experience of picking her brain was just invaluable.

WRIGHT

So what sets you apart from a traditional coach?

BROWN

Great question and I hear that a lot lately. A traditional coach—the way coaches are being trained right now—is they come to their clients and they offer no answers, they ask questions, and when the client is stuck, they will tell the client, "Well, you have the answer inside you, we just need to find it." What sets me apart from a traditional coach is that I bring consulting into the mix. So when my clients get stuck I actually help them explore answers, not just sit there and wait for them to find the answers, which sometimes can take several sessions with a coach. But if you've got some answers and you can start working with them right away and find the one that actually works for the client, you've just saved them time and heartache. That's the one thing I hear from my clients, especially the ones who have used a coach in the past; they love the fact that I'm not afraid to give them an answer and let them explore it further. So that's really what sets me apart from a traditional coach.

WRIGHT

Do you often give advice?

BROWN

If I give advice I always let them know that this is my opinion so that they don't think it's something that they have to use—you're asking me for my opinion, I'm going to give this to you, we can now look at it and explore whether to take it one step further and use it. I believe that clients should use their coach as resource. We have so much information and experience to share, why let us hide it away? So in that instance, yes, I do give advice.

WRIGHT

What is it about mindset that you feel is important?

BROWN

When the movie *The Secret* came out, I was hearing a lot of potential clients, and even some of my own clients tell me that they were going to follow this 100 percent and they were just going to change the way they thought. I asked them, "Do you think if you just think things in the positive that it's going to change how things happen to you—if you just sit here and think it, it will happen?"

"Oh yeah," comes the usual reply, "because that's the way it works."

Well the reality is that there is another component to that. Yes, mindset is very, very important. I've met people who have had a bit of a negative outlook—the glass half empty type of people. What happens is they see everything from that negative perspective and it closes them off to the positive that is happening around them. In that case, mindset is very important to be able to go forward in the positive, but it's also really important to combine it with action. You can't just sit and have a positive attitude, you have to have the positive attitude and then take positive action.

WRIGHT

What are the benefits your clients derive from working with you?

BROWN

Well, one of the big benefits of working with me is that I am a really off-the-wall, fun coach with a quirky sense of humor. You may ask if that is a selling point. Well, it really is.

I had a client meeting this morning and it was getting a little intense. I told her story and we just started laughing, like giddy school girls, but it broke that tension. I watched her and I could see she was so tight. Then, after I told the story, she just suddenly relaxed, leaned back in her chair, took a deep breath, and said, "Okay, so I'm not so overwhelmed anymore."

I think a sense of humor is a very important benefit. If you can bring humor into what's going on around you, it can help when tension starts to shut down what you should focus on. A good sense of humor really is important.

One of the stories that I tell clients is a story the minister told at my mother's memorial service. He talked about how my mother loved to go camping. Well, the family was all in the front row so you couldn't see us but you could see our shoulders shaking, and I'm sure the others in the room all thought that we were sobbing. The reality was that we were laughing hysterically because the joke in our family was that my mother's idea of camping was a Motel 6—you didn't get room service.

The big benefit of working with me is being able to take that step back, find the humor, find the fun, and then watch how your business will grow because you really love it and it doesn't become a chore that you don't hate—you're still in love with it because you know you're going to have fun with it.

WRIGHT

I know that success means different things to different people, but would you tell our readers what success means to you?

BROWN

The short statement on what success means to me is that I have done what I love to do, and I've done it in a way that I still love it. That is what I consider to be a success. I don't identify success with money; I don't identify success as owning a huge corporation where I have managers and tons of employees. For me success is when I wake up in the morning and I think about what I'm going to do that day and I know I've got maybe five clients to meet with. That's success for me because I still love the thought of meeting with these folks because every day is different. I might have an idea of what I'm going to talk to a client about based on what we've done in the past, but that doesn't necessarily mean it's going to happen.

So that's my definition of success—my success is that I do what I love. There's an old money/career saying that has many versions but goes something like this, "do what you love, love what you do, and the money will follow." Well, I think I would change that to, "do what you love, love what you do, and success is secure."

WRIGHT

So what are your thoughts about change and how do you use it to benefit your work with your clients?

BROWN

That's funny, as President of the Silicon Valley Coach Federation, I just posted a quote of my own, "Growth is change—if we don't change we can't grow." For me, change is important. When I'm interviewing potential clients I let them know that we will be making changes and if they're not going to make any changes, the chances are we're not going to work together because it's really the only way to grow a business.

Think of it from a planting point of view or story. If you put a seed in the ground and you do absolutely nothing to it, that seed will stay just that—a seed—it will never change. But if you put that seed in the ground, keep it warm, feed it, and water it, it then suddenly starts to change. The next thing you know, you've got that little green sprout coming up. Even that is going to change because you're going to take care of it, you're going to continue to feed it, continue to water it, maybe you're going to weed it, and pinch off some blossoms so it grows even sturdier. If you don't do that, no changes can happen. That's the big thing about change. I encourage my clients to change—to really embrace change—to try new things, because that's where they're going to see the best results and the fastest results.

WRIGHT

Do you consider yourself a risk-taker?

BROWN

If you would have asked me this question ten years ago, I would have said no, but in looking back at the past ten years, I've taken some major risks, and I've made changes in my life. I've taken chances that I never, ever thought I would. I've taken chances where family members have looked at me and said, "Linda, why don't you just get a nice, safe, secure job?" I had one friend say, "Linda, we need a bookkeeper, you can learn bookkeeping."

I have found that I am not the kind of risk-taker who would go and bet everything on black in Las Vegas. I take calculated risks, but I am still going to take that chance. I look at it this way, when I'm on my death bed, I want to look at my family and say, "I had the best life. I did everything I wanted to do and I tried—I tried everything. I know I've tried some things weren't successful and that's okay, because I found out that I really didn't like them." This refers back to how I define success—I have to love what I do. So yes, I'm a risk-taker.

WRIGHT

A brilliant man once told me that if I was walking down the road and saw a turtle sitting on top of a fence post, I could bet my bottom dollar that he didn't get up there by himself. So who do you consider to be the most influential people in your life and what lessons did you learn from them?

BROWN

One of the most influential people in my life was my mother. She had a ninth grade education, but to talk with her and to read the things she wrote, you would never know that. You would have thought she was college educated, and yet she always felt less because she didn't have that education. She gave me the strength to try different things; she gave me the strength to be who I am, to become the secure woman, and the self-confident woman that I became. Did she know this? Not until I told her.

I remember a friend asking my mother one day, "How did you get two successful daughters?" At that time my sister was in college and I was a sales manager with a high tech company. My mother looked at her and said, "I have no idea where these girls get their drive, it certainly wasn't from me." I looked at the woman and said, "Oh yes, it was. Look at my mother—she had the courage to go on as a widow with three children. I will gather that strength and I will make that my own as well." So she was one of the most influential people in my life.

Along the road I have met mentors who have instilled in me the courage to try and move beyond what I know. I was working as an inside sales assistant in high tech. The man I was working for—the salesman—came to me and said, "I want to move you outside. I want to make you a sales rep in the field."

My answer was, "Oh no, you're not putting me out there."

"You can do it," he said.

I kept saying, no, I was not interested, I love the inside, working behind the scenes, and didn't want to be out there. He just kept talking and he kept coming back. He wore me down.

"Okay," I finally said, "but what happens if I fail?"

I will always remember what he said, "You will never fail because I'm here to make sure you don't, because if you did I'd look bad, and I'm not going to let you make me look bad."

I thought, "Oh, this is a great way to learn."

So I used that when I started mentoring salesmen myself. When I am asked, "What if I fail?" I reply, "You won't fail, I'm here to help support you and to help you succeed because if you do fail, I'll look bad and I don't want to look bad."

WRIGHT

You have a unique belief about storytelling and how it can be beneficial in coaching. Would you explain your perspective to our readers?

BROWN

Oh, I'd love to. It's another one of those things that sets me apart from a traditional coach. Traditionally, coaches are encouraged to not allow storytelling—to stop the story and get to the point, the bottom line. I found very early on that I tell stories and use them as examples. That's how I process and get my information in a logical progression; it's also how I can relate to my information. I found that if I allow my clients to tell me their story, I got a lot of information from them that they didn't think they were giving to me. It's one of those skills that a really good coach can develop. It involves picking up the nuances of the unspoken point that your clients might be hiding, because they really don't even know that they're hiding them. Yet when you listen to their stories, you start to pick it up. I encourage my clients to tell me their story.

One of the benefits of doing that is I let them know that's their story now and if they're not happy with it, it's up to them to change their story. When you change your story, you change the way you live, and you change the way that, possibly, you run your business. So for me storytelling is very, very important. It will always be a very important part of my coaching style.

WRIGHT

What does "plan to be surprised" mean to you?

BROWN

If you are a client and you come to me thinking that you're going to do something a certain set way, I can almost guarantee that there is going to be a surprise in there and we're going to end up doing it a totally different way. We may even change the whole focus or outlook of your business because we're going to expect the unexpected and play with it. I always let my clients know, that if they come in with a set perspective I'm going to shake it up. Part of that is to make sure that it may be the way you really, really want to go, I'm going to make sure that you're really, deeply set with that idea, and if you're not, the surprise will change your mind and move you in the direction that you really want to go in, you just don't know it yet. So there is always a surprise.

With all the clients I work with, I never expect them to be run–of–the–mill or the same. I just know that every single one of them is going to be different, and for me that difference is the surprise. So not only do my clients get to be surprised, but I get to be pleasantly surprised, too.

WRIGHT

I was talking to a coach a week or two ago. She first asked me who I thought was the greatest golfer today, and I of course said, "Tiger Woods."

"Do you know he had a coach?" she asked.

"Yes I did," I answered.

"Well, since he is the best, why does he need a coach?"

I'm sure her question was rhetorical.

Do you think that everybody who is running a business needs a coach?

BROWN

My quick answer is yes, you bet. Do they need a coach? Will they benefit 100 percent from working with a coach? Yes. The majority of the successful executives and business owners out there have benefited from having a coach, a trusted advisor, or a mentor. I really think that business owners will find that their business can be improved faster, more economically, and they would see even bigger results if they had a coach to work with them.

WRIGHT

I think that's a great perspective. I really appreciate all the time you've taken with me this afternoon to answer these questions. You've given me a lot to think about and I know that the readers are going to be challenged by some of the things you've said.

BROWN

Well, thank you very much, David. I appreciate the time as well.

WRIGHT

Today we've been talking with Linda J. Brown, a business coach and consultant. She helps women entrepreneurs develop successful businesses. She offers support and helps build a structure and develop the strategies that will make their businesses thrive.

Linda, thank you so much for being with us today on *Stepping Stones to Success*.

BROWN

Thank you, David.

ABOUT THE AUTHOR

LINDA J. BROWN brings the experience of more than thirty years in industries ranging from retail to high tech sales. She has worked the retail sales floor, human resources, accounting, employee training, and outside sales. As a Senior District Sales Manager for Motorola Semiconductor Inc., she was responsible for a $90 million Fortune 500 company. In 2003 she started a successful Real Estate support service company that she closed in 2007.

Today Linda works with small business owners and solopreneurs, partnering with them toward greater success by helping them get clear on their vision for their business, developing the structures and strategies for making the vision a reality, and providing support and accountability along the way.

Linda is a graduate of the Coaches Training Institute, a member and certified coach with the International Coach Federation, a founding member of Women Teaching Women, and currently is President of the Silicon Valley Coach Federation. Linda graduated from the University of Utah with a BA in Theatre.

LINDA BROWN
Linda Brown Coaching
Los Gatos CA
408-314-3169
coachlindab@lindabrowncoaching.com
www.lindabrowncoaching.com

CHAPTER EIGHTEEN

Become Who You Are:
The Secret of Fail-safe Success

An Interview with . . . **Mike Jay**

DAVID WRIGHT (WRIGHT)

Today we're talking with Mike Jay. In his work as a professional coach, Mike has designed the Flawless Living System, a simple program to help people break the addiction of believing they can be anything they want—a self-defeating, vicious cycle in which too many people either sacrifice happiness for success, or they live with what makes them happy but have lives that don't give them all of what they need to live well. Flawless Living is an approach that relies on your inborn talents, your understanding of your life requirements, and the creation of a design that allows you stay in the flow state longer. It is a step-by-step program to leverage each additional effort you make into an effortless system of action, where even non-action can sometimes be key as you learn what to say "yes" to and what to say "no" to.

Mike Jay, welcome to *Stepping Stones to Success*.

MIKE JAY (JAY)

Thanks, David. I'm glad to be here.

WRIGHT

From what I understand, you've identified a series of steppingstones to well-being. What is the underlying foundation or the guiding principle of your approach?

JAY

Well, I think I should just set up the philosophy. What we're living in today is what has come out of the psychology of the twentieth century—now, people are afraid to lean toward determinism. It was this kind of thing that created phenomena like the Nazi extermination of what they saw as inferior races. In reaction, people have leaned so far away from it that they are now under the impression that anybody can be anything they want to be. What we're raising is a relatively controversial idea that you actually *cannot* be anything you decide to be and in fact, you don't really want to.

We're taking on this "blank slate" idea that we all come into the world born with equal potential. Yes, we do all have equal rights, but that doesn't mean we're all the same. This fact that we're individually different is the key philosophy behind the Flawless Living System. For if you spend your entire life trying to be like somebody else, or somebody you're not, you're going to spend a significant amount of time working in your weaknesses and limitations while neglecting your own strengths. Quite frankly, that's not ever going to help you become happy, even though you may feel that you're making progress.

Our whole system is designed to say, "Okay, we're all different. I'm different. How am I different and how can I leverage that difference?" That's where we started with this process. I now feel that the blank slate idea that you can become anything you want to be has become an addiction. This is why I've created this twelve-step program—to help people who are addicted to the blank slate idea rescue themselves and others from it.

WRIGHT

What do people who are following your program have to do first?

JAY

There is actually a key piece to understand, which is that a particular potential for happiness is born into us. Yet most of what happens to us during our life is that we conform to some standard set by someone who's powerful or some motivational speaker or someone we see as successful, and that diminishes our happiness. That being said, there will always be some people who, because of the way they are born and because of the particular set of requirements they're born into, fall into natural alignment with the standard in question.

We see a lot of these people become motivational speakers because they say, "Well, gosh, if I've done it, I can teach other people to do it, so here's what you need to do." That's not so bad for them. But the problem is, even in Stephen Covey's work promoting the seven habits of highly effective people, most people found that they couldn't replicate that success in their own lives.

What I'm saying is, "Wait a minute! Before you decide on a set of standards, let's look at how you're born into happiness based on your intrinsic strengths, values, and motivators. Let's look at the way this plays out in your life. Does it put you in accord with or at odds with the requirements of your life?"

I believe that maybe 1 to 5 percent of people are born naturally into a success paradigm where they just get up in the morning and they'll be successful. I'm sure you've met some people like that. I know I have. But for the rest of us—the other 95 to 99 percent—it's a struggle because we keep trying to be like those successful few. We keep trying to do what they recommend, but we're very unhappy. We give up our happiness to be successful.

What the Flawless Living System says is that you do not have to give up your happiness to be successful, but you do have to understand who you are and that happiness is natural. You have to understand what you can wake up every day doing that will help you become happy. Then you have to understand how that's different from your life requirements and go from there designing your life in a new way. That's the first thing people have to do—understand that happiness is natural.

WRIGHT

What is the key to aligning a person's natural happiness with his or her success?

JAY

The idea is actually fairly simple, although it's not always easy to put into place. We call it "success by design," which means we look at three things: The first is your natural capability and how the trajectory of that changes over time as you mature. The second thing we look at is what are likely to be the differing sets of requirements that you will be exposed to, or that you will expose yourself to, depending on how sacrifice-of-self you are. In other words, each of us is born into a mode where we're either go-getters or we're waiters. It's not really quite that simple, but the idea is that the go-getter people will force the environment to become like them and the waiters will adapt to whatever is there, and we need to design accordingly. So we set up a formula involving capability, requirements, and design that keeps people from having to spend their whole lives trying to change to fit something they're not.

My earlier work has all been based on the idea that you don't have to change, but you do have to have the conversation around change and then change will come out of that. The conversation begins with capability—what are you naturally good at? Two, what are you forcing yourself to do or being forced to do? Those are your requirements. And three, how do you design around the fact that you're going to have natural limitations if you're not one of those 1 to 5 percent of people naturally hardwired for success? So we call it success by design, which then builds in that natural happiness factor.

WRIGHT

Is what you are naturally aligned with something that you can figure out on your own?

JAY

Great question. I will say this: In general, acquiring self-knowledge is going to move you in that direction. But since we're each different, this idea of self-awareness—of being able to gain a perspective on ourselves—is also a trajectory that you are born with, and not everybody has the same amount. Consequently, what we normally say is, yes, some people will be able to do this self-discovery work on their own, some will need help and nudging, while others will need significant help or what we call "scaffolding" to be able to know themselves in a way that gives deep enough clues to what they will be naturally happy doing over time.

In other words, many of us can look at a snapshot of our life right now and say, "I'll be happy if I have this" or "I'll be happy when I'm doing that" or "I'll be happy when I'm with this person or when I'm with my grandchildren" or whatever. Those requirements will actually shift over time. At our core, however, we don't change. Our happiness is born into us as a system—an architecture—and we're each unique. Each of us is going to have certain kinds of gifts, and we're going to have certain densities around those gifts that may make it effortless for us to employ them. Others of us, however, are just going to have to work harder. I was in athletics throughout my early life, and I played with some guys who could do anything. They just had wonderful, natural physical gifts. And then there were those of us who had to work damn hard at it.

The whole continuum of what gifts you're born with is really important, and that's what you have to know about yourself. Sometimes you can figure that out on your own; sometimes you have to peel back the onion with the help of another person. In that case, you should grab one of us who is familiar with this process of inquiry and let us help you peel away a few of those layers so you get down to the root of what really makes you happy. That is the key in this particular step.

WRIGHT

These principles seem to make a lot of sense in understanding why so many people aren't either as happy or successful as they could be. Why does the blank slate concept continue to be such a powerful driver in our society?

JAY

In some cases, in our collective unconsciousness, people don't ever want to commit the error that was committed during World War II, when so many people were sacrificed because they were of the "wrong" ethnicity. There has been such a shadow in our collective unconsciousness that people don't want to be told they're different or they can't do something other people can do. In addition, each one of us has personally known or heard of someone who came from absolutely miserable circumstances, fought through all the obstacles, and became something wonderful. The whole American dream is essentially built on that possibility.

In our collective unconsciousness we have this set of shadow dynamics that we're moving away from and we have this light that we're moving toward. Even with our current President, Obama's whole platform is built on hope. It is written in the Bible that where there is no vision the people perish (Proverbs 29:18).

What the Flawless Living System does is go beyond hope because we believe that this is an actionable system and you don't have to just keep hoping and waiting for it to come true—you can turn that hope into actual possibility. I phrase this particular step in a pretty no-bullshit kind of way and say, "Stop pretending—stop pretending that you can when you won't." How many of us know what we *should* do? How many of us know that we should lose weight and how to lose weight and yet we don't? How many of us know how we should raise our kids but turn around and do it differently? How many people know what they should be doing at work but don't do it? It's not the *knowing*. It's not the *can*. All of us *can* do these things, but we *won't* do them because we're not naturally motivated to, so stop pretending that we will!

Now, you have to get to a point of acceptance with that, and this is really the big step. The tipping point for getting out of blank slate is to finally accept that "I am different than other people. I don't act like them. I don't want to act like them. I have gifts. I want to act like who I am. I want to get up every day feeling good about who I am."

There has been this huge focus in our educational system on esteem. But what we're doing is giving people societal esteem. We're giving them the esteem that says, "If you look like this, if you dress like this, if you have this kind of car or this kind of house, if you do these kinds of things, if you have this kind of friend or go to this school, then you're okay. Everything else is not okay." That, in my view, is the lure of blank slate because we take those who are naturally born into these systems that breed success and make them exemplars and we try to model ourselves after them. We keep trying to change and mold ourselves. As long as we keep doing this, there is a tremendous lure that we can actually learn all these things and do all these things because humans are adaptable and can learn to do a lot of things. The problem is, we turn right around and keep doing what we've been doing.

The statistics indicate that approximately 95 percent of people who go on a diet actually start by losing weight and then end up heavier. What is that about? Well we *can* lose weight, but at the same time we're not willing to do the things that continually keep the weight off. It's not that we can't do it, it's that we *won't* do it.

The Flawless Living process involves finally admitting and finally looking in the mirror and saying, "I'm going to stop pretending that I will just because I can," and then getting back to what I *will* do and seeing how that begins to put me into a whole different paradigm. That's the tipping point, I'd say.

WRIGHT

Very, very interesting. So if we have the self-knowledge of what makes us happy and we understand that we can't fulfill all our life requirements by ourselves, is there anything else that is key to sustainability and success?

JAY

Let me do a little sidebar right here. There is one underlying lynchpin in being successful and that has been proven in Viktor Frankl's work all the way through the Hawaii Studies on hardy personality to what we've now come to know as resilience. In a world that is uncertain and turbulent, in a world in which we can no longer predict, in a world that will soon have change as its only constant, we will lose the ability to be able to predict our futures.

So how do we know how to do well when we're moving toward some place and we don't and can't know what it's going to be? There is a set of skills and a set of things you can do that underpins this whole system and it's under the rubric of resilience. And how do we get resilience? Well, there are four things that produce resilience. The most important step is that when you find, for example, that you're not willing to do the bookkeeping, you stop pretending, and you go get a bookkeeper or maybe you barter with someone to get it done. Somehow you find someone who will do the bookkeeping because if you don't do it, even though you can, you won't have accurate information and you will therefore make bad decisions.

The key step in building resilience is reaching out—it's developing the ability to reach out for the help you need. Now with introverts, we want to make sure that we don't put something on them that is very difficult for them to do because introverts reach in, not out. In that case, with the Flawless Living process, you begin by accepting, "Okay, I'm an introvert. I don't want to reach out. But at the same time my design can start to do that." What we're saying is, whether you reach out or in, you've got to reach, because if you think you'll do it all on your own, you're fooling yourself—you're living in an illusion—and if you stay in that illusion, you're going to be stuck between happiness and success. You'll always be trading one against the other. When what you normally do to make yourself happy doesn't meet your success requirements, you end up giving up happiness to be successful. Most of us have a life of constant tradeoffs because we're misaligned with what it takes to be successful.

If you can't meet the requirements on your own, what I'm saying is to reach out or reach in. Let's find the resources that will help you bridge the gaps that are naturally going to be present, given that you are unique to your circumstances. Reaching out is the one thing that we know promotes higher levels of resilience. In today's complex world of uncertainty, where you don't know what you don't know about where you're headed, when you get there you have to rely on these resilience skills to produce solutions in the environment you find yourself in. And that's where we're all headed, by the way. If you don't think you're in over your head now, just wait a while, because things are becoming so complex, so difficult.

I read recently that there is more information in the *New York Times* on any one Sunday than was available to people during the entire eighteenth century. We're headed to very complex environments, and yet we're running off 25,000- to 100,000-year-old genetics—the same kind that kept us picking berries and away from tigers. Now we're in this complex technological world and trying to use those old genetics to navigate. We can adapt, but we don't adapt fast enough, which means we now have to enter a truly collaborative frame. This is the idea behind reaching out. If you truly want to become collaborative and you're an introvert, you'll design a system to support your reaching out. Or, if you're an extrovert, you'll begin to understand how to more effectively reach out to help other people.

Wealth systems use the OPM—other people's money—plus other people's effort plus other people's time plus other people's ability. The successful people who are naturally born into this know that's what you do naturally. For most of us, however, the first place we go when we reach an obstacle or problem is we withdraw. We don't want anybody to see how stupid we are or we don't want to show weakness or we don't want to appear helpless. Yet as long as we do that we're going to be less resilient.

This entire process rests, number one, on stop pretending, and number two, on realizing that you can't do it alone—that we're here to help one another. Once you get past the tipping point on stopping the pretending, you get the blossoming of what this Flawless Living System really can do. You release yourself from the blank slate and from the notion that you have to do it all by yourself.

WRIGHT

How about the thornier issues such as what if what we think we want and need doesn't align with our values-based happiness?

JAY

You know, this is a real tough one and our forum today is not conducive to being able to explain this fully. But most of us don't really know what we want because we live in a society that has created an artificial standard of what we should want—of what supposedly will make us happy or successful.

There is an interesting story told in a BBC documentary series done back in 2002 titled *The Century of Self*. They show the actual beginning of public relations. There was not even a term for public relations until it was invented in the 1920s by a guy who was a nephew of Sigmund Freud. His name was Edward Bernays, and he is credited with what we now call public relations and all of the Madison Avenue advertising systems that surround us all over the world in signs, movies, videos, audios, and everything we touch. We get twelve thousand exposures a day telling us what we should want. It is flat difficult, if you haven't taken the time to find out who you are, to avoid being mesmerized by the tremendous subliminal tricks that advertising has us play on ourselves and instead to see that we don't know what we really want. We therefore don't know what to value, yet values really matter because our particular values are the means to our happiness and success.

On one hand, we have to discover our core values that give us our ends and, on the other hand, to understand how we are getting there and whether it is efficient, effective, and sustainable. Are we using convoluted means to get to and, in fact, serve our ends? Most of us are, and that's very inefficient.

Several years ago, I put forward the notion that if you really want to reduce greenhouse gases in the atmosphere, know yourself. Why? Because you'll stop shooting with a shotgun and instead you'll shoot with a rifle. You won't have to consume but two-thirds of what you're consuming right now because, at the minimum, one-third of what you consume is stuff you don't need. Go look in your garage if you think I'm wrong. We're buying stuff that we look at five or six months or a year later and ask ourselves, "Why did I buy that? What in the heck am I doing with this stuff?" Our consumptive lifestyle has produced all that CO_2 in our environment because we don't really know what we want. We get tricked into buying what we don't really want or need because we don't know who we are.

This is a thorny issue because who's to say what anybody really wants? You have to decide that for yourself. At the same time, if you're not careful, you'll be right back in the illusion of blank slate, trying to be anything that the advertisers want you to be.

That's what they talk about in the BBC series *The Century of Self.* They show how this advertising paradigm, through time, has actually guided society in directions that it doesn't really need to go in and that are not healthy. That's the reason for the problems of overconsumption that we have today and that we think will make us happy. Now, it's true that some few people actually can be happy with that level of consumption, but most of us do not need to over-consume. It's just that we think we want something and we do whatever it takes to get it. Then we go through the experience of finding that it really wasn't what would make us happy—it was the hoping that it would or thinking that I'm "in" because I have this now when, in fact, the consumption is serving others' needs. That's the convolution in our wanting.

WRIGHT

How do you remove the noise in the system, whether it's internal or external?

JAY

I have a very simple question that has clicked with people since I first used it. I ask them, "Do you know what to say 'yes' to and what to say 'no' to?" Normally that will eliminate most of the noise because of what we just talked about. If you've got all these things coming at you—twelve thousand hits a day, twelve thousand opportunities to be persuaded—but if you don't know what to say "yes" to and what to say "no" to, and if you go along with what other people are trying to get you to do, you're going to constantly find yourself being drawn away from who you are toward what they are or what they want you to be or where they are going to benefit from your being something else. The key point is, what do I say "yes" to, what do I say "no" to, and why? That then begins to help you escape the slippery slope. As soon as you can tie your own individual happiness to the individual decisions that you make every day, saying "yes" and "no" to people, places, things, relationships, interviews, whatever it is, you have a sense of who you are and you operate from that place.

Now, there is a little key for the people who are developmentally oriented that I'll just slip in here and that's self-authoring, which is a subject-object place. When we say we're subject to something, it means we're embedded in it. We're like the fish that doesn't know it's in water. It's just a part of us and we can't differentiate it; we don't have a relationship with it. When something is an object for us, we have a relationship with it. Well, when you have a relationship to "yes" and "no" and you know why, you begin to self-author; in other words, you make decisions out of who you are and what your principles say you are. That consistently pulls you along a path or trajectory that is closer to having built-in returns for your happiness. The key, then, is whether that path is going to take you away from success, and if it does, we're going to have to design away that gap.

WRIGHT

Is there some system people can use to help implement their design?

JAY

Actually, every system we're in has a scoreboard—a set of requirements—whether you go to elementary school or whether (like me) you're talking and working in Moscow right now. Every system has a scoreboard and that's what you have to understand. How does the system keep score? Am I clear on what it takes to get a win?

Let's say I know who I am, and let's say I know what my requirements are, or I think I do. Well, if I know that being myself naturally won't get me on that scoreboard, then I've got to be able to reach out to or work with someone who can get me there. I've got to be able to tell that person what it means to ring the bell or whatever it is I can't do so the person can reach up there and ring that bell for me.

If I'm not clear on how the score is kept, then I'm going to be inefficient and ineffective, and the system won't be sustainable because I'm using up resources. In other words, when I'm not doing something myself, I'm using external resources, and most of the time those external resources have costs. We want to be very efficient with those resources so we've got to know how to ring the bell, or we've got to know how the bell is rung, in order to reach out and tell people, "Hey, I need this specific help right now. I need you to do this for me right now. I need you to gather a team and we're going to do this together."

So the key thing at this step is to know how the score is kept, how the bell is rung, and how to tell other people how to ring that bell.

WRIGHT

Sometimes our systems become closed loops and don't move us forward. Is there some way to guard against that?

JAY

Another short sidebar: Ilya Prigogine won the Nobel Prize in 1977 for this concept called "dissipative systems." He said that a dissipative system is one that is organizationally closed but energetically open, and somehow or other that applies to everything—to any living system where energy is coming and going. The key thing here is that most of us decide at some point and continuously throughout our lives what reality means to us—what is real and what is not real. However, because our perception is limited or our inductive bias moves us in a particular direction (as Malcolm Gladwell talked about in his book *Blink)* we only see what we see. We don't see the whole picture. What we need to do to go along with this system—to create an adaptive approach that allows us to keep learning and growing and also to be happy and successful—is a system of feedback.

This is called a "cybernetic system." A simple system involves input, throughput, and output. But the system doesn't become self-informing until you add the feedback loop; once you do that it becomes cybernetic. It gives information back to the system by which you can figure out whether or not it's doing what it's supposed to do.

Each of us has this inductive bias. We go through life only seeing what we're seeing. We need feedback to know if what we're seeing is really the reality or if we're mistaken. Most people don't want to get the feedback, and the reason is because they see it as a personal threat, as direct criticism. They see it as something that is basically somebody else's opinion and to be ignored. Or, when they get to a certain point of receptivity they might say, "Oh well, that's an interesting idea. I might consider that."

What we're suggesting is that if you want to leave the trajectory of blank slate, you have to become a cybernetic system. You already naturally are; however, you have to open that up so you can give and receive more effective feedback. That's one of the keys to stopping pretending. It's one of the keys to knowing yourself and to knowing the scoreboard.

How do different people go through life day after day giving the same amount of effort, and yet some people end up really happy and successful and others don't? What is going on with that? Well, some people see something one way and some people see it the other way. Our idea is that it's going to take more than just your own perspective; it's going to take additional perspectives. How are you going to get those? You're going to reach in, reach out, and you're going to ask other people, "Hey, am I doing the right thing? From your perspective am I going in the right direction? Am I ringing the bell as loudly as I could? Am I really being who I am? Do you see me being happy in what I'm saying 'yes' and 'no' to?" The idea is to get this type of feedback—we call it external referencing—and not just to work off your own self-referencing. Get the external-referencing system in place so that you can get help from people.

WRIGHT

Given the rapidity of change, how can people make their designs more adaptable?

JAY

There is an easy metaphor to remember here. After the Exxon Valdez oil spill in Alaska, people started to learn a lot about oil tankers. What happened with the Exxon Valdez is that it didn't begin to prepare for turning at the right time. That gave rise to the metaphor, "How long does it take to turn an oil tanker?" Well, if anybody has ever driven one or knows anything about it, you have to start thinking about turning an oil tanker way before the turn because those things don't turn on a dime. Our lives are the same way.

You see, we have so much cost invested in who we are and what we're doing—we bought this house, we bought this car, we have this job because of this education we have—that it's not really easy to just turn our lives around, although we know that some people do it midlife.

To use another metaphor, we know that during the Apollo moon shot the missile was off course at least 85 to 90 percent of the time. So how did it get to its destination? NASA constantly recalibrated it. They constantly said, "It's a little off target, bring it back this way. It's a little off target, bring it back that way."

Likewise, we have to recalibrate our own lives often because we don't know whether we're going in the right direction all the time. We use external referencing, we stop pretending, we know ourself, we begin to reach out, we understand that happiness and success are natural by design, we get a design in place, and we know how to keep the score. But if the environment is going to throw us off—it's going to be windy, it's going to be cloudy, it's going to rainy, it's going to be bumpy—what we have to do is recalibrate often. Check to see where you are and where you're headed. See if that fits with who you are and what you're doing. *Stop and take a happiness check.* If it's not there, let's figure out where you went off track and recalibrate. So that's a key thing as you get deeper and deeper into the last two steps of this system.

WRIGHT

There's something we haven't touched on yet. Is there some aspect of spiritual alignment that fits into the Flawless Living process?

JAY

The backdrop to this process is that we consider it to be genetically guided because we have the firm belief—and there is plenty of research now to show this—that we come into this world with a type of architecture—a use-it-or-lose-it type of system—that is motivated by something we showed up with, something that makes each of us really different. So while Bernays said the only way is up and we're all going to climb the ladder (and even Covey said you've got to understand whether your ladder is against the right wall), I say, "Wait a minute! The whole ladder metaphor is wrong. We don't need to be going up, we need to be going in."

In the East and in many of the religions all over the world, they talk about this idea of knowing yourself, of reaching in and understanding who you really are, of going to God in there. While the Flawless Living process itself does not have to be seen as a spiritual goal, it actually is spiritually entwined because what we're trying to do is to use what God gave us or to use what's evolving, whichever way you understand it. This actually becomes a very spiritual process—the spirituality is built into the system. It's like your computer where you don't see Microsoft running in the background or Linux or Leopard; you're using these applications that run transparently in the system that you know are in the background.

It's the same thing here. This system is spiritually guided because it is a process of becoming more wholly ourselves, more wholly whole to the unique idea that we are—and of understanding that we have these gifts, and that the greatest gift of all is to live in that uniqueness and share it with others. The idea isn't that you have to go somewhere to be spiritual. We're saying that all you have to do is breathe to be spiritual, to know yourself, to stop pretending, to look at how happiness is natural. Spirituality is interwoven into the system—you can't *not* be spiritual if you follow this system. That's what integrates it at an unconscious level to allow you to escape this blank slate velocity.

WRIGHT

Are there other elements that come into play in fully aligning your happiness and success?

JAY

Let's talk a second about epigenesis, which means nature and nurture and the combinatorial effect that changes both. Over time those twenty-five-thousand-year-old genetics are being changed by culture; they're being changed by environment. We talk a lot today about gene expression, in other words, not just that we have genes, but which ones are expressed? How do some of them know when to turn on and when to turn off? How do some become gifts and at the same time diseases? We ask these kinds of questions. Epigenesis is really important because it is, in effect, the evolution that is occurring in the creative process.

What we have to understand is that culture is a huge part of that process, especially for the folks who are adaptive, rather than the go-getter folks who are making the culture that adaptive people are responding to. I suggest that there are probably a lot more adaptive people than there are people who are actually working to make things happen. The world works better that way.

The point is that you have to be aware of what culture is doing to you. If you look at *The Century of Self* documentaries you see what culture is doing to you all over the world. I spend a lot of time traveling—as I said, I'm talking to you today from Moscow—and when I look at all the messages that culture is sending to people here, it's not unlike walking down the street in New York or Tokyo or Amsterdam or Madrid or Berlin. Culture is a messaging system and a series of messages. What we call scaffolding is what you use to build support into your life design, and in doing so, you've got to be aware of how culture affects you, what you plan to do about cultural norms, what you expose yourself to, and whether you have a choice in all this.

The key thing in escaping blank slate (and it's a tricky one) is, on one hand, to understand how you're subject to culture and, on the other hand, that you have a relationship with it. Once you can objectify culture and its role in your life, you can begin to understand how you have unconsciously been controlled by it. That subject-object dance is something all of us go through in our life. It was written about by Robert Kegan in his 1980s book, *The Evolving Self*, and his 1990s book, *In Over Our Heads*, as well as in some of his more recent writings. But the story really is this: How are you subject to your own culture? How does that help or hinder you in designing your means and your valuing process to reach your inborn ends?

Remember that 95 percent of us, left to our own devices, do not know what our true desires are. So this is a process of inquiry, a process of choosing to do this work. It's a process of becoming more objective about what has us and what is running our lives, and culture is a big part of that. We can't deny it, and we don't want to deny it; we want to make sure it works for us and not against us. So as we're saying "yes" and "no," and as we're looking at our happiness quotient, and as we're trying to understand success and the scoreboard and pretending and all of these things that we've talked about, we have to weave in culture.

Now, since I do put these in a twelve-step program, there is a tendency to think that you should do these steps sequentially. You can, and we've tried to organize them in a way that they are in a natural sequence. But in actuality, you should be doing them all in parallel.

One more thing before we close—each one of these steps has a behavioral set that has a certain density in each of us. We can actually measure this. We'll have an assessment for people to take; it measures their density in each one of these behavioral sets. We can map that density against the requirements of your life situation. We can begin to see the gaps that are created by how a person's behavioral sets are occurring right now, in real life, and we can either increase or lower the frequency through design to diminish the gap. This becomes a cool part of the process as you begin to understand the effects of culture and how you yourself have built up a somewhat resilient density in one way or another to cope, to manage, and to get through things.

In the Flawless Living System we give you a kind of survival kit—it's like having a Swiss army knife with everything you need and being able to pull out the tools you need at the same time. So you're using all of them at once, and all of them together become a toolkit.

Finally, in this process, you have to understand the integration. You have to understand that all of these things are already occurring in your life, but they may not be occurring at the right density. What we do is look at that and then, through the process of inquiry, we can begin to understand what the density *can* be in your life, what it *should* be in your requirements, and how to pick up the slack through design.

WRIGHT

Well, as always, Mike, this has been very, very interesting. It's something I thought about a long time ago—this idea that you can be anything you want to be. Sometimes I hear folks say that to people and I think it's putting a lot of pressure on those who are being told that. I don't believe it—on the front end I don't believe it. But we'll have to let readers make up their own minds. This has been a very interesting conversation for me, one in which I learned a lot. I know it will be an interesting chapter for our readers. I really appreciate your taking the time to answer all these questions for me today.

JAY

Thanks, David. I really appreciate the time you took to ask them in a way that makes it easy for me to tell my story. So thanks for allowing me to do that.

WRIGHT

Today we've been talking with Mike Jay. Mike has designed a Flawless Living System in twelve steps. It's a step-by-step program to leverage each individual effort into an effortless system of action, where even non-action can sometimes be a key in learning what to do—what to say "yes" to and what to say "no" to.

Mike, thank you so much for being with us today on *Stepping Stones to Success*.

JAY
Thanks, David. I'm happy to be a part of the project.

ABOUT THE AUTHOR

MIKE JAY is a professional business coach, consultant, and *happeneur*. An award-winning United States Marine and collegiate athlete, he initially parlayed his leadership experience into agribusiness innovation and management success in medicine, hospitality, and business services. In 1999, he founded a world-class business and executive coach training system. Through more than ten thousand hours of coaching sessions, Mike has served business leaders in twenty-seven countries. He is consistently on the leading edge of leadership innovation, culture change, and "emergenics"—a field he created to explore the nature of creating fewer problems than you solve. Mike coined the term "*generati*" and has dedicated his life to generative leadership.

MIKE JAY

1132 13th Ave
Mitchell, NE 69357
877.901.Coach (2622)
generati@msn.com
www.mikejay.com

CHAPTER NINETEEN

Productivity to the Max!
An Interview with . . . **Alicia Trigo**

DAVID WRIGHT (WRIGHT)

Today we're talking with Alicia Trigo, Chief Executive Officer of An Amazing Organization Inc. An Amazing Organization is a consulting firm specializing in revenue growth and productivity. For over a decade, Alicia has served as an enabler for businesses nationwide. She is known for her innovative strategies and robust network. Her endeavors cover an array of industries such as technology, international business, healthcare, retail, media, sales, marketing, public relations, and small businesses. Alicia is the creator of "The Amazing Method" a seven-segment program that enables a complete assessment that identifies areas to increase return on investment. Today, Alicia is a recognized speaker and has been praised for her motivational affect on her audiences.

Alicia, welcome to *Stepping Stones to Success*.

ALICIA TRIGO (TRIGO)

Good morning to you.

WRIGHT

So what is the affect and implications of productivity in the business place?

TRIGO

Productivity is the foundation of your business; it is where success is measured. Despite how well your business plan has been created or what a great financial forecast is in place, without excellent productivity there is no success.

The accountability for productivity is a strategy from A through Z with an evergreen prospective in an effort to improve your organization as you deliver products and services. Productivity enablers are the metrics to ensure accountability toward everything you do such as creating your goals, improving your products and overall customer service experience. The when, how, whom, what, if's, etc. are the grounds of productivity.

WRIGHT

So what are the key factors of productivity and success?

TRIGO

The key factors are very, very simple. It is my belief that the intricate part starts when you establish your productivity plan—that's when the work begins. Below I will highlight three key factors of productivity. These are the baseline of any productivity plan. A good productivity plan will have anywhere from ten to twenty key factors. The first three key factors are as follows:

KEY FACTOR NUMBER ONE:

Be Proactive. Think about the unthinkable—the good and bad. This is the only way to prepare. Normally, plans are prepared toward a goal; I prefer to prepare toward a profitable goal. The upfront and ongoing homework will be your best weapon to succeed. Remain fast, focused, and flexible at all times— fast to act at the right time, focused on productivity, and flexible to change when needed. Be ready, because around the corner there will be a competitor doing something new or you might need to deal with the lack of productivity in execution performance within your team. So first of all be proactive.

KEY FACTOR NUMBER TWO:

Be Creative. You have to step out of your business and then dive in and out! The ability to be creative is imperative; for that, you need people to serve as enablers to come in and help you be creative—you can't do this alone. Within your organization I recommend that you reward your team based on the creative ideas implemented with a success story as evidence. I also recommend conducting focus groups within and outside of your industry. We can learn and increase our creativity by experiencing the "out of the norm" spectrum. Start by sending your team to look for the coolest practices they can find and then conduct brainstorming sessions to identify the possibilities of inclusion in your organization.

KEY FACTOR NUMBER THREE:

Persevere. Follow your program once it is in place. I find this to be the weakest link of all plans. Plans are prepared, a lot of work and hours add up, but execution of the plan fails—not the plan, but the execution of it. Perseverance is the biggest part where people really need accountability.

The solution is to have clear objectives with precise time frames. Start by creating a forecast. Once data is collected, then move into real data forecasts. This is the measurement that must prevail as you move forward. This data will be your key enabler to solve 90 percent of your roadblocks.

As the base of these measurements, ensure that everyone within your team has clear objectives with time frames. Most importantly, set every review ahead of time and do not delay or cancel reviews. Below is a list of factors to consider as you build your productivity plan:

- Sales Order entry
- Sales ratio
- Delivery
- Storage
- Business development activities
- Business hours
- Conference calls
- Team meetings
- Client meetings
- Sales events
- Inventory
- Vacation
- Sick time
- Shortage of product
- Shortage of personnel
- Traffic
- New products
- Focus groups
- Reviews
- Customer returns
- Customer referrals
- Visits per customer
- Follow up

WRIGHT

So Alicia, will you tell our readers how you discovered productivity as the main contributor to success?

TRIGO

After many victories and defeats, I've learned many ways to increase my success ratio considerably. As business owners and/or leaders, I believe we possess an increased level of multitasking skills and the ability to imagine a vision fairly clear—ownership carries a vision.

It is crucial to continue the road to knowledge empowerment, just like technology continues to evolve. It is important to have a keen eye for the past. I look back to analyze my personal business trends and I think about the actions and reasons within a year in which I was extremely successful.

For example, what were my common practices and routines? At that point, excellent practices and activities became the common denominators. One of my best practices is to keep every single one of my yearly agendas (actually, I keep them all), and I have about twenty-three years of agendas with all the details of my daily activities. What I've done is review and seek benchmarks in my career. I then review and repeat the success trends.

When I review these, I see enablers all around me. Most importantly, I see what was I doing—the activities. At one point I realized that a repetitive activity was a common denominator, hence it became an enabler, and I understood. To be able to gain, I was giving. I was volunteering with the community with nonprofit organizations, I was mentoring other people, and I was involved in projects with other people. Then I understood that it is crucial to give in an effort to gain.

I also noticed that being around other leaders helped me in many occasions. As a matter of fact, one of the biggest steppingstones in my career happened right after I completed the Six Sigma Black Belt Certification (CSSBB). The certification allowed me to be around a group of business savvy entrepreneurs and motivated leaders for three years. We were all going through the study together. So when I look back, I see how people around you enable you to be able to get to the next level. You must ensure that you have a great support of enablers.

As I always say, leaders are not alone—they surround themselves with people who are smart, who can enable and contribute to your goals. Those are the main components of these enablers—people you can count on. They will bounce back ideas because alone you're not going to have all the ideas. I surround myself with very intelligent groups of people and that's how I do my consulting services.

I feel that I'm very creative. I feel that I'm very intelligent, and I feel that I can do a very good job at anything I put my mind to; but if I don't have that group of people around me enabling me, success is out of the question. That's how I found productivity enablers throughout my career and experiences with the ability of looking back at real data and analyzing it with a cause and effect spectrum in mind. I pinpointed the factors, the guidelines, and the actions that enable success for me. Later on, I created a systematic productivity approach for my business and for any business. I called it The Amazing Method. That's how I discovered how to find productivity— imagine that!

EXAMPLE OF PRODUCTIVITY GUIDELINE:

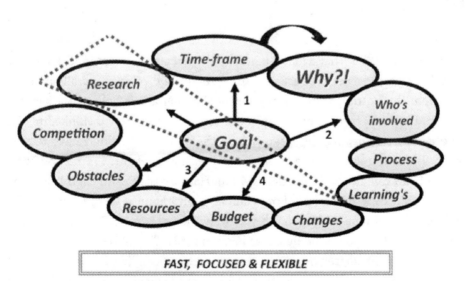

WRIGHT

So how can a business enable high productivity?

TRIGO

Number one: looking at the trends that they've had in the past. Don't go too far—you don't have to analyze twenty-three years; review the last two to three years. Then gather data of competitors' practices and see what they've been doing and how they have grown.

Research is key. Research first the results within and then research who has been doing what in your organization. It's very important that you invite people's talent, your talent as a leader, and everyone around you. You don't want people doing a job that does not highlight their forte—everyone needs to be working within their biggest asset.

I believe the first action is to conduct an assessment. Once the assessment is completed, then conduct a focus group. Gather all data and you will be able to pinpoint the weak and the strong areas. It is all about highlighting the strong areas—how you can do more of the strong and minimize the weak areas or make them stronger.

WRIGHT

Describe the productivity steps that you utilize to acquire your success today.

TRIGO

NUMBER ONE is that I have been able to create enablers, and I am very proud of creating a very robust network. When I say "robust," I really do mean this from the bottom of my heart. I'm not talking about how many friends I have in Facebook or how many people follow me on Twitter or Linkedin—I'm talking about someone who I can call on the phone and I don't have to start with, "*It's been a while!,*" That's not what I'm talking about. I'm talking about people I can call and say, "*Hi, this is Alicia. How are you?*" And then I can start the reason for my phone call. For example, "Can I bounce this idea with you?" or "Can you help me with—?" "Do you know this person?" "Do you know this company?" "Have you done business here and there?" Whatever I am asking, I get answers. Immediately I have a person on the other side who has become an enabler for me, and that is something that I have been very proud of. I have an intense robust network across the nation.

Working as a consultant for the last ten years, I've seen many different organizations grow from dozens to thousands and with that success, I've built enablers nationwide. So if I don't know something, I will definitely know who I can call to find out. If I do not have a relationship with a company or someone, I have someone who has. In my business, for my line of work, this is the number one key enabler of my productivity.

NUMBER TWO, I have a vision and, most importantly, I put it on paper. I establish my plan and I follow it. As I mentioned earlier, a key factor—the last one and the most important—is perseverance. If you cannot persevere with what you want to do, then you probably don't have a clear vision. You want to make sure that you know what is at the other end that you really, really want. At the same time you need a fast, focused, and flexible state of mind on your planning. You want to be aware of your surroundings, especially the competition and with economic changes.

For example, think about the economy in the United States for the last couple of years. A lot of people did not foresee the recession; therefore, being prepared is part of the plan. As I said previously, you need to prepare for the unthinkable, and when you prepare for the unthinkable you will not only survive, your business will continue to grow. To date I have spoken with several business owners who said to me *"The impact of the economy has not really done a lot of damage to us, I prepared and it's okay."* That is beautiful to hear, especially when more than 85 percent of businesspeople are complaining about how difficult it has been to survive in the last year. When you prepare and you think about the unthinkable, you become very successful.

To wrap these thoughts in a summary, the key is to have enablers, a plan, a direction, and infinite perseverance.

WRIGHT

How can a person increase the changes of improving productivity for his or her career growth success?

TRIGO

This is really important. I truly believe that once you have been able to establish your productivity plan, you have your strategy from A to Z, and you're able to communicate this through your team, you need to do a checkup on productivity every year. As an organization, you should conduct focus groups throughout the year.

Organize a group within your organization consisting of three to ten people. I highly recommend 50 percent of small clients, 30 percent of medium clients, and 20 percent of large clients. A consultant or a business friend who can host the event will be best. Conduct this gathering via a breakfast, lunch, or at dinner (I prefer breakfast). To prepare for this meeting, you need to have precise questions to ask, and ask them for honesty and confidentiality. Gather all of this information and conduct a team meeting to create strategic plans to increase the good habits and eliminate all the negatives. I recommend that you conduct these focus groups twice a year, minimum. Repeat the same tactic for an internal focus group, focused on operations and sales. Nothing can be good forever—you have to continue to grow.

WRIGHT

How can community engagement increase your productivity and your success?

TRIGO

It is imperative for us to be engaged in our community. Give; that is the motive of my life. You have to give to be able to receive, and it's pretty amazing how much you get when you just give—it's always times seven or ten. I think it's very important that you're out there communicating with people; you will be surprised how many enablers are out there.

I have been able to have a full-time job and be involved with four different nonprofit organizations as President while keeping a healthy family life. I was able to do all of this mainly because of the people I met in the community—enablers! They were giving to me as I was giving to them. So it's very important for you to engage. Once you put your name in the community and the people know you, not only are you going to be able to pick up the phone and get connections when you need them for your business, even focus groups. I encourage everyone that if you have a passion—whether it's a charity or for a nonprofit organization, an entrepreneurial group, a professional group, a minority group, and business membership centers—get engaged, get connected with your community. You will get more feedback than you can possibly imagine by doing so. It's a win-win situation for all.

WRIGHT

What are the metrics to achieve the productivity plan?

TRIGO

You must have metrics. For example, my weekly metric is called "Super 50." So, what is Super 50? Is a value activity metric. I set values for each activity that enables me to have success and the only way I can do this is via an assessment. I have to assess my activities, give a value to the ones that produce more results for me.

You can have five, six, seven, or ten activities and give points to each of these activities. You can give them values of five, values of three, or values of one. Then look in your calendar and see how many of these activities are scheduled into your week. Add your entire week, and if you get to fifty, that means you have great productivity for your week. Otherwise, you have a goal to reach. Having a goal is key to your success.

I explain this in detail at my seminars. There is a formula and criteria on how you want to provide value to each of the activities. It is important to know whether you have been productive or not. Everything has to have a value, everything has to have a weight, and it's the only way you can look back and see if what you're doing is creating results.

How was your productivity last week? Was it fifty or under fifty? Find out where you are and how you can make sure you are over fifty as soon as possible. There hasn't been a better time to be over fifty these days—productivity wise!

BELOW IS AN EXAMPLE OF A SUPER 50 WEEK:

	Mon	Tue	Wed	Thu	Fri	Sat
	Emails	Research Comp	SEMINAR	Read Biz Info	Research	
8						
9	Assoc. Meeting	Network Meeting	Leadership	Emails	Meeting w/ new biz	GOLF / SPA
10						
11	Review # 's	Phone Calls	Sales	Presentation		
12	Facebook		Customer	Twitter	Phone Calls	
1	Lunch w/ client	Presentation	Experience	Lunch w/ Spouse	Meeting w new biz	
2		Meeting w/new biz	Presence Skills	Charity Meeting	Review latest events & #'s	
3						
4	Email	Team Meeting		Phone Calls	Internet research	
5	Phone Calls			Meeting w/ new biz	Biz Expo	
6						
	Brainstorm		Phone Calls			
	LinkedIn		Emails			
		Meeting @ Biz Club				

WRIGHT

How can you increase productivity after completing the plan?

TRIGO

Innovation is critical, technology is your enabler, and assessments are your number one step. You need to know what's out there—what's new and can be an enabler for you. It's pretty unbelievable how people stay away from anyone knocking at their door trying to demonstrate a product. Listen, if you don't like it, simply say so and move forward. If you do not stay up-to-date with the products and technologies surfacing in the marketplace, you will not be able to grow. Someone else is going to open that door, listen to that vendor, and he or she is going to get ahead of your company. Act now. In your calendar, make time at least twice a month (secure an entire afternoon) to listen to some vendors and find ways to save money and innovate your company. You want to stay in tune with what is out there. Attend a business Expo show and see what is available so you can enable your company. As you move forward with great productivity, you can enable it to continue to transform as the technology changes. Never stop and always, always make time to hear what is new in the marketplace.

WRIGHT

During your consulting work at Amazing I'm sure you've discovered common errors business owners and professionals repeat across the board. Will you share with our readers some of these and how to avoid them?

TRIGO

There are some common denominators. I'll explain a couple that really hinder productivity.

A common denominator is lack of planning—"we don't plan to fail, but we fail at planning," I'm sure you have heard this before; it is the issue that I encounter many times. A goal is set and we think that is planning—this quarter we're going to do this, and that quarter we're going to that, and by the end of the year we're going to get there. Go people, get it! That's not the way we need to make our business plans. A strategy must be in place. This doesn't take as long as it seems, it really doesn't. It might be time-consuming to do research, maybe a week or two of research and the result is a good strategy for the rest of the year. It simply makes sense. You cannot start running without first trying to walk.

At Amazing, we help businesses with this very key factor. We conduct an assessment, pinpoint the areas, and we help business owners and leaders enable their plans. That's the number one basic factor where I see so many businesspeople failing; that's where the amazing method comes in and enables.

Number two is communication—they fail to communicate the entire strategy. I used to make the same mistake. I'm a visionary, hence, sometimes back in the day, I would fail to explain all the details involved in making my vision a reality. I learned the hard way, and it served me as a life lesson to ensure excellent communication. Now I'm 100 percent systematic with communication, and it is so much more efficient and results-oriented. Once communication improves and you have a very clear plan with the thinkable and unthinkable steps, you will be able to be extremely successful.

WRIGHT

You place a lot of emphasis on metrics for success. Why are these so important?

TRIGO

Metrics are critical because especially in today's environment we are extremely emotional due to the economy, home, and worldwide events. During the last couple of years someone very close to you has lost his or her job, decreased income somehow, or you know someone who has suffered or has died of an illness. Those are very significant events in our life. Our society is very emotional these days and the only way for you to be able to feel encouraged, to be motivated, and to be able to see the light is for you to sense, feel, and understand your progress. If you're not making progress, if you don't feel like you have been able to go from A to B, your energy level will decrease. I call this factor, emotional intelligence. The ability to understand each other while keeping in mind the reality of emotions is a great skill for a leader.

A little bit of progress is better than no progress at all. This is my main point when it comes to your own productivity and the Super 50. If you look at your agenda and you look at a total of thirty-two on your productivity and next week you're doing forty-five, you feel encouraged by your progress and will want to do more because you know you're getting closer to the goal. Every organization works the same way—if the numbers are negative it will not motivate the team. It's all about exceeding your plan; that's when you feel the fullest, the happiest, and you are at your motivational peak. Strategize to formulate the numbers, follow them closely and ensure that productivity is the main enabler of success.

WRIGHT

What are your favorite productivity enablers for success?

TRIGO

People, knowledge, and weekly metrics are my favorite productivity enablers for success. The intricacies that form our daily lives are inspiring to me. I'm always looking for good practices and things to avoid from every service industry out there. It helps me tremendously and equals knowledge.

From people, I receive an immense amount of assistance and answers. It is no surprise that I like to surround myself with intelligent, caring, and successful people. I keep the communication going constantly, via e-mail, phone, Twitter, Facebook, LinkedIn, breakfast, lunches, dinners, community events, gatherings, weddings, birthdays, and so on. After moving around in several states, and wanting to stay connected with great people I have met throughout my career, I use every tool available to stay connected and move forward with excellent communication.

Knowledge is key for successful people. I believe you should spend a lifetime on education. Our competitive landscape should be the biggest force to knowledge. The effect of not knowing could be devastating to any business. Hence attending seminars, business expos, financial classes, and technology tradeshows should be part of every businessperson's life.

The Super 50 weekly metric system keeps me real with my activities. I check every Friday and it is such a high when I'm over fifty. My weekend is so much better. Perhaps that's why the Super 50 is my favorite one.

WRIGHT

Well, Alicia what a great conversation. This is really important information. I love the question that asked what was I doing when I was successful. That is important for everyone to think about. I consider that I am successful now, but everyone has had times when success seemed out of reach. I also liked the point you made that leaders are not alone.

I really appreciate all this time you've taken with me to answer these questions. You've given me a lot to think about and I'm sure that our readers will feel just the same.

TRIGO

Well, thank you David, it's been my pleasure. This is my passion, I have a plan in place, and the productivity is over fifty. That means we are doing good!

WRIGHT

Today we have been talking with Alicia Trigo. Alice is the Chief Executive Officer of An Amazing Organization Inc., which is a consulting firm specializing in revenue growth and productivity. She is the Creator of The Amazing Method, a seven-segment program that enables a complete assessment identifying areas to increase everyone's return on investment.

Alicia, thank you so much for being with us today on *Stepping Stones to Success*.

TRIGO

Thank you, David.

ABOUT THE AUTHOR

ALICIA TRIGO is Chief Executive Officer of An Amazing Organization Inc. Amazing Organization is a consulting firm specializing in revenue growth and productivity. For over a decade, Alicia has served as an enabler for businesses nationwide. She is known for her innovative strategies and robust network. Her endeavors cover an array of industries such as technology, international business, healthcare, retail, media, sales, marketing, public relations, and small businesses. Alicia is the creator of "The Amazing Method," a seven-segment program that enables a complete assessment identifying areas to increase return on investment. Today Alicia is a recognized speaker and has been praised for her motivational affect on her audiences.

ALICIA TRIGO
813-597-4072
alicia@amazingorg.com
www.amazingorg.com

CHAPTER TWENTY

Coaching for the Survivor's Soul

An Interview with . . . **Debbie Kiefiuk**

DAVID WRIGHT (WRIGHT)

I'd like to welcome Debbie Kiefiuk to *Stepping Stones to Success*. Debbie Kiefiuk, MEd, serves as a speaker, writer, and life coach. Degreed in sport psychology and exercise physiology, Debbie empowered world class figure skaters to achieve sports excellence through team-building workshops, mental skills training such as imagery, goal-setting, focus, and concentration, sports nutrition, and how to get the winning edge by psyching up, not out during competition. She has been published in international and national magazines such as Weider's publications, *Muscle & Fitness Hers*, *Professional Skater Magazine*, columnist in *Go Figure* ("Gold Medal training"), and writer for trade journals for fitness professionals. Her career has also included working in the healthcare industry as a sales representative. Applying what she learned in sports to her career, she finds that successful people have the winning attitude, intentional focus to achieve goals, and the discipline and determination to turn obstacles into challenges. Her coaching comes from Coach-U, ICF ,WellCoaches, and Coachville (ICF accredited programs). She agrees that in order to coach the game successfully, you've had to play the game. Debbie shares with us today several powerful lessons on how coaching can change your life.

DEBBIE KIEFIUK (KIEFIUK)

Thank you, David, I'm glad to be here.

WRIGHT

Well, Debbie how did you get into coaching and choose the path of an empowerment coach?

KIEFIUK

In my teenage years, I got turned on to motivational programs. *The Subliminal Winner* by Denis Waitley, and a book by Dr. Joyce Brothers, *How to Get Whatever You Want Out of Life,* inspired me for an upcoming figure skating competition. I found that these motivational programs and my sports imagery kept me very focused. They helped to keep me very purpose-driven, extremely focused, and motivated when I was in training. In fact, I found them to be so effective, I remember a time that I not only won a figure skating competition but I placed first—a clean sweep from all six judges, straight across the board! I'll never forget that moment, David, because what it taught me was the power of these motivational programs and my ability to stay focused during a time of adversity in my life to be able to pull off a win.

It wasn't really winning that was the most thrilling part of this experience. It was the fact that during this competition I had a landed a difficult jump and I had a peak performance. In the zone is when everything clicks and comes automatically. That was my first experience of what it was like to be "in the zone," where you do things that you normally haven't done before and you are extremely successful. This proved to me that the tools I used to engage me in this winning process empowered me to excel.

So indeed, early in on in my life I learned the power of applying these coaching tools. Later, when coaching became popular, I decided to participate in an International Coach Federation accredited program called Coach U. This is how I became turned on to coaching. My earlier success in sports with coaching enhanced my ability to achieve success in my life. So essentially, sports coaching is how I got into life and business coaching.

WRIGHT

That's fantastic. What was the life-altering experience and how did it affect your life?

KIEFIUK

This life-altering experience that I will share is quite a story. I have refrained from sharing in the past, but as Maya Angelou poet, civil rights activist, writer, and teacher said so well in her quote, "there is no agony like bearing an untold story inside of you." So this is why I want to tell my story.

I was a rape survivor and as much as I dislike using that word "victim," I was a victim. Later I became victimized all over again when I went to seek help. This was actually during the time when I was a figure skater. I went to seek help from those in the medical profession—those whom I trusted, those in positions of power, those whom I thought would have answers to help me. David, I believed them to be competent, or at least to have some sensitivity about my issue, but instead there was a lack of sensitivity, empathy, compassion, and knowledge about my personal experience.

I had gone to a doctor as a young adult to address two health issues. I had an eating disorder and I had been sexually assaulted. I told the doctor that I wanted to get to the root of my problem—that of being assaulted by my chaperone at the age of seventeen on my senior class trip.

Instead of helping me, the doctor laughed at me. He dismissed me. I will never forget his words. He said, "That is so farfetched." He used his power over me; he not only dismissed me, but he misdiagnosed me, and later he subjected me to improper medication. He actually violated the Hippocratic Oath to "do no harm."

I didn't really know what to expect from psychology and psychiatry, David. I didn't know what to expect from my appointments with him, but things never seemed right. During this time I was actually in training for the Boston Marathon. How I wished I had consulted a sports psychology professional. These professionals would have worked on the human side of performance and take me seriously in my pursuit of excellence in my life. They would have also helped me during this difficult time in my life. When this doctor crossed boundaries with me in a sexually suggestive way, I left. I trusted my intuition; he was not there to help me.

I was very disappointed in those who were not able to help me. I was self-responsible, I continued to go the normal routes to get help, but I continued to blame myself and feel shame, even though I was the one being self-responsible and doing everything I could to overcome my eating disorder and the trauma I was experiencing that was often suppressed because I was dismissed.

Now, years later, I did learn how to overcome my eating disorder as well as the trauma. Even though I was successful and a highly functional individual, my traumatic experience had a profound effect on me later in life because I never dealt with the root of the issue. Years later, when I entered the corporate environment as a pharmaceutical rep, I was sexually harassed by a manager. I dislike using the term "sexually harassed." I really wish the term would be "worker harassment" because so much of this problem stems from sexist attitudes toward competent professionals. This leads to behaviors that don't necessitate a sexual involvement but creates a negative image of the victim.

I was also sexually assaulted by a doctor behind closed doors. This was during the launch of a new product—Viagra. Although I did not sell this product, it created numerous uncomfortable situations as a rep. I was also experiencing a problem with my boss who got his job through nepotism, not necessarily by his own merit. When he began to verbally abuse me, I felt that the right thing to do was to go to human resources. The company had a zero tolerance policy to sexual harassment. Instead of adhering to their own zero tolerance and policy, they retaliated against me. Even though I had documentation that included a tape recording of my boss admitting to me that he knew he was sexually harassing me, it didn't matter—the problem only got worse—so I quit.

I went on to another job, once again repeating these experiences in my life over and over again—putting myself in the position of a victim and not learning how to empower myself. I went to another job and I experienced more of the same disrespect. My boss would pick up a basket of rolls at the lunch table when I was having a business meeting with another male colleague. When I wanted to engage in conversation, he would whack it up and down like a gavel on the middle of the table saying, "Down girl, down girl, have another biscuit." Rather than being engaged in the meeting I just sat back, not daring to say anything because the last time I had spoken up, I had been the victim of retaliation. I didn't want it repeated.

I then decided to go on and open my own business. I also decided to seek legal counseling about the first company, because I did not feel it was right that I had to start my career all over again.

Again I experienced more of the same. I'd go to these lawyers and they would say, "Oh, your situation isn't bad enough to fight legally." "Oh, it's hard to fight those kinds of cases because you're not suicidal." They had all sorts of excuses. I said, "Listen, I'm not suicidal but what is happening is wrong." The lawyers wanted a case where they could make money (there would have been no punitive damages in my case). To me, it was about my having justice and a career; it was not about money, but my voice was falling on deaf ears.

I was trying to be empowered by something outside of myself. I didn't know about living in a problem-free zone and how to avoid these situations. I expected others to help me and that they would have all the answers. When I did fight for my rights, I kept hitting a wall, experiencing rejection. I had to tell my story repeatedly. It was as if I was getting re-traumatized by having to retell my experience.

Fighting was stressful and it opened up old wounds, so I decided to seek counseling. Since I never got closure and recovery from my past traumatic experience, I was encouraged to get closure and focus on my past by a therapist. At the suggestion of the therapist, I wrote a closure note to the doctor who dismissed my sexual experience years ago—the one I thought had caused me more harm than the rape itself. The therapist didn't suggest that I actually send the closure note, but I did. My emotions were very overwhelming. I wrote about the harm that I was experiencing at my place of work, the rape he dismissed years ago, and his behaviors toward me. I admit my behavior of delivering the letter and defacing his front door was inappropriate.

Fighting for my justice and hitting the wall made me go on the downward spiral, quite the opposite experience when I was an athlete in the zone, and on the up and up. It was the opposite of winning because something outside of my control made me lose control of my emotions.

To make a long story short, I found myself on the other side of the law. The doctor I had written the note to decided to press charges against me. He took my words and distorted them out of proportion. This comes as no surprise. His values were much different than mine because he wasn't there to help or understand people. He had a different way of operating. He had no sensitivity with women's issues and a different attitude toward me.

The lesson I learned about fighting people who had more power, money, and clout than I had was very evident, and I can understand why statistics show that 60 percent of sexual assaults are not reported to the police; since 1993 this has increased only by one third. My experience happened in the 1980s. If one in six women are sexually assaulted and one in thirty-three men, according to statistics from RAINN today, there is still a long way to go to empower others to break their silence, to not experience retaliation because of it, and to have the healing power they so rightfully deserve. Too often we see media messages that put the victim in the light of something negative.

As I mentioned, I found myself on the other side of the law. I needed a criminal defense lawyer; I was still in my desperate moment. I was still in the victim mode mentality. I was frightened, disempowered, and I was again making poor choices about whom to trust. Just moments before I was to appear before the judge, the lawyer I had chosen (who did not work with me and did not discuss my case prior my court appearance) took me out in the hall in isolation, and told me I should plead no contest. He coerced me and instilled fear that if I did not plead no contest that I could go to jail. My anxiety heightened and I was not concentrating, so just moments before I was to come before the judge, I chose to obey what this lawyer told me to do. Instead of even collecting the evidence or even convincing the doctor to change his accusation against me to a lesser charge, my rights were swept under the rug. I never did have my day in court. Instead, I served two years on probation, followed by another five years before the charge was removed from my record.

This was quite some time ago, and I certainly survived the experience and moved forward a long way. I had just wanted this doctor to believe me. It was a way for me to express my anger and frustration. Women often feel safe when they write.

This had become a life-altering experience for me because I had trusted those I should have been able to trust to help me, but they betrayed that trust. This became my calling. I have a renewed sense of purpose in my life—to empower others to run their own lives, to make wise choices, to prevent problems before they happen, to connect with a positive community in a time of need, to have resources available to you when you need them, and ultimately to be able to avoid betrayal from those who are in positions of power who have violated and abused their responsibility.

WRIGHT

How did this life-altering experience create a paradigm shift for you?

KIEFIUK

Fortunately, my skills and athletics—my success in my figure skating and running—enabled me to draw on my inner strength, a strong desire to excel, to go beyond surviving to thriving, and to not be defined by my experience.

I experienced an epiphany on the first day of my two-year probation, when I sat there in the waiting room. There was a sign on the wall that read, "Attitude is a thing that makes a big difference." I thought at that moment, "Here I am, on probation, and all of my perpetrators got away with their crimes. This does not seem fair—I'm not a criminal," I thought. And in that moment, I decided I was not going to let anyone get the best of me.

I thought about my situation and how it could have been a lot worse. I thought of Holocaust survivor Dr. Viktor Frankl. He saw the positive in his tragic experience and he empowered himself by creating Existential Psychology.

I truly learned in that moment the importance of attitude and self-empowerment. The other skills I learned from sports psychology and human potential development programs like coaching.

Coaching changed my life because it taught me how to build a strong personal foundation. I really enjoyed going to my class because I was safe in an environment that accepted me unconditionally. Getting on a spiritual path and learning about the laws of attraction and the laws of the universe were also a part of what created my shift. In surviving the charge I took responsibility for the consequences of my choices in life. It also enhanced my conscious awareness of the way things were and my need for change.

WRIGHT

What empowered you?

KIEFIUK

Through coaching I learned that instead of looking outside of myself for the answers, for someone to change the way things are in the world, I learned to find power within—the power I had when I had won the skating competition. I had great coaches. Coaching taught me skills such as how to build a strong personal foundation, how to live in a problem-free, drama-free zone, how to set boundaries, build reserves, and how to create an environment where I could thrive, not just survive. Essentially, life coaching put me on a new path to self-discovery and human potential.

Other programs that also empowered me include Toastmasters, Dale Carnegie, and of course motivational programs from Denis Waitley of Nightingale-Conant, certainly Jack Canfield's Chicken Soup of the Soul Series, and Deepak Chopra's programs. All have these programs have served to benefit me in my journey, as well as my parents, friends, and family.

I also had some excellent coaches, Brad Bandemer, from Inside Out Freedom, who taught me about the power of forgiveness. He talked about the cost and pain involved when someone harms you. His formula for forgiveness was extremely empowering to me. To forgive doesn't mean that what the person did to you is right. Brad had a very successful formula that helped me move past and through that rut. I had another coach who empowered me in the workplace. Susan Cantwell helped pull me out of the rut of my defensive role as victim by saying, "Play in the league that you were meant to play in," and "play on the offense and not the defense." Those words enhanced my awareness of empowerment rather than succumbing to the role as a victim.

Journaling was also a very useful method for me to empower myself. In journaling my life lessons, I had titled a book *Run a Marathon in These Shoes*. It is about how recovery after trauma is like running a marathon. I think this is important because I think there are going to be a lot of military individuals suffering from post traumatic stress and other individuals who experience adversity in their life who can benefit from this self-discovery tool. This book not only talks about the dark side—the depression and anger—it also talks about the bright side and how to empower yourself. I share my journey and that of others every step of the way—a total of twenty-six chapters, each representing the twenty-six miles in a marathon. Each chapter has a song relating to it with a theme to create sensory rich images. The chapters fully express what I was experiencing in each moment. I also share stories of others. It is similar to the movie *Forrest Gump* when he's running to music and experiencing his life's challenges. This book is unpublished to date.

Additionally, in my experience, I had created a vision for my own purpose and calling.

All of these things helped to empower me and created my paradigm shift. Coaching changed my life.

WRIGHT

Is getting on a personal path of self-empowerment an easy process?

KIEFIUK

That's a really good question, and the answer is not necessarily. I think that sometimes we gravitate to the things that we're told in life. Having a good coach can make the process a lot easier.

WRIGHT

A strong personal foundation is a program you mentioned, tell us more about that.

KIEFIUK

Well, the concept of a personal foundation is analogous to house being made up of very strong materials like cement and steel so it won't crack or collapse under severe weather. Our personal foundation is a structural basis that supports our living a very exceptional life that includes our body, mind, and spirit. We need protection against stress and other things that can destroy our foundation. There's a quote that illustrates this concept: "A skyscraper doesn't start at street level. In fact, the taller the building, the deeper the foundation." This holds true for people, too.

There are certain programs that Coach U has created. One of these is called the Personal Foundation Program. You acquire skills such as "Handling and Eliminating what You are Tolerating," getting clear of your past, living with integrity, getting your needs met, getting wants and values met, living life by your values, setting boundaries, strengthening your family and your community, improving your attitude, building reserves, and so on. Having a strong personal foundation can help us live a more meaningful life because we'll be able to use our skills and resources, which will naturally help us to attract things that we want.

WRIGHT

What do you do that is different from what a therapist does?

KIEFIUK

Essentially, what I do is help people to be present-future focused. I don't often focus on the past, but certainly if somebody needs some clinical attention

I suggest that they research and find a professional to help them. What I help people do is to move forward in their life. Sometimes therapy can keep people stuck because the therapist may not be engaged in the process of self-actualization or growth themselves, which can stunt your growth. I found coaching to be highly effective for me. My journey of personal empowerment has enhanced my own wisdom and finding my own voice. Essentially, I help people empower themselves in that way.

WRIGHT

I have to agree with you.

KIEFIUK

Someone said to me, "Oh, you're insurance is really good." and at the same time was totally dismissing me and just looking forward to that paycheck. One therapist told me that he thinks therapists are going to be a dying breed fifty years from now. I wasted a lot of my time by going down that path. Coaching is a much better answer for me.

WRIGHT

When I hear those words from a health care professional, "Oh, your insurance is great," I take it to mean that I'm going to be stuck in a five-year contract with that person.

KIEFIUK

That's right. And the other thing is there is no exchange of dialogue of who that person really is—you don't know what his or her beliefs are and if the person has a certain belief, or stereotypes others, or, most importantly, they're not on a path of personal growth themselves, they can keep you stuck.

WRIGHT

What is the difference between power and empowerment?

KIEFIUK

Power can be good or bad. Power, as in "power over others," is used to dominate, discriminate, or discourage others from reaching their life's potential or purpose; this is not a good thing. Empowerment involves self-awareness, consciousness-raising, and life skills for successful living that not only benefits the individual but also adds value to society. Empowerment is good power. Oprah Winfrey is an example of a person who is both empowered and powerful—she's empowered. She uses her power to empower others, not to have power over them.

Recently, in our society, we have seen the effects of those who abuse their power and how it's caused psychological, mental, and spiritual harm through greed. Power alone that focuses on gaining external things like money and status has been harmful to everyone.

Empowerment is more of an intrinsic thing, not an external thing. Empowerment is spiritual and it enhances well-being. A person with a strong personal foundation is an empowered individual who doesn't look for external things to bring him or her happiness.

WRIGHT

So how does what you learn in sports apply to life in coaching others?

KIEFIUK

I believe there are intrinsic qualities that make a person successful. Athletics teaches those things, which includes team-building, discipline, being goal-oriented, driven, self-motivated, focused, and self-efficacy—all those wonderful things I've learned and applied from my sport psychology classes. There is an athlete in all of us and mental training skills learned from sports psychology is very useful, not just in sports but also in business and in life. I like to apply this analogy to sales professionals.

I like to help women and men in the workplace empower themselves. For women, I like to use athletic role models to empower them using their own personal power and enhance their self-efficacy or their belief in their ability to choose success. Role models can serve as powerful reminders that anything is possible; they can inspire people to excel.

An example of a wonderful woman role model I like is Kathy Switzer. Kathy serves as a role model for runners and women because she was the first woman to run in the male-only Boston Marathon. Jack Semple, a Boston Athletic Association official, tried to physically pull her off the course during the April 20, 1967, race but was unsuccessful. The next thing you know she had paved the way for other women so that now both men and women can run the Boston Marathon. There are many role models who can be useful to empower people to overcome adversity and achieve excellence. It's also important for women to understand their own personal power in making their own paradigm shift to achieve excellence through their stories.

In my coaching I also use skills from Dave Buck's coaching program, "Your Winning Season." In this seminar, he talks about your inner game and outer game. I think that's good terminology for awareness enhancement, inner game and outer game. In performing powerful imagery in the class, I cultivated a calling and, like my skating competition, it empowered me and helped me achieve sales success at a new job. I worked on my inner game. It was my outer game—things beyond my control—that I had to be aware of and learn to let go.

I find that the application of what you learn in sports applies to life in so many ways. The important distinction is a philosophy from sport psychology—being "mastery oriented" versus having a "win at all cost" mentality. Athletes who are very mastery oriented have intrinsic qualities based on talent and application of skills learned. A "win at all cost" philosophy is a win, not based on ethics or morals, but based on a lie and self-deception of self and others. It can be compared to when athletes take steroids. That's not what we want. I think that by teaching people the inner skills of success and to be mastery oriented is really what it's about. We can learn a lot of these things through valuable lessons from sport psychology and coaching.

WRIGHT

Well, Debbie, what's next in your career?

KIEFIUK

As one of my coaches stated, "A dream you can achieve on your own isn't big enough." After working on myself from the inside out, I'm ready for a new adventure. In addition to speaking, writing, and coaching, I'd like to play a bigger game and work with others in making a positive change in society. I'd like to use my experience to empower others. Essentially, I find it hard to both fight for one's rights and recover at the same time. So I'd really like to empower others to break their silence, because when they do, that's when true healing begins to take them beyond surviving and thriving to living the life they so rightfully deserve.

I also have a life purpose to empower others to make personal shifts for positive change within themselves and ultimately make paradigm shifts in our society or, as Laura Berman Fortang, author of *Live Your Best Life*, has stated so well, "To change the world one person at a time."

My vision is still the same and when I was in my angry stage I did envision doing the whole media circuit thing—making my rounds at all the talk shows like *The Oprah Winfrey Show*. I envision myself sitting there with Whoopi Goldberg, Joy Behar, Barbara Walters, Sherri, Elizabeth on *The View*, talking about hot topics in the arena of women's issues. I'd still like to do this. I'd also like to be on media talk shows that help expose some of the gaps in the law as civil rights expert Gloria Allred has pointed out. (By the way, she gave me a very positive letter when I was looking for attorneys.)

Catharine McKinnon wrote *Women's Lives, Men's Laws*. She is the Elizabeth A. Long Professor of Law at the University of Michigan Law School and Visiting Professor of Law at the University of Chicago. Catharine really opened my eyes and healed my heart so that I could understand that it was okay for me to feel angry. I'm past that angry stage. As activist Gloria Steinem said, "The truth will set you free, but first it will piss you off." I think it's okay to be angry because it does reignite commitment. I'd like to be coached by leaders like this, learn more about how I can make a difference, and serve in an activist role to empower others. Self-empowerment is what it's all about—to live life on your own terms.

ABOUT THE AUTHOR

DEBBIE KIEFIUK, MED, serves as a speaker, writer, and life coach. Degreed in sport psychology and exercise physiology, Debbie empowered world class figure skaters to achieve sports excellence through team-building workshops, mental skills training such as imagery, goal-setting, focus, and concentration, sports nutrition, and how to get the winning edge by psyching up, not out during competition. She has been published in international and national magazines such as Weider's publications, *Muscle & Fitness Hers*, magazines, and trade journals for fitness professionals. Her career has also included working in the healthcare industry as a sales representative. Applying what she learned in sports to her career, she finds that successful people have the winning attitude, intentional focus to achieve goals, and the discipline and determination to turn obstacles into challenges. Her coaching comes from Coach-U, WellCoaches, and Coachville, ICF (International Coach Federation) accredited programs. She agrees that in order to coach the game successfully, you have to play the game.

DEBBIE KIEFIUK, MED

Speaker, Writer, Wellness Coach
17212 N. Scottsdale Rd., #2423
Scottsdale, Arizona 85255
Phone/Fax: 480-588-7081
Debbie@EmpowerYourselfToExcel.com
DebKiefiuk@cox.net